The language theory of Mikhail Bakhtin doe
– "dialogism," "Marxism," "prosaics," "au...
foundation of his writing rests ambivalently between phenomenology and Marxism.
The theoretical tension of these positions creates philosophical impasses in Bakhtin's
work, which have been neglected or ignored partly because these impasses are
themselves mirrored by the problems of anti-foundationalist and materialist
tendencies in literary scholarship. In *Mikhail Bakhtin: between phenomenology and
Marxism*, Michael Bernard-Donals examines various incarnations of phenomenological and materialist theory – including the work of Jauss, Fish, Rorty, Althusser,
and Pecheux – and places them beside Bakhtin's work, providing a contextualized
study of Bakhtin, a critique of the problems of contemporary critics, and an original
contribution to literary theory.

Literature, Culture, Theory 11

Mikhail Bakhtin

between phenomenology and Marxism

Literature, Culture, Theory

❖❖

General editors

RICHARD MACKSEY, *The Johns Hopkins University*

and MICHAEL SPRINKER, *State University of New York at Stony Brook*

The Cambridge *Literature, Culture, Theory* series is dedicated to theoretical studies in the human sciences that have literature and culture as their object of enquiry. Acknowledging the contemporary expansion of cultural studies and the redefinitions of literature that this has entailed, the series includes not only original works of literary theory but also monographs and essay collections on topics and seminal figures from the long history of theoretical speculation on the arts and human communication generally. The concept of theory embraced in the series is broad, including not only the classical disciplines of poetics and rhetoric, but also those of aesthetics, linguistics, psychoanalysis, semiotics, and other cognate sciences that have inflected the systematic study of literature during the past half century.

Titles published

Return to Freud: Jacques Lacan's dislocation of psychoanalysis
SAMUEL WEBER
(*translated from the German by Michael Levine*)

Wordsworth, dialogics, and the practice of criticism
DON H. BIALOSTOSKY

The subject of modernity
ANTHONY J. CASCARDI

Onomatopoetics: theory of language and literature
JOSEPH GRAHAM

Parody: ancient, modern, and post-modern
MARGARET A. ROSE

The poetics of personification
JAMES PAXSON

Possible worlds in literary theory
RUTH RONEN

Critical conditions: postmodernity and the question of foundations
HORACE L. FAIRLAMB

Introduction to literary hermeneutics
PETER SZONDI
(*translated from the German by Martha Woodmansee*)

Anti-mimesis from Plato to Hitchcock
TOM COHEN

Mikhail Bakhtin: between phenomenology and Marxism
MICHAEL F. BERNARD-DONALS

Mikhail Bakhtin

between phenomenology and Marxism

MICHAEL F. BERNARD-DONALS

University of Missouri-Columbia

CAMBRIDGE
UNIVERSITY PRESS

Published by the Press Syndicate of the University of Cambridge
The Pitt Building, Trumpington Street, Cambridge, CB2 1RP
40 West 20th Street, New York, NY 10011-4211, USA
10 Stamford Road, Oakleigh, Melbourne 3166, Australia

First published 1994

Printed in Great Britain at the University Press, Cambridge

A catalogue record for this book is available from the British Library

Library of Congress cataloguing in publication data

Bernard-Donals, Michael F.
Mikhail Bakhtin: between phenomenology and Marxism / Michael F. Bernard-Donals.
p. cm. – (Literature, culture, theory; 11)
Includes bibliographical references and index.
ISBN 0 521 46098 0 (hardback) – ISBN 0 521 46647 4 (paperback)
1. Bakhtin, M. M. (Mikhail Mikhaïlovich), 1895–1975. 2. Literature – History and criticism
– Theory, etc. 3. Language and languages – Philosophy. 4. Communism and linguistics.
5. Phenomenology. I. Title. II. Series.
P85.B22B45 1994
801'.95'092–dc20 93-47123 CIP

ISBN 0 521 46098 0 hardback
ISBN 0 521 46647 4 paperback

For Hannah

Contents

Preface

This book's premise begins with two simple and related questions. First, why should we study aesthetic constructs, and what kind of knowledge does that study yield; and second, what does the work of Mikhail Bakhtin offer to such a study? The questions can be made more precise: how can aesthetic knowledge be said to have social significance; and, if literary analysis does affect or change human social relations, what is the nature of that change? Bakhtin's project – which he called a "sociological poetics" – is at once an analysis of how social structures are comprised of language, and of how aesthetic objects are uniquely formed social structures, and so is uniquely positioned to intervene in the space delimited by these questions.

Yet at the foundation of Bakhtin's work lies an ambivalence about the way the human subject is constructed. In his earliest work – which bears a close relation to Husserl's phenomenology, Gadamer's hermeneutics, and the aesthetic theory of the neo-Kantian resurgence of the 1910s and 1920s – Bakhtin proposes a human subject that is defined by its *relation* to other subjects, and the ways in which that relation is manifested in the creation of signs. The "phenomenological" works emphasize the inescapability of language, and suggest analyses of (aesthetic) language based on the complexities of one subject's relation to another. As his work progresses, however, Bakhtin pays more attention to the material conditions of the human subjects whose language is under analysis. Bakhtin reframes the question of language production (and the production of signs generally) as a question of the re-production of signs as ideological material, thereby effectively shifting the analysis of subject-formation away from questions of interpretation and "bias" toward an examination of the "characteristics and forms of the social intercourse by which this meaning is realized" (Bakhtin/Medvedev, *The formal method* 9). This shift of emphasis to analyze broader processes of subject-formation brings Bakhtin's work closer to the work of traditional historical materialist analyses of culture and history.

Mikhail Bakhtin: between phenomenology and Marxism accounts for the incongruities between these "individual" and "social" analyses. What is most interesting about these incongruities is *not* that they prevent "Bakhtinian" analyses of language, culture and aesthetic objects. The boom in Bakhtinian studies in all of these areas over the last ten to fifteen years is powerful evidence to the contrary. Rather, the disparity between the "individual" and "social" theories of subject-formation in Bakhtin points to a difficulty in the *nature* of the knowledge such theories yield. Though understanding language as a way to "change the minds" of its users is certainly valuable, the question remains as to how one moves from such new knowledge to less (or, if possible, un-) biassed knowledge of one's material conditions and, armed with such knowledge, how one might effect real, measurable, change in those conditions.

One might ask why one needs yet another book on Mikhail Bakhtin. Quite simply, it is because in his work the perennial problems of subject-formation, the nature of the aesthetic, the possibility of the human sciences, and epistemology generally, are closely intertwined. More specifically, there are two reasons why I think this project is a valuable one. First, no one in the "Bakhtin industry" has adequately discussed Bakhtin's language theory in terms other than a *single*, unified theory. There are literary and cultural theorists who understand Bakhtin's work as fellow-travelling with historical materialism (Hirschkop; White; Bennett; Shepherd). There are others who see it as closer to a theory of prosaics (Morson), or a theory of dialogism (Bialostosky), or a theory of "authorship" (Holquist), but it has never been fully acknowledged that Bakhtin's influences were many and contradictory. Moreover, the fact that there have been so many attempts to reconcile Bakhtin's work under one "umbrella" theory suggests that no single unifying theory is sufficient. *Mikhail Bakhtin: between phenomenology and Marxism* undertakes to study the complexities of his work, particularly in relation to the problematic early "phenomenological" essays. Second, the ambivalence in Bakhtin's work reflects a similar ambivalence current in the literary and theoretical academy today. Are literary works aesthetic constructs that, by their very aesthetic nature, deserve attention from the public and media? Or are these works simply another cultural construct borne by the historical forces that create and affect the public and media? By whose definition are such constructs "aesthetic?" Bakhtin's phenomenological works tried to get to the heart of the nature of aesthetic response. When those attempts dissolved into unanswerable questions of how subjective response is created culturally and how aesthetics can be considered a branch of material culture, he turned to materialism. There, Bakhtin considered *how* the work was material, and how its language — no longer considered strictly aesthetic, but part of the intercourse of culture — could act as an instrument of social change (either for the better or for the worse). All these questions, of course, are relevant today, during a time when theoretical approaches to language and literature are being interrogated for what value they can bring to the public in general; when questions are being asked about whether there is a need for a science of the underpinnings of texts when those texts are assumed to have value by definition; and when the very category of "the aesthetic" is seen as a questionable cultural commodity.

The book is broadly divided into three main subject areas, and in each I provide an exposition of the earliest manifestations of Bakhtin's work on the construction of the subject by way of the "other." These appear primarily in *Art and answerability*, "The problem of the author," "Discourse in life, discourse in art," and "Epic and novel." In these texts, Bakhtin's phenomenology — the subject of the book's first three chapters — most resembles the neo-Kantian position developed in the 1910s and 1920s, notably by Hermann Cohen, as well as Husserl and Gadamer (and to some extent, Ingarden). At stake in this exposition and subsequent comparisons is the extent to which Bakhtin's "individualist" construction of the subject — and the resulting application of such a theory for the value of doing aesthetic or cultural analyses — confronts or elides the problems encountered by these "phenomenological" theorists. Specifically, I discuss the ways in which Bakhtin's notion of how to define the object of investigation (the literary text or aesthetic object) improves on Husserl's; whether it is possible for Bakhtin's phenomenology to give a better account for divergent and competing readings of texts; whether he provides a method for adjudicating such divergent readings; and, finally, whether Bakhtin's concept of "negotiating" the network that defines an utterance's context is sufficient to ground such adjudications.

The next two chapters provide an exposition of the "social" theory of subject-formation found in the more "Marxist" Bakhtinian works, such as *Marxism and the philosophy of language*, *The formal method in literary scholarship*, his later *Speech genre* essays, and in certain sections of *The dialogic imagination* essays and of the Dostoevsky book. In these texts, Bakhtin pre-empts the phenomenological theory of the subject by producing a broader concept of subject-formation at the level of societies. Moreover, Bakhtin casts his argument in terms of ideology rather than simply language, making the case that ideological construction is in fact material and does contribute to subject-formation, but that one's historical situation also – and distinctly – contributes to such formation. I investigate what is an integral problem for language study generally and for Bakhtin's work specifically: namely, that there may be a distinct method for the study of the material/historical placement of the subject, and that that method is *scientific*. Here I provide a description of how Bakhtin's materialism is like and how it is unlike other versions of historical materialism – specifically Althusserian and post-Althusserian versions (Laclau and Mouffe, Pecheux, Coward and Ellis, and others) – since it is these latter versions that have had to wrestle with the possibility of the liberatory nature of a materialist *science*, and since Bakhtin ultimately shrank from the claim that such a science would work.

The final two chapters negotiate what might be possible for a materialist project modelled on Bakhtin's. Given the problems of both the "individual" and the "societal" descriptions of subject-formation, how does Bakhtin – who works at the margins of both – negotiate these problems successfully, if at all? Bakhtin's project might finally be called a "materialist rhetoric," which begins – like current anti-foundationalist language theories (such as Stanley Fish's and Richard Rorty's, the two main antagonists in this section) – by acknowledging and providing an analysis of the complex ideological network that interpellates subjects (a process which is much like Bakhtin's phenomenological project). It also accounts for the material/historical base for such a network, positing a proximate scientific method for the analysis for those specific historical, economic, and social articulations that overdetermine them. This *derives* from the Bakhtinian model, but not directly, since Bakhtin in fact never followed through on this analysis, though he often called for it (see White, "The struggle over Bakhtin"; Hirschkop's essays). It remains to be seen if such a "materialist rhetoric" can be constructed, and whether it can be successful.

Acknowledgments

This work is indebted to many people and many institutions. For their help in getting the earliest versions of the chapters of this book written, and for beginning the dialogues that would bring it to print, thanks go to Helen Cooper, Taisha Abraham, Dean Casale, Ellen Gardiner, and Kevin Railley. Michael Holquist, Bruce Bashford, and Sandy Petrey all read the first draft of the manuscript and made valuable suggestions about what to add, what to subtract, and where to go for additional information. Don Bialostosky has read some of the material in this book and has helped tighten some of the loose screws. I must also thank anonymous readers at *PMLA*, *Critical Inquiry*, *Cultural Critique*, *Pre/Text*, *Philosophy and Literature*, *MLN*, *boundary 2*, *College English* and *Comparative Literature* for their helpful comments on later drafts of Chapters 1, 2, 5, 6, and the Conclusion. Parts of Chapters 2 and 4 were published in substantially different form in *Studies in the literary imagination* (Spring 1990); parts of Chapters 1 and 7 were published in *College English* (February 1994); parts of Chapter 6 were published in *the minnesota review* (Fall 1990). Grateful thanks are owed to the Humanities Institute at the State University of New York at Stony Brook, whose Director, E. Ann Kaplan, provided me with a fellowship in 1990/91 which gave me some much-needed time to research this project further. Thanks also go to the Modern Language Association, the Society for Critical Exchange, and the Society for the Study of Narrative Literature, for providing forums for me to present – and amend – some of the ideas in this book. I am grateful for the support of colleagues both at the State University of New York at Stony Brook and Mississippi State University, who helped keep up my morale at some of the more trying points in this project. I must also thank Linda Frost, Ellen Gardiner, and Rita Kranidis for their friendship and support with this and other projects that looked like they'd never get off the ground.

Two other special notes of thanks: First, to Michael Sprinker, without whose help I would never have been in a position to write this book. I didn't realize, when I walked into his class on Marxist aesthetics in the winter of 1986, that I was in for a wild ride into literary and cultural theory that I now hope doesn't stop anytime soon. More than just providing a wild ride, though, he has vigorously supported my work (even when he most seriously questioned it), he has in one way or another helped me in my academic travels from New York to Mississippi and now to Missouri, and he has given me invaluable advice. More importantly, however, he has given me a great deal of friendship and support that I hope one day I can begin to give back. In many ways this book is a tribute to him.

I also thank my family: Hannah, my wife; Shoshana and Miryam, our children. Only Hannah knows the nature of the roller-coaster ride this particular project has been, and I thank her for letting me lean on her when the ride got especially bumpy; and I thank her also for sharing with me the rewards that go along with those bumps. Most of all, though, I couldn't have made it through this project without her encouragement, her support, and her intelligent advice. Thanks to Shoshana and Miryam for smiling, for putting up with quick baths and the occasional slow response to requests for milk or juice, and for asking me where the pictures are in this book. They have helped me keep things in proper perspective.

Abbreviations

AR	Wolfgang Iser, *The act of reading* (Baltimore: The Johns Hopkins University Press, 1978)
CD	John Brenkman, *Culture and domination* (Ithaca: Cornell University Press, 1987)
Doing	Stanley Fish, *Doing what comes naturally: Change, rhetoric, and the practice of theory in literary and legal studies* (Durham, NC: Duke University Press, 1990)
FM	M. M. Bakhtin/Pavel Medvedev, *The formal method in literary scholarship: A critical introduction to sociological poetics*, trans. Albert J. Wehrle (Cambridge, MA: The Harvard University Press, 1985)
For M	Louis Althusser, *For Marx* (London: New Left Books, 1969)
IR	Wolfgang Iser, *The implied reader: Patterns of communication in prose fiction from Bunyan to Beckett* (Baltimore: The Johns Hopkins University Press, 1974)
LM	Rosalind Coward and John Ellis, *Language and materialism: Developments in sociology and the theory of the subject* (Boston: Routledge and Kegan Paul, 1977)
LP	Louis Althusser, *Lenin and philosophy* (London: Monthly Review Press, 1971)
MPL	M. M. Bakhtin/Valentin Voloshinov, *Marxism and the philosophy of language*, trans. Ladislav Matejka and I. R. Titunik (Cambridge, MA: The Harvard University Press, 1986)
RC	Louis Althusser and Etienne Balibar, *Reading capital* (London: New Left Books, 1970)
TAR	Hans Robert Jauss, *Towards an aesthetics of reception* (Minneapolis: University of Minnesota Press, 1982)
Text	Stanley Fish, *Is there a text in this class?* (Cambridge, MA: The Harvard University Press, 1980)

I

Problems with Formalism

"Bakhtin and the Formalists were made for each other." This is the way Katerina Clark and Michael Holquist begin the chapter entitled "The Formalists" in their biography of Bakhtin (*Mikhail Bakhtin* 186). The gist of the comment, borne out by the rest of the chapter and in fact by a good part of that book, is that the Formalists allowed Bakhtin to formulate the ideas that he had worked on up to that point in his career. Others more substantially tie Bakhtin's work to Russian Formalism. Although Victor Erlich does not tie Bakhtin specifically to Formalism as it was developed in the Soviet Union in the 1920s, he nevertheless says in the Introduction to his *Russian Formalism* that, were he "writing this book today, [he] would undoubtedly pause before the achievement of Mikhail Bakhtin ..." whose work "attests to a strong affinity for the mature phase of Formalist theorizing" (10). And Gary Saul Morson, in "The Heresiarch of the *Meta*," suggests that "to leave Bachtin [*sic*] out of an account of Russian Formalism is profoundly to misunderstand the nature and objectives of the movement ..." (408). Finally, Tony Bennett devotes a good portion of his *Formalism and Marxism* to pursuing the link between Bakhtin and his circle to both Formalism and to Marxism.

I mention the prominence of the ties between Mikhail Bakhtin and Russian Formalism not to dispute it. On the contrary, I think that there is a great deal of other evidence to link the two, and so in some ways Bakhtin and Formalism *were* "made for each other." That is, they grappled with similar questions of the nature of literature, and they came to prominence during a time in the history of Russia and the Soviet Union that is considered by some a time of renaissance for Russian literature and theory. However, for my purposes, what is most interesting in Bakhtin's quarrel with Formalism is that it sheds light on the two forces that would consistently pull at the work of Bakhtin throughout his career, namely phenomenology and Marxism. I am suggesting that if one takes a close look at the work of Mikhail Bakhtin at any stage in his theoretical development, one can see at once two identifiable strands in his work: one that could be roughly identified as an outgrowth of the neo-Kantian philosophy that was current in the late nineteenth and early twentieth centuries, and which was developed in different forms by Husserlian phenomenology and the work of Husserl's followers (see Holquist and Clark, "The influence of Kant"); and one that could be called Marxist (though perhaps it might be more accurately called "sociological," since – as we will see – it is far from any identifiably orthodox kind of Marxist theory), that stresses the liberatory nature of language and was developed in Bakhtin's close collaboration with Pavel Medvedev and Valentin Voloshinov. (In this work, I will leave the question of the origin of the disputed texts unaddressed: I will, however, cite the pertinent works as though they were coauthored – that is, as Bakhtin/Medvedev – since, despite Gary Saul Morson and Caryl Emerson's recent arguments, I am more persuaded by those who see them as the work of several different hands, among them Bakhtin's. See Perlina, "Bakhtin-Medvedev-Voloshinov"; Clark and Holquist, *Mikhail Bakhtin*; Morson and Emerson's *Mikhail Bakhtin* and *Rethinking Bakhtin*.)

The reason I undertake this study is that so many scholars from so many different "camps" have such difficulty in reconciling the various Bakhtins to one writer, or one set of ideas. The reason for this difficulty, I would suggest, is precisely Bakhtin's ambivalent position between phenomenology and Marxism.[1] One can begin to see the problems in such an ambivalence if one quickly looks at the object of study of each of these undertakings. Phenomenology generally studies the ways in which individual humans come to cognition of objects. More specifically with regard to the work of Roman Ingarden and to some extent the earlier work of Edmund Husserl, phenom-

---

1 Phenomenology and Marxism are certainly not, in the context of contemporary critical theory, mutually exclusive. In fact, theorists since Bakhtin have built literary and cultural theories on a foundation that imbricates these two methodologies. The example that comes most quickly to mind is Jauss's *Rezeptionsaesthetik* as it appears in *Towards an aesthetics of reception* as well as in his famous essay on "the idealist embarrassment" in Marxist aesthetics.

  I do want to suggest, however, that Bakhtin – who never read Jauss, or Merleau-Ponty for that matter – understood phenomenology as having for its object of knowledge a radically different set of data from those of historical materialism. I could make an arguable case that what I will go on to describe might be seen not as an impasse between phenomenology and Marxism but rather an unexplored potential connection that would make Bakhtin's work all the richer. The fact remains, however, that Bakhtin, from what I gather, never made the connection, and the contradictions that appear in his work are the result of this lacuna, one that must be accounted for prior to any project that would seek to present a single Bakhtin.

enological studies suggest how humans can make aesthetic judgments, and come to some aesthetic understanding, of works of art. In following this notion, Bakhtin proposes a human subject that is defined by its relation to other subjects and the ways in which that relation is manifested in the creation of language. The emphasis in this "strand" of Bakhtin's work falls on the shared, common purview of the interlocutors in any situation, and it seeks to discover how signs have been interiorized by these individual subjects and subsequently reuttered based on the relation of the subjects' position to one another.

In contrast to this, the Marxisms which I will discuss here have as their object of study the ways in which human social formations are constructed, and the ways in which ideology plays a part in those constructions. Phenomenology deals with the construction and nature of individual human consciousness, the latter with the construction of human social relations. The way in which the Marxist strand becomes apparent in Bakhtin's work is in his examination of the "characteristics" and "forms of the social intercourse by which ... meaning is realized." The emphasis here is on an analysis of the broader processes of subject-formation, focusing on the ways in which language-production and sign-production yield knowledge of social formations. The ambivalence between phenomenology and Marxism can be seen in Bakhtin's earliest encounter with Formalism – which itself was influenced both by phenomenology and Marxism, though in often abstruse ways – and it is with this encounter that I will begin my study of the pull in Bakhtin's work between phenomenology and Marxism.

From its inception before the Russian Revolution, the primary concerns of Russian Formalism were two: first, to establish the study of literature as a scientific study, one which had at its disposal its own autonomous methods and procedures; second, these methods were to be used to find what constituted "literariness." Specifically, Formalism wished to determine aesthetic and linguistic properties that distinguished literature and poetry from other forms of discourse, particularly from prosaic or "ordinary" language. These concerns were in reaction to what were seen by the Formalists as illegitimate trends in literary scholarship. The first of these trends was a "confusion" over just what constituted true literary study: at the time, much attention was given to the "external circumstances in which literature is produced" (Erlich, *Russian Formalism* 172), such as authorial-biographical studies, psychologistic studies, and cultural history. Boris Eichenbaum suggested that "the literary scholar qua literary scholar ought to be concerned solely with the inquiry into the distinguishing features of the literary materials" (*Literatura* 121). In order to make these features clear, the Formalists suggested that, rather than study the reader's or the author's psyche, scholars should determine the nature of what was in the work itself (Erlich 173).

The Formalists' attempt to solve the problem of how a work is "literary" suggests ways in which both a phenomenological approach and a sociological or Marxist one might be seen as alternatives to that problem. As Victor Erlich suggests, Gustav Spet and Victor Zhirmunski took great pains to distinguish between "literariness" that is the result of the material and construction of a work, and the "content" of the poetic work, what might be called its "imagery." It isn't what one is able to see in a literary work that makes it literary, they argue, but rather the *way* in which the author has made it be seen. For Zhirmunski, the visual images evoked by poetry are vague and subjective, as they hinge to a large degree on the single reader's individual – and perhaps idiosyncratic – associations. Nevertheless, since the "material of poetry is neither images nor emotions but words ..." (Erlich, *Russian Formalism* 174), it has at its disposal "the whole nexus of formal-logical relations inherent in the language and incapable of expression in any other branch of art."

In this way, Formalism moves the emphasis of literary study from its content to its form, or, more specifically, its language. The notion of the "device" thereby became the central tool for literary analysis, since it is by means of the device that readers become aware of objects in works, the technique that makes the thing perceivable and artistic. "The device of art is the device of 'defamiliarization' of objects and the device of the form made difficult, a device that increases the difficulty and length of perception; for the process of perception is in art an end in itself and must be prolonged" (Shklovsky, "Art as technique" 12). This estrangement effect does two things. First, it focuses on how the poet uses language in ways other than the "everyday" to force the reader to negotiate unfamiliar phrases and to make the necessary mental connections in order to do so. The artist tears the object out of its normal context by bringing together, for example, disparate notions in a single phrase or stanza of poetry, thereby avoiding cliché and the regularized responses of the reader or interlocutor. This, in turn, acutely focuses the reader's or interlocutor's awareness on things and their sensory texture (Erlich, *Russian Formalism* 177). Or, as Erlich suggests, "The distinctive feature of poetry lies in the fact that a word is perceived as a word and not merely a proxy for the denoted object of an outburst of an emotion, that words and their arrangement, their meaning, their outward and inward form acquire weight and value of their own" (177). Second, estrangement – in drawing attention to the form of the language in a work – compels the reader to ignore the ideological implications of the device, or in fact of the work as a whole. In "Art as Technique," Shklovsky cites several examples from Tolstoy, among them instances of inconsistency and hypocrisy in human behavior. Though Formalism generally did not completely disavow the connection between their own science of linguistics in a given text and that text's connection to the larger social world, the effect of Formalist study was to de-emphasize such concerns. And, in fact, the theory of literary evolution advanced by the Formalists based on the replacement of worn-out devices with different, new ones – explaining why Sterne's radical departure from traditional narrative technique became outmoded in the eighteenth century and why it had to be replaced by a new device – relies on purely literary categories without reference to historical and social changes generally.

This dichotomy between "everyday" and "poetic" language – and the attendant distance between ideological concerns and more purely poetic ones – can be seen in the early Formalist negotiation, as a result of this distance, of "form" versus "content." For, if Formalism's main concern was the study of those devices immanent in a work – more precisely, those devices that would force the reader's attention to their "difference" from ordinary language – then how could such a study begin to take account of something (that is, ordinary language) that was extraneous to literature? Attendant to this problem is one that asks from what experience a reader judges whether something is "different" or not. In other words, if literary works are defined by their literary nature, then just what is the material out of which such works are made? That there was no unanimity on this score, as Erlich suggests, suggests not just confusion but a real crisis in the theory. Erlich goes on to quote Shklovsky on the nature of material, and in the contradiction that follows is a telling critique of Formalism generally. Shklovsky suggested that "The outside world is for the painter not the content, but merely material for his painting" ("Art as technique"

189). The same applies to psychoideological components of literature usually classified under the heading "content." Ideas and emotions – and, one could add, history, depictions of the socioideological world – "expressed in a work of literature, as well as events depicted in it," are treated as "building materials" for the job of artistic construction, phenomena of the same order as word-combinations ("Art as technique" 189). Just before this Shklovsky notes that "it seems obvious to me that for a writer words are not a necessary evil, or merely a means of saying something, but the very material of the work. Literature is made up of words and is governed by the laws which govern language" ("Art as technique" 188–9).

Here is the contradiction: which is it that makes up the material for the literary work of art, words or things? Needless to say, "things" don't appear in literary works of art, but the fact remains that Shklovsky seems to want to treat words – that is, the way in which language functions, following rules of semantics and so on – in the same way that he treats linguistic depictions of objects, people, situations. In a sense this is a fundamental misunderstanding of a concept introduced by Husserl – someone to whose work the Formalists had access, mainly through Gustav Spet – namely the difference between the "object" (*Gegenstand*), the non-verbal phenomenon denoted by the word, and the "meaning" (*Bedeutung*), the way in which the object is presented. This confusion illustrates several problems for the Formalist position.

First, without some underlying theory of how aesthetics in general function, it was difficult to say how human cognition was able to distinguish between "everyday" constructs and "aesthetic" constructs. Without some idea of how the human mind processed information about objects or other people, Formalism was not able to discern the difference between human reaction to "normal" or everyday stimuli, and those that were supposed to be estranged. Moreover, what is everyday to me might not be everyday to some other reader or interlocutor. Terry Eagleton's example of the sign "Way Out" in a London underground station may seem quite everyday to a Londoner on his way home from a pub, but to someone from California, also in the underground on his way home from a London pub, this sign might be seen as a kind of commentary from on high on his present condition (*Literary theory* 7). The point is that without knowing the difference between how the Londoner and the Californian process the information, we can't say categorically whether this language is in some way "aesthetic" or not.

A second problem with the Formalist position is how to deal with language. In the Husserlian scheme – much as in the Saussurean one – language is not the same as the non-verbal object of language. This does away with the distinction between "form" and "content," a distinction with which the Formalists were eager to dispense, but it blurs the commonsense line between the sign that says "Way Out" and the language we use to make reference to it. To treat material objects, as the Formalists did in their early stage, as phenomena of the same order as words or word-combinations is to reduce everything around us to language, which is surely not the case. (It may be – as it will be tempting for Bakhtin to suggest – that objects are not discernible outside of our ability to conceive of them linguistically. See Bakhtin/Voloshinov, *Marxism and the philosophy of language* 11.) I can know that the word-processor on which I am writing this can exist independent of my being able to talk about it; moreover, the material circumstances of its existence are not dependent upon, nor are they defined by, the language I may use to describe them.

Finally, though the Formalists did begin to theorize the ways in which literature is a three-way relationship between not just writer and text, but between writer, text and reader (by discussing the ways in which the device bridges the gap between reader and writer [Holub, *Reception theory* 18]), there is no broader discussion of the ways in which the everyday language of one reader might be "estranged" differently from another's. Quite apart from the Londoner and the Californian happening upon "Way Out" and discovering that they read differently, one can easily imagine two native English speakers reading the same book and coming to quite different interpretations of it. The different readings may be the result of one reader having a different "language background" from the other, but explaining things in these terms raises larger questions, such as are there extra-aesthetic reasons for such a difference? If the answer to this question is in the affirmative, then the Formalist solution of severing linguistic concerns from various other social concerns seems a hasty one.

In fact, these kinds of problems were very similar to some Bakhtin had with the formal method. In two seminal works – Bakhtin's "The problem of content, material and form in verbal artistic creation" (1924) and Bakhtin/Medvedev's *The formal method in literary schol-arship* (1928) – Formalism is addressed by Bakhtin and his circle on these very terms. And it is in these two works that one can begin to see the dual strands of phenomenology and Marxism at work in Bakhtin's attempted solution to the problems not only of Formalism but of literary study in general. Moreover, it is these two strands of Bakhtin's thinking that will come into contact throughout his career and that will cause such difficulty for those who would like to see in his philosophy of language a unified theory.

It is the second of these two strands that he and Pavel Medvedev address in the fourth chapter of *The formal method of literary scholarship*. Though I will pay a great deal more attention to this text in later chapters, it is important at this early stage to lay out the specific challenge Bakhtin/Medvedev makes to Formalism in Russia, and to see the beginnings of the Marxist language he uses in that challenge. Early on in that chapter, Boris Eichenbaum is quoted with approval for what he sees as the problems with contemporary scholarship: "'Academic' scholarship, having completely ignored theoretical problems and sluggishly made use of outmoded esthetic, psychological, and historical 'axioms,' had by the time of the formalists' debut so completely lost contact with the actual object of research that its very existence had become phantasmal" (55-6). Bakhtin/ Medvedev praises Formalism for having brought literary scholarship back into contact with literary texts, which it had often ignored, and for having raised the level of discourse in literary studies to a degree it had not previously reached in Russia. But there is more emphasis on the problems with Formalism than on praise for it, and one of the greatest of these problems is that Formalism, in its "struggle against idealist detachment of meaning from [the] material ... negated ideological meaning itself. As a result the problem of the concrete materialized meaning, the meaning-object, was not raised, and in its place we find the mere object, which is not quite a natural body, and not quite a product for individual consumption" (64). The concentration on the device which would make a work "literary" led away from concerns of what kind of ideological material was used to construct that work. Bakhtin/Medvedev concludes that if the Formalists were led to "show the significance of constructive devices by putting 'everything else to the side as motivation,' then it is now absolutely necessary to return all this 'everything else,' i.e., all the richness and depth of ideological meaning, to the foreground of research" (65). Certainly, suggests Bakhtin/Medvedev, "[i]t is necessary to be able to isolate the object of study and correctly establish its boundaries," but these boundaries must be established in such a way that they "do not sever the object from vital connections with other objects, connections without which it becomes unintelligible" (77). Bakhtin/Medvedev established early on that literary works are works of ideological creation: they are material things, part of the practical reality that surrounds humans because they are constructed linguistically, and language is part and parcel of the ideological material that surrounds – and creates – humans (7).

The point here is that poetic language is only one aspect of language in general. Moreover, the linguistic study of poetry – or of any literary object – is only one way to study such an object. Though it is certainly the case that the way in which a work is constructed may serve to define it as literary or non-literary, it is also the case that any utterance may also be constructed in just such a way, and may also be seen, in certain cases, as aesthetic or not aesthetic. Formalism's mistake, then, was to have separated aesthetic objects from all other utterances, and to have studied only the former. All definitions – aesthetic, non-aesthetic, beautiful, everyday – "only pertain to the organization of the utterance and work in their connection with the functions they fulfill in the unity of social life and, in particular, in the concrete unity of the ideological horizon" (Bakhtin/Medvedev, *The formal method* 84).

What is missing from the Formalists' conception of language is history. Language isn't spoken in a void, but is borne by concrete historical and social conditions at the time and place of its utterance. More importantly, the "meaning of the word- utterance is also joined to history through the unique act of its realization, becoming a historical phenomenon" (Bakhtin/Medvedev, *The formal method* 120). History must be discerned through an analysis of the particular time and place of an utterance's generation, but also of the individuals engaged in a given discourse. This social evaluation "actualizes the utterance both from the standpoint of its factual presence and the standpoint of its semantic meaning," not just "the word, grammatical form, sentence, and all linguistic definiteness taken in general abstraction from the concrete historical utterance" (121). It defines the "choice of subject, word, form, and their individual combination within the bounds of the given utterance. It also defines the choice of content, the selection of form, and the connection between form and content" (121). Certainly, suggests Bakhtin/Medvedev, this kind of analysis is not solely the province of aesthetics; nevertheless, complete aesthetic analysis cannot go without such a social evaluation. The deeper and more fruitful social evaluations are "determined by the economic existence of a class in the given epoch of its existence. One may say that the major historical aims of a whole epoch in the life of the given social group are formed in these evaluations" (121).

Formalism misunderstands what the poet does. She or he does not choose linguistic forms – or poetic devices – but rather "selects, combines, and arranges the evaluations lodged in [those forms] as well. And the resistance of the material we feel in every poetic work" – what Formalism in some cases might call estrangement – "is in fact the resistance of the social evaluations it contains" (Bakhtin/ Medvedev, *The formal method* 123). Bakhtin/Medvedev asks that we imagine two different social groups who have at their disposal the same language-material with the same lexicon, morphology, syntax and so on.

Under these conditions, if the differences between our two social groups arise from important socioeconomic premises of their existences, the intonation of one and the same word will differ profoundly between groups; within the very same grammatical constructions the semantic and stylistic combinations will be profoundly different. One and the same word will occupy a completely different hierarchical place in the utterance as a concrete social act.   (123)

Each group lives under a different set of material conditions, brought about by their niche in the economic hierarchy. One might picture members of two groups reading a report in a Sunday newspaper about a debate on state funding for abortion counseling. One reader is of the working class, perhaps has parents who never went to college, and feels very strongly about "family values" and "the life of the unborn." Another is a member of the upper class, whose parents went to college and who herself found a position after college working for a bank, and who has begun to subscribe to the philosophy that governments should not interfere in personal and business decisions. In reading such a report on the controversy in the very same edition of the very same paper (assuming that they both subscribe to the same paper, which might not be the case), each might have very different reactions to such an utterance, and might in turn have quite different things to say. What is important here is not what each member of the different "groups" will say, but that such a social evaluation is necessary to be able to say something about the language of the text each is reading.

Moreover, this kind of analysis shows that what is at stake is not necessarily the nature of the language of the text. What is more important is the way language functions differently for different groups, and the different ideological material that goes into the judgments each makes about given utterances.

Formalism ignores the fact that all utterances are part of a broad and complex social intercourse in which language plays an important role. Poetic texts are part of such intercourse, though they may be defined as a separate genre of utterance apart from various others. Nevertheless, poetic utterances come into contact – since the author of such utterances is part of the social intercourse, as is the reader, whose language functions along with that of the author – with that everyday language. This is in a sense the primary rule for Bakhtin/Medvedev: all language is material and is part of the ideological stuff of which humans make decisions about the world they live in. And this gives literary scholars a way to make decisions about how literary language diverges from "everyday" language but is at once affected by it. It provides access to the poetic utterance in a way that Formalism did not. This "Marxist" solution resolves, at least partly, the first Formalist problem.

The second strand of Bakhtin's thinking, phenomenology, can also be seen in his encounter with the Formalists. In fact, the early essay, "The problem of content," in which he addresses Formalism directly, is seen by some as an early version of *The formal method* (see Clark and Holquist, *Mikhail Bakhtin* 189). What is interesting, aside from the problem of the authorship of the second volume, is the stark difference in the ground of the argument with the Formalists between the first and second volumes.[2] Whereas in *The formal method* Bakhtin/ Medvedev was concerned with the way language in general, and aesthetic language in particular, could be studied by examining the ways social intercourse was determined by the material (including language) out of which that intercourse was constructed, the "phenomenology" of "The problem of content" stresses the ways in

---

2 This is not to say, however, that the "phenomenological" ground of "The problem of content, material and form" is not also covered in *The formal method*. In fact, both pay attention to the ways in which Formalism suffers from a lack of a theory of general aesthetics. However, in the later volume, that lack is discussed within the context of a Marxist aesthetics, one which, at some points in his career, Bakhtin saw as the resolution to the "crisis" of literary studies.

which individual human subjects come to perceive the aesthetic object itself.

The problem that leads the Formalists into self-contradictory notions of the nature of language and the construction of the aesthetic object is "the product of an incorrect or, at best, a methodologically indeterminate relationship between the poetics they are constructing and general, systematic, philosophical aesthetics" (Bakhtin, *Art and answerability* 258). Bakhtin puts it this way:

[W]ithout a systematic concept of the aesthetic in its distinctness from the cognitive and the ethical as well as in its interconnectedness within the unity of culture, it is impossible even to isolate the object to be studied by poetics (the works of verbal *art*) from the mass of verbal works of other kinds.

(259)

It is this work of isolating the individual object of study, of course, that occupied the Formalists in their earliest incarnation. In order to recover the ability to systematize the study of the aesthetic object, Bakhtin suggests that literary scholars should start from the beginning and create "an aesthetics of artistic verbal creation" (260).

What is needed, suggests Bakhtin, is a more accurate definition of the material used in artistic creation. Aesthetic creations are collections of material – not simply language – organized by the artist toward some intention. Bakhtin uses the image of a sculptor working with marble: certainly the sculptor is working with his material, but it is not the material that is important in defining the statue as aesthetic, nor in understanding how the sculptor or the contemplator have cognition of that statue. Rather,

the sculptural form created is an *aesthetically* valid form of *man and his body*: it is in this direction that the intention of creation and contemplation proceeds, whereas the artist's and the contemplator's relationship to the marble as a determinate physical body has a secondary, derivative character, governed by some sort of primary relationship to objective values – in the given case, to the value of corporeal man. (265)

The marble shape of the human form is the "external work"; the aesthetic object is the totality of the material and the intentional activity directed toward the work, including cognition and creation. Left out of the Formalist equation of literary study, then, are (1) the non-coincidence of the aesthetic object with the material that is used to produce that object, and (2) the corresponding non-coincidence of the contemplator's and creator's intention toward such an aesthetic object and the intention toward the material. What is accessible to Formalism – what Bakhtin here calls a "material aesthetics" (since it deals only with the material out of which an aesthetic object is constructed) – is "the second of the tasks of aesthetic analysis." The first of these is the aesthetic study of the distinct nature of a given work and its structure, or a work's consummation, which Bakhtin calls the "architectonics" of the aesthetic object. The second task is "the study of a work as an object of natural science or linguistics," or the "composition" of a work (267-8). To give just one example of the difference between the architectonic and the compositional, "*Drama* is a compositional form (dialogue, division into acts, etc.) but the *tragic* and *comic* are architectonic forms of consummation" (269). "Architectonic forms are forms of the inner and bodily value of aesthetic man, they are forms of nature – as his environment, forms of the event in his individual-experiential, social and historical dimensions and so on. They all are achievements, actualizations ... They are forms of aesthetic being in its distinctiveness" (270).

At this point there are similarities that should be noted between Bakhtin's "Marxist" quarrel with Formalism and the beginnings of this "phenomenological" one. In the first place, Bakhtin takes the Formalists to task here for separating the object of study from "the broad highway of unified human culture." Instead, they "cling to linguistics, fearing to move more than one step away" (261). This is precisely the same complaint Bakhtin/Medvedev makes in *The formal method*. Second, Bakhtin here stresses that Formalism should not take as its beginning premise the separateness of artistic and "everyday" language, suggesting that "verbal creation" should subsume aesthetic studies within itself. Again, *The formal method* called for just such a subsumption. What should be noted here, for our purposes, however, are not the similarities between the calls for a broader conception of aesthetic analysis, but the differences between how these analyses are formulated. Finally, as in *The formal method*, Bakhtin stresses that sociological analysis – what he calls "aesthetic vision outside of art" – is not properly the unique domain of aesthetic analysis; nevertheless aesthetic analysis cannot be complete if either sociological analysis or aesthetic analysis outside of art is not considered.

It is precisely the "aesthetic vision outside of art" that occupies Bakhtin in the longest of his early essays, "Author and hero" (in *Art and answerability*), one of the most thoroughly "phenomenological" texts in the Bakhtin canon (see Bernard-Donals, Review). What unifies aesthetic activity, both within the realm of art and outside it, is the act of human cognition, which is the crux of the study of general aesthetics ignored by the Formalists. For Bakhtin, there are three aspects to human aesthetic activity. The first of these is cognition, which is the act of finding reality "already organized in the concepts of prescientific thinking" ("The problem of content," in *Art and answerability* 275). That is, cognition is the faculty of the human mind that organizes objects without regard to axiological relations to other humans or, for that matter, to any action that might be taken with regard to their organization. It is purely scientific, organized knowledge that, similar to the Husserlian idea of cognition, refers to "essences," those concepts that are universal from human mind to human mind. The second aspect of activity is the ethical, which is the range of actions that can be taken in response to the cognitive understanding of some event or object. Bakhtin suggests that "it is usually expressed *as the relation of the ought* [sic] *to reality*" (278), but then does not go on to elaborate. The third aspect is the aesthetic, which actualizes the cognitive understanding and the ethical action into a consummation of the two. In a sense, aesthetic activity in humans gives form or shape to cognitive–ethical unity by transposing the identified (by cognition) and evaluated (by ethics) reality "to another axiological level, subordinat[ing] it to a new unity and order[ing] it in a new way: it individualizes, concretizes, isolates, and consummates it, *but does not alter the fact that this reality has been identified and evaluated*, and it is precisely toward this prior identification and evaluation that the consummating aesthetic form is directed" (278). To put this another way, aesthetic consummation completes cognitive and ethical aspects of an object by placing those aspects into relation with the individual human subject, the acting consciousness.[3]

3 The author's relation to the aesthetic object is unique in this equation, and will be discussed in relation to the position of the perceiver in subsequent chapters. At this point, however, I will quote at length a section on the author's relation to the aesthetic object, since it is important to understand that all subjects involved in the phenomenological reception of a work must occupy a position *outside* that object:
    The artist, understood "in the world in connection with all the values of cognition and ethical action" "unit[es], individualize[s], render[s] whole, isolate[s], and consummate[s] ... the comprehensively experienced axiological makeup of reality – *the event of reality*.
    "Aesthetically valid form is the expression of an essential relation to the world of cognition and action. However, this relation is not cognitive and not ethical: the artist does not intervene in the event as an immediate participant in it, for then he would become someone who is engaged in cognition and who acts ethically. The artist assumes an essential *position outside* the event as a contemplator who is disinterested but who *understands the axiological sense of what is coming to pass* – as a contemplator who does not experience the

To return to the Formalists, Bakhtin notes that the principal result of not having a theory of general aesthetics from which to build their analyses of literary objects is that the term "content" is confused. This makes difficult the distinction between the material of the object (that is, language) and the object's content (that is, the depiction of material reality in a work, a depiction of which humans can have cognition, but which is not immediately coincident with language). One has to distinguish clearly between the cognitive ethical moment of an aesthetic object – which for Bakhtin is defined as content, the "constitutive moment in a given aesthetic object" (*Art and answerability* 285) – and judgments and ethical assessments that one can construct in order to say something *about* content. These latter assessments and utterances about the content of the object are not part of the aesthetic object. Moreover, content – which is devoid of the aesthetic consummating activity of the perceiver or of the author – can be talked about separately from the aesthetic object, since it is not related axiologically to the perceiver or author. Content is paraphrasable; the aesthetic object is not. Similarly, ideological material is also paraphrasable and analyzable; the aesthetic object is not. Thus this "phenomenological" remedy resolves the second Formalist blind spot.

By suggesting that ideological material is paraphrasable and analyzable, but that the aesthetic object is not (at least on the same terms), we have pinpointed the crux of the problem for Bakhtin's body of work. The materialist or "Marxist" component of his work, in which he discusses the ways in which various languages come into contact and reveal difficulties and contradictions in verbal material as well as other ideological material, seems to be at odds with the phenomenological component, in which he discusses the individual subject relations that construct utterances. Certainly one would think that the two are compatible: if one simply applies the work on individual subject relations and cognition to the work on broader social relations constructed by and with language, then one can conceivably build a unified and consistent Bakhtinian language theory. And there are those that have tried to do just that.

However, when one looks a bit closer, one finds that this kind of extrapolation is not so simple. The most notable problem is the

event but co-experiences it, for, without co-evaluating to some extent, one cannot contemplate an event as an *event* specifically" ("Author and hero" 281–2).

disjunction between the way in which language functions as ideological material to form humans – an idea that is present both in the "phenomenological" and the "Marxist" work – and the importance of the real material conditions of existence of human subjects individually and as social entities. In "The problem of content," Bakhtin goes a long way toward proposing how human mental activity can "aestheticize" everyday activities, what Michael Holquist calls "the work we all as men do, the work of answering and authoring the text of our social and physical universe" ("Answering as authoring" 70). And, in "Author and hero in aesthetic activity" Bakhtin goes on to suggest how human subjects are constructed specifically through their interiorization and subsequent reuttering of language, a process that is similar in many ways to "phenomenological" and subsequent reception-oriented aesthetic theories (see especially 4–42; see also Shepherd, "Bakhtin and the reader"). But "answering and authoring" our social and physical universe is a different order of activity altogether from changing – let alone improving – the social and .physical universe. Texts in the Bakhtin canon – notably the essays included in *The dialogic imagination* – suggest that the dialogization of language and literature can lead and in fact has led to social change throughout human history; the Rabelais book seems to suggest that dialogization and carnivalization of various speech and literary genres can work toward overthrowing monologic and authoritarian modes of discourse as well as modes of government. Both the phenomenological and the Marxist tendencies make use of the doctrine of "unfinishedness," the former with regard to the creation of the human subject, the latter with regard to the formation of the social world. It is uncertain, however, as to whether the constant dialogization and interlinguistic changing of individual human subjects will or can lead to social change of the kind implied in the Rabelais text.

Though Bakhtin has pinpointed the problem the Formalists had in confusing content with material (that is, the ideological material of the work and the language of the work), he makes a similar error in failing adequately to distinguish between language (which is ideological material) and ideological material in general. And those who would want to unify these aspects of Bakhtin's work into some holistic philosophy of language make the same error by conflating language and ideological material. One can go along with the idea that the interiorization and dialogized reutterance of language can change human cognition without subscribing to the view that this change in cognition will necessarily lead to a change in the material conditions of existence for those human subjects. It is one thing, for example, to dialogize the term "poverty," but it is altogether another to be able to dialogize the material condition of poverty into the material condition of plenty. Bakhtin's encounter with the Formalists placed him in a difficult position. On the one hand, he attempted to construct a philosophy of language that would suggest ways in which the utterance would not be divorced from the verbal aesthetic object. On the other, he had to suggest a way in which the aesthetic nature of such an object could be studied in relation to the human faculty of cognition. Bakhtin/Medvedev accomplished the former by suggesting that the subject's material conditions have much to do with one's understanding of any utterance, in a sense beginning to construct a materialist theory of social construction. Bakhtin accomplished the latter by centering his theory of general aesthetics around a theory of cognition, in a sense beginning to construct a philosophy of language.

It remains the task of this book to examine the ways in which this contradiction – perhaps a better term would be ambivalence – in Bakhtin's work between "phenomenological" and "Marxist" analyses of human interaction and subject construction play themselves out. In this examination I will take a closer look at how Bakhtin's immediate predecessors influence his work and in what ways that influence contributes to his ambivalent position; and I will examine the ways in which this position sheds light on contemporary phenomenological/reception theories and historical materialist accounts of language and ideology.

2

Neo-Kantianism and Bakhtin's phenomenology

Bakhtin's interest in phenomenology – or, more specifically, the way in which the human mind comes to consciousness in a relationship with objects or other human subjects – stems from his immersion at the beginning of the twentieth century in neo-Kantianism, the dominant school of philosophy at the time. In the 1910s and 1920s, neo-Kantianism was largely imported from Germany, in particular from Marburg; at one time or another at the turn of the century almost all the chairs of departments of philosophy, both in Germany and in Russia, were occupied by neo-Kantians. Of the philosophers from the Marburg school, the most influential for Bakhtin was Hermann Cohen. In general, what interested Bakhtin and his colleagues during their gatherings in the years immediately following the Revolution was Kant's concern for founding a relationship between a theory of knowledge and a theory of ethics based in *The critique of pure reason* and *The critique of practical reason*. In the first of these works, Kant shows that human understanding cannot go beyond the phenomena of sensory experience, and thus questions about transcendent objects – God, for example – will necessarily be unanswerable. If one takes this transcendent knowledge as ultimate reality, then reality is unknowable, and as a result there can be no rational metaphysics. In the second book, Kant's aim was to remedy the problem established in the first. In order to provide access to what were now unknowable objects by way of theoretical reason, Kant suggests that the activity of consciousness that directs humans' moral life, practical reason, removes knowledge in order to make room for faith. Kant emphasizes the primacy of consciousness – the activity of the mind – in the process of gaining access to phenomena. Kant insists on a necessary interaction between the mind and the world by arguing that thought is a synthesis of the two sources of knowledge, namely sensibility and understanding.

It is primarily this relation of the mind and the world – or, in other terms, between the "I" and the "other" – that will characterize Bakhtin's relationship to neo-Kantian philosophy in particular and to phenomenological theories of the human subject in general. More directly, it is Bakhtin's relationship with the thinking of Hermann Cohen that will establish the seminal concept of "dialogue" or "dialogism" that is featured so prominently in Bakhtin's thought. Speaking of Cohen, Katerina Clark and Michael Holquist, in the Bakhtin biography, suggest that "perhaps [he is] less a neo-Kantian than an anti-Kantian insofar as he abhorred the dualism in Kant's account of how internal thought relates to external experience" (58). Despite the prominence of these two concepts – and their evolution over the course of Bakhtin's writings – it is rather the relationship between the "I" and the "other" (the foundation for the notion of dialogue) that is the most distinguishing import from Cohen's neo-Kantianism. It not only characterizes a phenomenology of aesthetic contemplation for Bakhtin, but more broadly characterizes all of human activity. It is this relationship to which Bakhtin clings in the remainder of his writings – though this relationship is less often explicitly named than it is submerged as a given in any of his texts – and which serves as an important touchstone in his philosophy of language, a touchstone that will serve to complicate and problematize that philosophy as well as the critical theory of all who deploy Bakhtin's work for their own ends. It remains the task of this chapter to examine briefly the roots of Bakhtin's neo-Kantian phenomenology; to lay out Bakhtin's theory of "I-and-other" as it exists in the early essay entitled "Author and hero in aesthetic activity" (*ca.* 1920); and to suggest the points of convergence and divergence in Bakhtin's phenomenology and that of Edmund Husserl.

I

Kant's notion of thought is in fact a synthesis of two different kinds of knowledge. The first of these, sensibility, is the realm of physical sensation. The second, understanding, is roughly equivalent to what rationalists assumed to be the sole basis of knowledge, the realms of concepts in the mind. The ability to make judgments requires both forms of knowledge, which Kant brought together in a "transcendental synthesis": a priori concepts do exist in the mind, but they can be used actively to organize sensations from the world outside the mind. The realm of things-in-themselves really does exist, but so does the mind in order to give shape to it (cited in Holquist's introduction to *Art and answerability*, xii).

Cohen deplored the division between mind and world, and hoped to unify the two. To do so, he discarded the thing-in-itself in favor of the mind, the realm of concepts which is only logical. The overthrow of the thing-in-itself was in part a result of a reaction to positivism, the philosophical school that had held sway in Germany since the advent of left-Hegelianism in the middle of the nineteenth century. Cohen proclaimed that "theoretical idealism has begun to shake the materialism of the scientists and perhaps will soon finally overcome it" (cited in Holquist and Clark, "The influence of Kant" 304). Instead, "the world is not given but conceived," was a slogan aimed to suggest that the world was not a prefabricated object of human thought. Consciousness instead consists of our coming upon some object, and then – by applying formal categories of thought in a series of syntheses – turning that object into a subject of human under-standing. The object is not the thing-in-itself but the limit of conceptualization; as such, coming to an understanding of it is never complete but always approximate. This "incompleteness," however, is not a negative aspect of understanding; on the contrary, it is in the constant process of conceptualization and understanding that humans renew themselves and the world.

However, in order to find a "unity of cultural consciousness" one has to solve the problem of solipsism: if all human understanding is an interaction between objects of knowledge exterior to the mind (which nevertheless are not the things-in-themselves and as a result are cognized "approximations") and the organizing principles or concepts of the mind, then there is a danger that the neo-Kantian "phenom-enology of mind" would dissolve into an abstract philosophy without any relation to the real world. In trying desperately to do away with the materialism left over from the nineteenth century, Cohen and his colleagues ran the risk of going over into the other extreme, in which all that mattered was the way in which the mind functioned and having little, if anything, to do with the way the world itself functioned as an object of that knowledge.

In order to come to terms with this potential problem, one of Cohen's colleagues, Paul Natorp, suggested that "both, namely thought [which is equivalent here to the operation of the mind] and being [which means here objects of knowledge exterior to the mind], exist and have meaning only in their constant, mutual relations to one another. Being is not something static, set over against the activity of thought; it exists only in a process of becoming which is intrinsically related to its activity" (cited in Holquist and Clark, "The influence of Kant" 304). What is thus most important is how humans come into being in their *everyday* relations with one another and with the world, and with this formulation Kantian practical reason makes axiology "the queen of metaphysics" (Holquist and Clark 304). In a way, Bakhtin was more true to this aspect of Kantian thought – that "philosophy can live only as the science of values" (304) – than was Cohen: whereas Cohen favored the mind while still giving some degree of emphasis to exterior objects (including other subjects), Bakhtin – as we will see shortly – tried to claim a greater role for the world in the mind/world balance.

Kant, as we know, was never able to resolve the distinction between mind and world; later in his life the gap between mind and world took the form of a gap between God (as object of theological belief) and human (or, more precisely, the human mind). This unbridgeable gap as it appears here between "belief" and "under-standing" was taken up by Hermann Cohen, and this had a significant effect on Bakhtin's philosophical genesis, only on different terms. Cohen struggled in his work between a defense of God as an intellectual concept and the desire for a more direct experience of God which Holquist suggests "can be felt in every page of Cohen's *Religion and reason*" ("The influence of Kant" 308). Cohen saw two traditions – one, the tradition of western metaphysics, the culmination of which was Kant; the other, the Hebrew tradition, the origins of which lie in the Torah. The first of these was a tradition of pure reason, the second a tradition of everyday lived experience. In his view, these two needed to be united. I will not suggest that Mikhail Bakhtin continued Cohen's search for a union between humans and the Godhead – though this is something for which Holquist makes muffled claims – simply because, in the bulk of his work the references to the way God makes his presence felt in human activity are used *as examples to illustrate* how his aesthetic theory functions (see Bernard-Donals, Review 1118-19). Nevertheless, Cohen's search for the experience of God is important for understanding Bakhtin's phenomenological thinking. Bakhtin sought God – or, perhaps more accurately, an experience that one could liken to that of the divine in the everyday – in the space between humans that might be bridged by the word, by utterance. This space can be bridged only through energy and communication.

For Cohen what was seen as a divergence of two levels of experience – the holy and the everyday – was for Bakhtin a difference between an "aesthetic" experience and an experience based solely in cognition.

In "Author and hero in aesthetic activity," Bakhtin suggests that aesthetic activity as it appears both in the language of verbal artefacts and in the everyday activity of humans is by and large the same kind of activity. In the same way that, in literature, the author of a work gives certain characteristics and actions – in Bakhtin's terms, "intonates" – to the hero or heroine and other characters, so too in life humans "react valuationally to every self-manifestation on the part of those around us" (4). We "define" those around us, but it's not so much a definition as a proposal or "a prognosis of what we can and what we cannot expect from him ... [W]e are interested not in the whole of a human being, but only in those particular actions on his part with which we are compelled to deal in living our life and which are, in one way or another, of special interest to us" (5). The way in which we do come to such a prognosis is "through our relationship to it [or him]: it is our relationship that determines an object [or other human subject] and its structure, not conversely" (5). This relationship is one that is "consummated," or completed, by assembling all the determinations and valuations of the object or other and forming them into a unitary and unique entity that is "a concrete, intuitable whole, but also a whole of meaning" (5).

II

As I suggested earlier, Bakhtin was more willing than was Cohen to see ways in which objects or beings in the world played a part in the "phenomenology of the mind" that grew out of neo-Kantianism. Bakhtin stresses the axiology of human relations as the basis for a theory of human understanding, whereas Cohen, in his eschewing of the material of everyday life, had difficulty not only in reconciling understanding to the objects of understanding, but also with broader questions of how humans could form intersubjective relations (for Cohen, "experiences of holiness"). Moreover, Bakhtin grounds his ideas of human subjective relations, and the ways in which they are "consummated" through language, in a materialism that was discarded by the Marburg neo-Kantians, in this case the science of biology.

When humans come into contact, they are necessarily oriented in time and space differently from one another: in the simplest terms, each can see different things, and so each understands his or her situation differently, by dint of their discrete locations. I. I. Kanaev – a member of Bakhtin's circle in the early and middle 1920s, and whose name appears on an article on "vitalism" which has been attributed to Bakhtin – suggested that biological organisms are defined as having (or not having) life in terms of their reactions to surrounding stimuli.[1] If an organism reacts, for example, to light, then that organism is "defined" by the reaction. If an organism, on the other hand, does not react to stimuli, then that organism is said to be dead. "Whatever engenders a particular response of the organism in a specific situation ... is the center of its life. This is what at a higher level of complexity, in human beings, is called the self" (quoted in Clark and Holquist, *Mikhail Bakhtin* 66): the combination of one's biology with its capacity for reaction.

It is in the correlation between the human capacity to "author" signs in order to consummate objects of knowledge, and the author's function in consummating the hero in aesthetic works, that we can begin to discuss the phenomenology of everyday life that Bakhtin constructs in "Author and hero." It should be noted that, very early on in this essay, Bakhtin makes an important distinction between two objects of study. "An author is the uniquely form-giving energy that is manifested not in a psychologically conceived consciousness, but in a durably valid cultural product, and his active, productive reaction is manifested in the structures it generates – in the structure of the active vision of a hero as a definite whole" (8). In a sense, we are given two distinct problems, one phenomenological, the other material. The first is a problem of how the author, at the moment of creation, consummates this other. The second is the problem of how a perceiver – in a very real sense, another "author," since he or she is giving form to an object – constructs this "durably valid cultural product." In that the problem of aesthetics is largely a problem of how one comes into contact with – how one reads – cultural products, Bakhtin's essay is concerned with the way in which the author's relation to the hero as it appears in literary works can be made the object of systematic study. But this is a categorically different problem from the purely phenomenological one. "An author creates, but he sees his own creating only in the object to which he is giving form ... At the time

---

1 The article, entitled "Contemporary vitalism," appeared in 1925 in two issues of the journal *Celovek i priroda* ("Man and nature"), 1:33–42 and 2:9–23.

the author was creating, he experienced only his hero, and he put his whole essentially necessary relationship to the hero into the image of the hero. When, on the other hand, he begins to speak about his heroes in an 'author's confession' ... he voices his present relationship to them as already created and determined" (6–7).

Thus there are two relationships involved, both of which must necessarily be part of literary study. Traditional literary study, Bakhtin argues, has only taken into consideration the second of these two problems. Moreover, Formalism hasn't bothered to inquire into either one of these areas: it has not formed a theory of human subject relations, of which the relation between author and hero is but one division; and it has not taken into account "such factors as the critical response to [the author's] work, [the author's] own present world view ... various practical considerations," in sum, the material history of a work (7). Bakhtin himself, in the bulk of the long essay here under consideration, undertakes to study the verbal material by which the author's relationship to the hero is constructed. And it could be argued that this is the kind of work he does in the so-called "literary" texts, where he studies the verbal material in Rabelais's, Dostoevsky's, and others' novels. But it is the actual moment of consummation that begins the aesthetic process (and, in general, the process of subject relations). And, though Bakhtin implicitly suggests that, having begun to lay out such a theory of aesthetic consummation, one can turn one's attention to the problems of material verbal constructs, it is the difficulty in reconciling the phenomenological and the material objects of study – the same problem that Kant, and the neo-Kantians (particularly Hermann Cohen) experienced – that creates problems in Bakhtin's *oeuvre*.

The author, for Bakhtin, is "the bearer and sustainer of the intently active unity of a consummated whole" ("Author and hero" 12), either the whole of a hero or of a work itself. The relationship between the author and hero is one where "the author occupies an intently maintained position *outside* the hero with respect to every constituent feature of the hero – a position *outside* the hero with respect to space, time, value and meaning" (14). Because of this exotopic relationship, the author sees and knows more than each hero individually and all the heroes collectively, "something that is in principle inaccessible to them" (12). Bakhtin calls this an "excess" of seeing and knowing. In concrete terms, we could conceivably call excess of seeing – in purely aesthetic terms – the "idea in the author's head" about how characters in a book will act, their motivations, desires, and so on. Though the author's idea will change and evolve over the course of writing his or her book, the individual moments in the creation of the book will constitute the author having "consummated" the heroes and characters in it.

Human subject relations are also characterized by just such an excess of seeing and knowing, but in different terms. "If I am consummated and my life is consummated, I am no longer capable of living and acting" ("Author and hero" 13). In order to live, one needs to be unconsummated – a person needs to be open for herself, one needs to be "axiologically yet-to-be, someone who does not coincide with his already existing makeup" (13). In fact, such self-coincidence is not possible: at the moment, for example, that I say that I am "I," that I am the person to whom I am referring, my circumstances have changed, time has passed, and the person to whom I refer has disappeared (or, more precisely, has ceased to coincide with the part of speech represented by the pronoun "I"). I can consummate "moments" in my relationship with some other (or some object), but, as we will see, these individual moments do not comprise the whole or completed human subject.

Bakhtin makes certain that aesthetic understanding – wherein objects or subjects are consummated (either in whole, as in aesthetic works, or in part, as in human activity) – is differentiated from cognitive–ethical understanding. "Cognitive and ethical objectivity is the impartial, dispassionate evaluation of a given person and a given event from the standpoint of an ethical and cognitive value which is or is held to be universally valid or tends toward universal validity" ("Author and hero" 13). In this sense, cognitive–ethical understanding parallels the neo-Kantian idea of essences: it is assumed that there are mental constructs that function the same way from individual to individual; further, any action taken (the ethical moment of cognitive–ethical understanding) will be the result of a certain universally understood process of reason and will occur within a certain range of actions. Cognitive–ethical understanding is not subordinated to an organized whole – in Bakhtin's sense – whether that be the (consummated) whole of an individual's life or to some greater whole (say, a divine plan, in which it could be imagined that God or some such divinity could act as an "author" and consummate the "heroes" and characters of its creation – something, I should add, in which Bakhtin, who was highly sympathetic to the Russian Orthodox church, believed). "By contrast, the center of value for aesthetic objectivity is the *whole* of the hero and the event of his lived life, and all values that are ethical and cognitive must be subordinated to that whole. Aesthetic objectivity, in other words, encompasses and comprises cognitive–ethical objectivity" (13). This is true of the lived life of human subjects as well. As I have suggested, though an entire life cannot be consummated, individual moments can, and the cognitive–ethical understanding of these moments is subordinated to the aesthetic consummation *at that moment*.

In order to consummate individual moments of one's lived relation to some other (or in order to understand aesthetically the moments of one's own lived life), one "must become *another* in relation to himself, must look at himself through the eyes of *another*" ("Author and hero" 15; my emphasis). Human subjects evaluate themselves in terms of how others might apprehend them, and it is through this "extrapolation" – you might call it a "best guess" as to how others see us – one tries to understand the elements that constitute one's consciousness. One takes into account the value of one's outward appearance as it might make an impression on the other, even though this appearance is not immediately available to the apprehending subject. Moreover, one has also to take into account "the background behind our back, that is to say, all that which in our surroundings we do not see and do not know directly and which has no axiological validity for us, although it is seen and known by others and has validity for others" (15-16).

But this is not the last move in aesthetic activity. "[T]hese moments or constituents of our life that we recognize and anticipate through the other are rendered completely immanent to our own consciousness, are translated, as it were, into its language: ... they do not disrupt the unity of our own life – a life that is directed ahead of itself toward the event yet-to-come, a life that finds no rest within itself and never coincides with its given, presently existing makeup" ("Author and hero" 16). We might be able to complete either a "reflection" of ourselves as seen by some other, or comprehend the other in the same way, but these reflections are not coincident with our selves as they are experienced by us. The second and more important step in aesthetic activity is to return the "reflection" to our own consciousness. As Bakhtin suggests:

Even if we succeeded in encompassing the whole of our consciousness as consummated in the other, this whole would not be able to take possession of us and really consummate us for ourselves: our consciousness would take that whole into account and would surmount it as just one of the moments in its own unity (which is not a unity that is *given* but a unity that is set as a *task* and, in its essentials, is *yet-to-be*).   (16; Bakhtin's emphasis)

We cannot consummate our own lives, or "say to itself the word" that would do so: consummating one's life is completing one's life, and in Bakhtin's terms, anything that is completed – in later terminology, what is monologic – is dead. After looking at oneself through the eyes of this other, the subject then returns to understand this reflection in one's own consciousness, so that, "as it were, [the] recapitulative event takes place within ourselves in the categories of our own life" (17).

In effect, individuals must take account of "reflections" of their lives "on the plane of other people's consciousness" even to the point of trying to extrapolate from those reflections their complete (consummated) lives. As I have tried to make clear, this consummated moment of our lives, as we try to make sense of these moments as others might make sense of them, is quite different from the way in which we are in fact truly presented to others. Moreover, it is quite different from the way in which we experience our own lives. Cognitive–ethical moments are distinct from aesthetic moments: with the former, humans are able to make decisions about the nature of objects based on universal concepts, and to act according to those universally valid apprehensions. Cognition constructs "a world independent in every respect from that concrete and unique position which is occupied by this or that individual ... However, this unitary world of cognition cannot be *perceived* as a unique concrete whole ... For what the actual perception of a concrete whole presupposes is that the contemplator occupies a perfectly determinate place, and that he is unitary and *embodied*. The world of cognition and every constituent in it are capable of being thought, but they are not capable of actually being perceived" ("Author and hero" 23–4). Aesthetic understanding of the same object or moment renders them complete, insofar as we know their individual components and are able to understand in what way those components function together as a whole. One can thus see how Bakhtin sought not only to solve the problem of the Formalists – which he saw as their inability or unwillingness to theorize a phenomenology of the mind in which the poetic elements of a given text might be seen to function together not simply as a poetic whole but as a whole in a subject's consciousness – but to construct a broad phenomenological theory on which to base an aesthetics that understands "durably valid cultural products." In one move, Bakhtin managed to define the consciousness that completes – that, in his own terms, "authors" – aesthetic wholes, to construct a typology of the forms in which such wholes appeared (which constitutes the bulk of the remainder of the "Author and hero" essay), and to establish (if only implicitly) a means by which human subjects consummate already written verbal cultural constructs.

Missing from this early stage of Bakhtin's thinking is the role language will play in the relationship of human subjects. As I noted earlier, "The problem of content" does deal in some ways with how verbal aesthetic constructs can be analyzed with respect to language, but Bakhtin pays much greater attention in that essay to the shortcomings of Formalism and to the broader relationships between content, material, and form in written texts. But the specific function of language in both phenomenological subject relations and in written texts will not be addressed until *The formal method*[2] (Bakhtin/ Medvedev, 1928) and *Marxism and the philosophy of language*[3] (Bakhtin/Voloshinov, 1929), texts I will take up in later chapters. Nevertheless, I should here raise the question of how language functions in relation to phenomenology, if only briefly, since it will play an integral part in how Bakhtin's phenomenology works in relation to other, more contemporary phenomenological theories.

As noted earlier, Bakhtin grounds his theory of the subject in the materialism of biology, based on the work of his colleague Ivan Kanaev. Organisms are said to have life based on their reaction to stimuli; in humans, this capacity for reaction is what Bakhtin calls "addressivity." Humans respond to influences outside their bodies, including reaction to physical objects such as the natural world, the human-created world (including the forces of production, as we will see later on), and other humans. This relationship, as I have intimated, is directly related to Bakhtin's neo-Kantian origins: the mind must have some kind of relationship to those things exterior to it. In order to escape solipsism, there needs to be a mechanism in place so that

2 Citations from M. M. Bakhtin/Pavel Medvedev, *The formal method in literary scholarship: A critical introduction to sociological poetics*, trans. Albert J. Wehrle (Cambridge, MA: Harvard University Press, 1985) will hereafter appear in the text abbreviated *FM*.
3 Citations from M. M. Bakhtin/Valentin Voloshinov, *Marxism and the philosophy of language*, trans. Ladislav Matejka and I. R. Titunik (Cambridge, MA: Harvard University Press, 1986) will hereafter appear in the text abbreviated *MPL*.

these exterior phenomena can be processed (understood) by consciousness in such a way that they are not simply seen as elements *of* consciousness. Hence the necessity, in aesthetic understanding, of the relationship *outside* of the self. Humans react to this outside stimulus differently from other organisms: they produce *signs*. For Bakhtin, signs are ideological material:

> side by side with the natural phenomena, with the equipment of technology, and with articles for consumption, there exists a special world – the *world of signs*.
>
> Signs also are particular, material things; and ... any item of nature, technology, or consumption can become a sign, acquiring in the process a meaning that goes beyond its given particularity. A sign does not simply exist as a part of reality – it reflects and refracts another reality. Therefore, it may distort that reality or be true to it, or may perceive it from a special point of view, and so forth. (*MPL* 10)

This suggests that, in the lived life in which humans come into contact with one another (or with objects) and react to the other (or material), we produce ideological material that may or may not be coincident with that other, but which in any event is the result of the double movement of aesthetic understanding.

Bakhtin makes it plain that aesthetic understanding or consummation is only possible in a relationship between self and other: "An aesthetic event can take place only when there are two participants present; it presupposes two noncoinciding consciousnesses" in which one consciousness "delimits" or completes the other from the outside. There are two ways to read "noncoinciding" here, and both seem to fit into the phenomenological scheme Bakhtin sets up. Most explicitly with relation to aesthetic activity, the author does not coincide with the hero, even in autobiography, since they are on different "planes": the author, a real person, is "bestowing" upon the hero – who may have characteristics much like the author himself – a completed personality (for lack of a better term); yet this hero is not the author for the obvious reason that the hero is a fictional character and does not exist independent of the author. More to the point, even if the author gives the hero traits that mirror nearly exactly traits that exist in the author, the hero is "consummated" in the language of the text, and once the author finishes writing the life of the hero, the author's life continues: the "I" of the aesthetic construct and the "I" of the author are markedly different. The first is the I-for-myself, the consummated whole; the second is the I-for-the-other, the yet-to-be-completed, cognitive–ethical life.

In terms of lived relations, however, human subjects are non-coincident because they occupy different time and space from one another. As a result of this non-coincidence, each person's orientation to his or her surroundings (Bakhtin's "background") and his or her capacity for response will also be non-coincident. There exists that "excess of seeing" that results in a difference in the "experienced horizons" of each subject. "[A]t each given moment, regardless of the position and the proximity to me of this other human being whom I am contemplating, I shall always see and know something that he, from his place outside and over against me, cannot see himself" (such as the world behind his back, the look on his face, and so on). "It is possible ... to reduce this difference of horizons to a minimum, but in order to annihilate this difference completely, it would be necessary to merge into one, to become one and the same person" ("Author and hero" 22–3); in body this is patently impossible. Were it possible to merge consciousnesses, aesthetic understanding could not be achieved. Because each subject has an "excess" of vision, the ideological signs which will be produced will also necessarily be different.

Humans apprehend different things from one another because they have interiorized distinct ideological material, distinct language. Put another way, our apprehension of ourselves – and as a result our apprehension of our surroundings – has been formed "by the manifold acts of other people in relation to me, acts performed intermittently through my life." As soon, in fact, as humans begin to experience themselves consciously, that experience comes explicitly from the outside: from the actions of parents, and from the language of all those around them. Even a child's name in some sense begins to form the ideological material of that child. (Once again, it should be noted that the child's name is not coincident with the child herself; as the child grows, this distinction will become more visible to her. "I don't like being Patty," a child might say. "I want to be Patricia.")[4] "The words

4 Bakhtin's notion of the development of children and the role language plays in that development in some ways parallels Lev Vygotsky's, whose work appears translated into English in two volumes: *Thought and language*, ed. and trans. Eugenia Hanfmann and Gertrude Vakar (Cambridge, MA: Harvard University Press, 1962) and *Mind in society: The development of higher psychological processes*, eds. Michael Cole *et al.* (Cambridge, MA: Harvard University Press, 1978). Vygotsky, of whose work Bakhtin was aware, experimented with young children and discovered that, from the beginning (in some cases before conception),

of a loving human being are the first and the most authoritative words about [her]; they are the words that for the first time determine [her] personality *from outside*, the words that *come to meet* [her] indistinct inner sensation of [her]self, giving it a form and a name in which, for the first time, [she] finds [her]self and becomes aware of [her]self as a *something"* ("Author and hero" 49–50).

As the language of the other becomes interiorized, the subject reutters that language as she encounters new situations. A process of evaluation takes place, in which the subject matches the interiorized language to the material data she has at her disposal. She must apprehend the material as the other might see it, and then return to her own interiorized language-data, as it were, and construct a distinct sign for that material. To use an oversimplified example, let us assume that a subject encounters an object. In perceiving that object, there are two options: she can have cognitive understanding of the object, in which case no aesthetic consummation will take place, though knowledge of the object and resulting (ethical) action based on that knowledge can take place; or she can aesthetically complete the object. In order to do this, the subject must explore the language that she has interiorized previously, and see if it matches the object she has encountered. This is similar to cognitive knowledge, in which there exist universally valid concepts to which each individual object could belong. In the aesthetic analysis, however, the subject observes that the object for which previous signs have been interiorized is different in some respects from those signs. Thus the subject, in examining those previously interiorized signs and coming to terms with which

children exist in a world of language. As children gain the capacity to articulate verbal signs, such sign-creation will accompany action, as when a child "talks through" an activity while he or she does it. In such cases the world of events is dependent upon language production in the sense that the child's world is understood almost completely within a linguistic context. As children become older, action-oriented speech is interiorized: speech which had accompanied action slowly becomes incorporated into the child's "background," or consciousness. As new situations and language are encountered, they are assimilated into this "inner speech," though these words and situations are not yet "the child's own," as they are still thought of in connection with the moment of experience. It is by this transition that children recognize "others" whose language is different from their own, and through which social play and negotiation emerge. For Vygotsky, thought and speech are exclusive of one another: there exists speech without thought (as in animals), as there is thought without speech. This is something to which Bakhtin would not accede, at least not in aesthetic understanding; utterances can, nevertheless, be constructed without aesthetic consummation, as in the ethical response to some cognitive understanding. See Caryl Emerson's "The outer world and inner speech" in *Bakhtin: Essays and dialogues on his work*, ed. Gary Saul Morson (University of Chicago Press, 1986), 21–40, for a discussion of the differences and similarities between the two thinkers.

might and which might not consummate the object in question, authors a unique sign for the object. What occurs is an utterance of a sign based on previous encounters with signs that belong to *others*. When the subject finally consummates the object – when she produces a non-coincident sign for the object – she has reauthored her self as well, since this new sign will in turn be interiorized to form a distinct background for future aesthetic negotiation.

In my encounters with others, language functions in a similar manner. Because our orientations in time and space are different, we can "see" things to which the other does not have access; because of our different language backgrounds (since we've interiorized different ideological material), our language will also be different, even though we may speak the same "national language" or come from similar material situations (class, race, gender, and so on). In order to find language with which to speak to this other, I have to "author" him, and in order to do this I have to author my self as well. That is, I must ensure that I can make myself understandable to him by creating out of what I've accumulated about the context of previous sign-production some extrapolation of how those signs can be made understandable to the other. In order to do this I have to "create" a non-coincident self by trying to determine how I am seen by that other. As was suggested before, I must investigate the other's consciousness (his social placement, how he may have interiorized signs, and so on); though I can never *know* that consciousness, I have to project it based on the "excess of seeing" to which I have access. Having consummated the other based on this apprehension, I then have to investigate my own language background and utter language – coherent in the current context – that will be understandable to the other.[5] In the process of constructing language, "we evaluate our exterior not for ourselves, but *for* others *through* others" ("Author and hero" 33).

---

5 Bakhtin, in "Author and hero," provides the example of a subject encountering a human who is suffering, and describes the way in which the subject consummates the other (25–7) which is illuminating to the present discussion. As with the entire essay, however, this example does not suggest the ways in which language plays a role in aesthetic activity.

III

The latter distinction between the I-for-myself and I-for-the-other brings up one of several problems with Bakhtin's phenomenology that should be discussed before we proceed further, since these problems figure prominently both in comparing Bakhtin to Husserl and in Bakhtin's intervention into more contemporary models of phenomenology. The distinction between the I-for-myself and the I-for-the-other suggests that there are two orders of phenomena in play when humans utter language. Bakhtin asserts that the I-for-myself, in which a subject consummates another subject or object (or, in fact, consummates the subject's self at a given moment) is a purely aesthetic moment. In distinction to this, the I-for-the-other, in which subjects direct activity toward some other or toward some object – like speech, or like written discourse (either aesthetic or prosaic) – is ethical, and thus cognitive and not aesthetic. It is true that, in order to construct aesthetic verbal artefacts (that is, literary texts), the author must consummate his heroes and characters, and construct the text in such a way as to effect some other (that is, the reader) to consummate those heroes similarly. But the act of writing itself – and the act of speaking, as when subjects encounter one another and actually perform some utterance – is a cognitive–ethical activity not-for-oneself.

The suggestion that follows from this is that the act of subject-formation that results from the utterance is *not* the kind of aesthetic act that Bakhtin here (in "Author and hero") delineates. The point is very clear:

We are not concerned in the present context with those actions which, by virtue of their outward sense [that is, I-for-the-other], involve myself and the other within the unitary and unique event of being, and which are directed toward the actual modification of the event and of the other as a moment in that event; such actions are purely *ethical* actions or deeds. Our concern is only with actions of *contemplation* – *actions* of contemplation, because contemplation is active and productive. These actions of contemplation do not go beyond the bounds of the other as a given; they merely unify and order that given. And it is these actions of contemplation, issuing from the excess of my outer and inner seeing of the other human being, that constitute purely *aesthetic* actions. (24)

There are two ways to read "toward the actual modification of the event": either Bakhtin means that, if the event of aesthetic contemplation were modified, then the result would not be aesthetic consummation but ethical action; or that the modification of the aesthetic event would constitute another, distinct and consequent event. In either case, there are two distinct events that occur either simultaneously or causally: one is aesthetic, the other is cognitive–ethical. Dialogue – the act of utterance – is thus not part of the aesthetic moment.

The terms "dialogue" and "dialogism" are often confused or misunderstood. Traditionally understood, dialogue begins when the self's non-coincidence with itself and with other selves requires a bridge between the notions of I-for-myself and I-as-other. Dialogue is not so much a discourse between two people (as in Saussure's notorious model of one interlocutor "pitching" and another "catching" meaning), as it is a metaphor for the welter of communication that exists in the social world generally. Rather than involving an exchange of meanings, there occurs an exchange of selves, since language is the medium with which subjects conceive of their world and their placement in it. As we have seen, dialogue also suggests the non-coincidence of the sign-as-interiorized and the sign-as-uttered: the moment a sign is uttered in a particular context, both the sign and the context are interiorized, thus producing a new context for future use. Moreover, the selves involved in such an "exchange" are also reconstructed, since their language (as ideological material for their "lives") has changed.

One of Paul de Man's last essays notes the difficulty with this notion of dialogue and dialogism, and rightly so. What bothers de Man about the concept of dialogism is that it is a "principle of *exotopy*: ... the function of dialogism is to sustain and think through the radical exteriority or heterogeneity of one voice with regard to any other." In this regard he cannot tell where the passage occurs, in Bakhtin's theory, "from otherness to the recognition of the other, the passage, in other words, from dialogism to dialogue" or whether, in fact, such a transition occurs at all (de Man, *The resistance to theory* 109–10).

In fact, the transition occurs in the space between aesthetic consummation and the utterance that results from it. Dialogism most certainly is a principle of exotopy, founded, at least in part, on the difficult situation Bakhtin's neo-Kantian predecessors left him (and the philosophical world), namely the division between mind and world. The world is exterior to the consciousness to which it is present. Not the least part of this exterior world are other human subjects, who are all in the same situation: they are all separate from one another, by dint of the separateness of their consciousnesses from their flesh-and-blood presence as beings. In positing a biological response in humans that takes the form of language, Bakhtin provides a way out of the difficulty: humans all react similarly, by producing language in response to stimuli. Stimuli are as apt to be other humans as they are to be objects in the world. Further, the reaction is to form signs that in some way correspond to the stimuli (though, as we've intimated, are not necessarily "true" to the stimuli; at no point in my reading of Bakhtin have I found evidence which suggests that Bakhtin clarifies what "being true" to that stimuli means).

Since all humans have the capacity for aesthetically "consummating" a given moment (or stimulus) over and above coming to cognitive–ethical consciousness of that moment, as well as the capacity for uttering language in response to that event, it could be said that "dialogism" is the way in which humans encounter one another and enter into a consummating relationship, as outlined by Bakhtin, above; while "dialogue" is the cognitive–ethical event that results from this consummation (as the novel is the cognitive–ethical resultant action of the author's having consummated his heroes and characters into an aesthetic whole). What should be obvious at this point is that de Man is right in suggesting that the passage from "dialogism" to "dialogue" is a problematic one: dialogue does not solve the problem of exotopy, since any utterance is in turn susceptible – and in fact, in the "proper" human relationship, which calls for aesthetic consummation, must be open – to consummation in its turn. The act of utterance, which is seen by some as a way to contravene the "radical exteriority or heterogeneity" of human subjects, in fact does not. Utterance is a dialectic of aesthetic and ethical moments, neither of which guarantees that individual humans subjects will be able to understand one another (or, if they are capable of understanding one another, of coming to any sort of agreement), since any cognitive–ethical action (that is, utterance) can be consummated differently depending upon the context and circumstances.

One could see this lack of completion as perfectly compatible with Bakhtin's stated aversion to ever "completing" a given subject or moment, and his emphasis on the process of human subject relations rather than on the product. Given his neo-Kantian starting point, however, this would seem not to be the case, since Bakhtin was specifically looking for some way to overcome the distinction between "radically exterior voices." Moreover, since utterances and aesthetic moments seem to be different phenomenological events, the artefacts resulting from the two would also have to be different. Specifically, if something is other-directed, such as an utterance (or, by extension, a text), that object must necessarily be material and therefore susceptible to material analysis. But if something is self-directed (such as a moment of aesthetic consummation), the only way to study such an event would be either to examine the subject for whom the event is taking place (or, perhaps, the event itself, including the various interlocutors), or the resultant object of such an event (that is, the text – the novel, poem, painting, etc.). As we have stated, such resulting "utterances," if you will, are in fact the result of cognitive–ethical understanding, and so we are left where we started: how is it possible to note the passage from what is "dialogic" to what is the result of "dialogue"?

If we agree with Bakhtin that the difference between an aesthetic verbal artefact and an ethical verbal artefact lies in the difference in the two of the "contextualized ideological material" (specifically, the degree to which characters and moments are completed in the language of the author), then we may be able to get out of this conundrum. In "The problem of content," Bakhtin suggests that non-aesthetic verbal constructs are those in which "the potential unity and indispensability of the world of cognition shine, as it were, through every constituent of the aesthetic object ... [B]ehind every word, behind every phrase ... one can sense a potential prosaic meaning, a prosaic slant, that is, a potential, total referredness to the unity of cognition" (286–7). The consummated whole of aesthetic unity – the way in which moments and the consciousnesses of heroes and characters are made whole by some other (exterior) consciousness (the author) – is visible in the language of the text, in which the ideas and the characterizations are made complete. The "dialogue" that results from such activity is in fact aesthetic because its elements are completed aesthetically. It remains to be seen whether this distinction – in relation to Gadamer and others – is supportable.

The problematic distinction between aesthetic "events" and the resultant ethical "utterances" suggests another difficulty for a term in the Bakhtin canon, namely "intersubjectivity." Detractors of Bakhtinian theory have noted that this term is vague since it describes a process that occurs *between* subjects, and is not discernible except in (and necessarily apart from) the results of such a relation; and that, moreover, intersubjective negotiation – either of language (or texts) or of selves – is never-ending to the point of uselessness. For Bakhtin it is not the sentence that is the smallest significant unit of language, but the utterance. This latter is defined as a series of created sign-relations given voice (or set into print) by some subject; utterances end when there is a change of speakers ("Discourse in life, discourse in art" 103). Yet even within individual utterances, one can perceive language that has been "previously owned," that is part of a context different from the current one, and that is related in some ways to that other context despite its current use. It is precisely in the "space" between utterances that a negotiation of the context of those signs takes place: this is what is meant by "intersubjectivity." Bakhtin provides an example of intersubjective negotiation in the essay, "Discourse in the novel" (in *The dialogic imagination*) in his discussion of how various speech genres are embedded in the language of Dickens's novels, and how those already used contexts play on the "language-backgrounds" of readers. In effect, each utterance is "negotiated" since the reader's projection of what the utterance means will not be coincident with what the utterance in fact does mean for that reader. Any reading will thus "miss" (it will not mean the same as might have been expected), and so the language must be negotiated. This also occurs when two readers encounter a similar text and read that text differently: agreement (or disagreement) must also be negotiated.

In a review essay of Clark and Holquist's biography of Bakhtin, Michael Sprinker suggests that negotiation does not end the problem of the "radical otherness" that can exist between selves and their uses of language. "Meanings are never completely formalizable because the context of any utterance can never be specified" (Sprinker, "Boundless context" 122). The result is that Bakhtin's conception of intersubjectivity and its relation to dialogism is similar to, if not the same as, deconstruction because (as Sprinker quotes Bakhtin) "There is neither a first nor a last word. The contexts of dialogue are without limit. They extend into the deepest past and into the most distant future" (127). Sprinker complains that at the very moment when various speakers or readers of a text might agree upon a particular reading or meaning of a text or utterance, there is no guarantee that such a reading will last, nor that someone will not at some later point produce a different reading that will throw the agreed-upon meaning into disarray and confusion.

As I have suggested, the reason for this slipperiness is Bakhtin's own imprecision about how the dialectic of aesthetic consummation and utterance is resolved. More specifically, it is difficult to tell whether one person's resulting utterance (aesthetic or prosaic) is correct, or even appropriate to the situation. Depending upon how uttered signs conform to a speaker's language background, they are said to be either "in accord" with it or "at variance" with it. If an utterance is at variance, it can either be interiorized and uttered dialogically, or interiorized and ignored, thus guaranteeing no change or progress in a subject's "creation of himself." Because there is no guarantee that a sign or utterance will "be true" to the context in which it is uttered, and since the consummation of lived human activity is always partial and never complete, there is no way to make reference to the material situation outside the language situation. As such, there is no guide against which an utterance might be measured in order to see it as untrue or invalid. Sprinker makes use elsewhere of an example that illustrates just this difficulty. Referring to Stanley Fish (with whom I will take issue later), we are asked to consider two groups of people. The first of these believes African-Americans are intellectually inferior to whites and should not be in professional positions for which whites are better endowed. The second group supports affirmative action programs because they believe African-Americans have not benefited in the past from equal employment, but they also believe that the pool of African-American candidates is so poor that standards must be lowered to make room for them, thus depriving qualified whites of a job. Sprinker suggests that "both views ... are racist, and yet it is far from clear that the people who hold the second are insusceptible to being persuaded that their view is racist in the same way as the view of the first group" (Sprinker, "Knowing, believing, doing" 47–8). My question, as regards Bakhtin's notion of negotiation, is this: how is it possible to negotiate the "selves" involved in this example in such a way that *both* views can be considered racist? It is Sprinker's suggestion, I think, that an individual holding the first view could be called a racist but not succumb to the view that he in fact is, for the reason that (following Bakhtin) the ideological material that the individual has interiorized is completely exclusive of such terminology. An individual in the second group, however, has at his disposal ideological material that includes definitions of racism that shape the paternalistic attitude that he holds. But this does not solve the problem of racism, nor the particular problem of whether acts of language negotiation can move an individual from the first group (let alone the second) from a position which on the face of it is materially (and common-sensically) wrong. If, over the course of time, it becomes clear to the first individual that the ideological milieu has changed in such a way that his attitude has become obsolete and that he needs to change his way of thinking, then there is the possibility for that self to re-author himself, as it were. But this depends on material conditions outside of the linguistic (and phenomenological) realm, and there is no guarantee that the material conditions will not change in such a way that racism will become *less* obsolete. Measuring utterances against other utterances makes for a painstakingly slow process of change in understanding, and it cannot ensure that such a change will occur at all. This would seem to run counter to Bakhtin's own view of language as teeming with potential for what he calls a subject's "renewal" (see *Rabelais and his world* 11).

IV

At this point it remains to be seen whether these problems in Bakhtin's phenomenology can be resolved by, or whether they will be complicated with relation to, the "Marxist" or historical strand in his work. What we might ask at this point, though, is whether these problems in the phenomenological construction of the human self are unique to Bakhtin, or whether they are symptomatic of phenomenology generally. It will be useful to see in what ways Bakhtin's phenomenology compares to Edmund Husserl's work, since that work is at the base of all subsequent phenomenological (often called "reading" or "reception") theories of literary analysis. The comparison between "reading" theories and Bakhtin's work has been made before;[6] my task here goes beyond comparison to see how the phenomenologies that form their foundations serve to strengthen or weaken those theories.

The philosophical position of Edmund Husserl was well known to the Russian Formalists (his *Ideas* was published in 1913 and was popularized by Gustav Spet), and Bakhtin was familiar with Spet's work if not with Husserl's. Husserl's position was at its base different from Bakhtin's: the latter took his starting point from Kant and those thinkers who followed him, namely that questions of epistemology

6 See especially David Shepherd's "Bakhtin and the reader" in *Bakhtin and cultural theory*, eds. Ken Hirschkop and David Shepherd (Manchester University Press, 1989), 91–108.

must necessarily come first in any inquiry into understanding, and, more specifically, to delineate the objects of scientific inquiry before such an inquiry begins. Husserl's starting point, by contrast, was to draw a line between sciences of a specifically philosophical standpoint (such as Bakhtin's) and those of a dogmatic standpoint. The first "are concerned with the sceptical problems relating to the possibility of knowledge. Their object is finally to solve the problems in principle and with the appropriate generality, and then, when applying the solutions thus obtained, to study their bearing on the critical task of determining the eventual meaning and value for knowledge of the results of the dogmatic sciences" (*Ideas* 87). The dogmatic sciences, on the other hand, have a different aim: "*The right attitude* to take in the *pre-philosophical* and, in a good sense, *dogmatic* sphere of inquiry, to which all the empirical sciences (but not these alone) belong, is in full consciousness *to discard all scepticism together with all 'natural philosophy' and 'theory of knowledge'* and find the data of knowledge there where they actually face you, whatever difficulties epistemological reflection may *subsequently* raise concerning the possibility of such data being there" (86).

One can begin to see the fundamental differences between Bakhtin and Husserl as regards the position of the Formalists. In the Soviet Union immediately following the Revolution there were any number of competing and mutually exclusive systematizations of knowledge that competed both for intellectual primacy as well as for the base of what were seen as new aesthetic theories. Husserl's point that it was difficult, if not pointless, to engage in inquiry concerning the philosophical underpinnings of such systematizations rang true, since in Russia – which was in flux – such an inquiry would prove pointless as well. Besides – as Peter Steiner remarks – "becoming embroiled in the philosophical fray would only distract [the Formalists] from what they considered their main objective: the advancement of a new literary science" (*Russian Formalism: A metapoetics* 250).

At least in part, Bakhtin and his circle were inextricably involved in the "philosophical fray" from the beginning, since they had been working with German philosophy for many years prior to the Revolution, and this partially explains the reason why Husserl's and Bakhtin's starting points were so different. Phenomenology took as its first problem to determine the nature of the encounter between the human mind and objects (and subjects) exterior to it, while neo-Kantianism sought first to find a bridge between mind and object before inquiries into such encounters could be undertaken. Certainly it could be said that Bakhtin's philosophy of language, emphasizing the way in which human consciousness functions in terms of its relation to something or some other consciousness exterior to it, could be said to rely more heavily than the Kantian (or, in fact, Cohen's) position upon the data of knowledge as they are experienced. It is the reliance upon the experience of human lived life that makes it tempting to see Bakhtin fall into a Husserlian (or "purely phenomenological") camp.

But there's more to the Husserlian position. Husserl complained that positivist science, which Cohen and other neo-Kantians also attacked for the same reason, suffered from a naiveté that conflated facts with phenomena. "The fundamental defect of the empiricist's argument lies in this, that the basic requirement of a return to the 'facts themselves' is identified or confused with the requirement that all knowledge shall be grounded in *experience*" (*Ideas* 74–5). If a scientist were to proceed with his research through pure experience he would be provided merely with knowledge of a single fact in a unique time and space with no relevance to anything beyond it: the science of accident. What one needs, in order to found a science, are broader criteria of relevance by which to relate a single phenomenon with categories of phenomena similar to it. "Category" exceeds the empirical realm, and it is not a result of direct experience; rather, it is grounded in what Husserl calls the "essential insight" that manages to locate the categorical idea common to all objects of the same category which in fact constitutes that object.

The "science which aims exclusively at establishing the 'knowledge of essences' and absolutely no 'facts'" is "pure phenomenology" (*Ideas* 40). It proceeds from intuition rather than from sense-experience by grasping directly the essences that underlie the phenomenal world that provide it with its categorical identity. It is here that, despite the different starting points of Bakhtin and Husserl, one finds similarities. Bakhtin also saw a need for some kind of unifying category of consciousness in order to discern in what way the aesthetic consummation of such categories differed, or, in other terms, in order to systematically inquire into the construction of aesthetic wholes. This category is the "cognitive–ethical" domain.

In "The problem of content," Bakhtin outlines this category at some length. "Cognition finds nothing to be already on hand; it begins from the very beginning – or rather, the moment of the prior givenness of something valid apart from cognition remains beyond it and passes into the realm of factuality – historical, psychological, personal-biographical, and other factuality which is fortuitous from the perspective of cognition itself" (276–7). The "givenness" of which Bakhtin speaks here is its "factness," or its presence in some material context. The "facts" that Husserl suggests positivism confused with the phenomenological experience of objects or subjects are intimately bound up with the "historical, psychological, personal-biographical, and other factuality" that differentiate one object from another similar object. More specifically, "the world of ethical actions and the world of beauty themselves become objects of cognition," but in doing so, neither the ethical nature of the action nor the aesthetic consummation of the object "impose" themselves upon the cognitive object.

In the world of cognition, like the world of essences, "*there are in principle no separate acts and no separate works*. Rather, it is indispensable to bring in other points of view in order to discover a way to approach them and to make essential the historical singularity of the cognitive[–ethical] act and the isolatedness, completeness, and individuality of a scientific work" (277). It is necessary, in order to establish a "phenomenology" of human action (for Bakhtin) or a pure phenomenology (for Husserl) to establish first what is essential to any object; but inseparable from cognition (essences) are the individuating historical data that "one can immediately see and lay hold of" (*Ideas* 78). What essences/cognition allows for is the principle by which different subject positions can be seen *as* different. For Husserl – but, more importantly, for those who follow his work, notably the Prague linguists as well as Ingarden and, in reaction, Gadamer – it forms the principle by which "*langue*" or a "canon" can be established so different signs and systems can be seen as diverging from them.

Despite the similarities in their concepts of the essences that establish the foundation for human relations of consciousness, a profound difference between Husserl's "pure phenomenology" and what might be called a Bakhtinian epistemological phenomenology, lies in the nature of language and its relation to human consciousness. This difference also goes back to the different beginning assumptions of Bakhtin and Husserl, but it has a further twist to it. For Husserl, it is not necessary to establish the epistemological foundation for the sciences, since any attempt to found such knowledge is at best fruitless and at worst impossible. One simply needs to begin the investigation of experience through what occurs phenomenologically, and then attend to any epistemological difficulties as they arise. For Bakhtin, the epistemological foundation of any science must necessarily come first. Bakhtin's foundation for his science of the text (if one chooses to call it that) is the I–other relationship that takes place between humans through the creation of signs (and, more specifically, with language). Cognition is an inseparable part – in fact, it is the irreducible part – of such a relationship, and yet it does not constitute the basis of real human knowledge, since the most accurate description for human relations of understanding is aesthetic consummation. In this way, Bakhtinian science has at its foundation a principle of variance, or, as de Man puts it, exotopy: humans are radically "other" in relation to each other, but it is this relationship that defines human understanding, and all epistemologies must come to terms with it, as Bakhtin's does.

Husserl, in eschewing such an epistemological foundation, plunges directly into the problems of human understanding and, more specifically, the problems involved in achieving that understanding through language and communication.[7] Husserl provided the cornerstone of his search for a universalist semiotic theory with the "expression," which he advanced in "Investigation I" of the *Logical investigations*. Only a repeatable sign, one that retains its essential self-sameness under all circumstances, can serve for Husserl as a vehicle of logical thought capable of embodying truth. Husserl saw the failure of psychologistic and physicalistic doctrines of representation as their lack of some concept of ideal sign; without such an ideal sign, any representation or sign that was merely a result of the perceiver's mental states, or of the objectivity it denotes, opened it up to the chaos of the phenomenological world. Taken to its most extreme conclusion, if every act of signification uses a sign in a new and unrepeatable time-space, then the sign used in such acts will necessarily be distinct, non-identical, and therefore useless for human understanding based in communication.

To avoid this problem, Husserl divided signs into two incompatible categories: the "expression," that is, "each instance or part of speech" and "each sign ... essentially of the same sort" capable of remaining self-same despite differing contexts; and the "indication," which lacks any such identity and thus represents a fluctuating state of affairs

---

7 Much of this discussion is based on Peter Steiner's analysis of Husserl in relation to Russian Formalism. See *Russian Formalism: A metapoetics* (Ithaca: Cornell University Press, 1984), 199–240.

(*Logical investigations* 275). But this did not explain why words (that is, "expressions") remain unaffected by the contexts of speech events, so Husserl had to discover, in the internal structure of expressions, some factor resistant to contextual change. "In the case of a name [for example], we distinguish between what it 'shows forth' (i.e., a mental state) and what it means. And again between what it means (the sense or 'content' of its naming presentation) and what it names (the object of that presentation)" (276). Both "showing forth" and "naming" are dependent upon empirical reality and so cannot retain their self-sameness when they are repeated in different contexts. The "content of an expression's naming presentation" (the meaning of a sign), however, is independent of phenomenal context, and thus this meaning, which is inherent in the word prior to its representing other entities, endows the expression with its identity. Once meaning is established in this way, the next question must be about the nature of that meaning. Husserl needed to come up with a situation in which the word would function as a pure meaning free of indicative relations, and also to account for the self-sameness of meaning in repetition. To meet the first condition, Husserl identified the mental soliloquy, since in an interior monologue the subject knows what he means, and his words don't serve him as indicators of his thought. Instead, the meaning of the expression merges with the subject's meaning–intention. To meet the second condition – and to do away with the implication that meaning is totally subjective, since it would thus dissipate into a multiplicity of meaning-intending acts – Husserl posited that meaning had also to exist intersubjectively as a universal object prior to and independent of its actualization in language. Subjective meaning–intentions would thus be individuations of a larger type or class.

The results of such a concept of meaning are problematic to Husserl and for all those who follow. Yet Bakhtin's alternative is no less problematic. Husserl's model of the soliloquy as the speech situation in which the sign is most ideally posited is indicative of the phenomenological problem. As Peter Steiner suggests of Husserl in relation to Saussure, "Once the word is addressed to someone and leaves the safe haven of a single consciousness, its identity is totally compromised, for 'all expressions in communicative speech function as indications' (*Logical investigations* I, 277)" (Steiner, *Russian Formalism: A metapoetics* 222). Though a subject can conceive of a sign's meaning within his own consciousness, once it is communicated to some other subject it becomes affected by the empirical situation, and as it enters the consciousness of that other, it may or may not be perceived as the ideal sign. The self-sameness of the sign in subject number one disappears, since that first subject must shape the utterance to make the sign an "indication," and subject number two is not guaranteed to accept that sign as the indication of what subject number one has in his mind. Husserl tries to do away with this solipsistic problem in *Cartesian meditations*, where he suggests that "pairing" of subjects is a "constitutive component of my experience of someone else" (141). In such a relation "we find essentially present here an intentional overreaching, ... a living mutual awakening and an overlaying of each with the objective sense of the other. This overlaying can bring a total or a partial coincidence, which in any particular instance has its degree, the limiting case that of complete 'likeness'" (142). The suggestion is that, in the relation between the "ego" and the "alter ego," there will necessarily be some overlap in understanding or in their "essential knowledge" of their phenomenal worlds which can be played off one against the other. But this suggestion does not do away with the problem that has developed in Husserl's notion of how language plays a part in phenomenology, namely that the unity that he posited for human consciousness in order to make differentiation possible linguistically has in fact not unified it at all.

V

As I have suggested, this problem goes all the way back to the root beginnings of the phenomenological project. Problems of epistemology can wait until the establishment of an investigation into experience has been completed. In (temporarily) ignoring the problem created by his notion of the self-sameness of idealized meanings, Husserl runs up against an epistemological problem that halts the semiotic project in its tracks: if meanings are ideally cognizable, how is it that different people understand the same utterance (or the same novel or poem) differently, especially since those verbal constructs are built of the same words? To suggest that the world of sense-experience (or, in other terms, the brute material world) compromises the ideal meaning both through its initial utterance and again in its reception only serves to complicate the problem, since it was this world of sense-experience that was the initial object of investigation to begin with.

Bakhtin's beginnings outside of "pure phenomenology" isolate his philosophy of language from the problem of ideal meanings. Positing cognition as the component of human understanding by which objects can be universally identified does not lead him to the problem of having to explain how meanings can be universalized. In fact, cognitive understanding is just one aspect of human understanding, alongside the ethical response to cognition and the aesthetic consummation of the cognitive–ethical act. Though cognitive understanding does serve as a unifying category for human consciousness, it is not its source. That source, for Bakhtin as it was for neo-Kantian philosophy, is directly opposite to Husserl's attempt to batten down a unifying semiotic system: humans are radically "other," they are first and always opposite one another, and yet they can't exist outside of some relation to one another. The way in which humans can bridge this otherness – if only partially – is through the aesthetic act of consummation, in which a subject enters into a symbiotic relationship with another subject, but then subsequently produces an utterance which occurs outside the aesthetic moment of completion and which may serve to distance the subjects more than unify their consciousnesses.

Husserl, beginning from sense-experience and resolving problems of how knowledge is possible later, unifies human consciousness by way of the self-identical ideal meaning. This will allow phenomenology to examine sense-experience for individual subjects, but it will produce difficulty for its followers in explaining how communication – and the transmission of signs through verbal artefacts (that is, literature) – is possible. Bakhtin, on the other hand, begins his investigation with an explanation of how human understanding is possible at all, and suggests that language is the vehicle for bridging the gap between the I-for-myself and the I-for-the-other. In building a model of human understanding on dialogue (rather than on monologue or soliloquy), language becomes the material by which humans construct subject-positions, but still does not resolve the problem of how those subjects can come to agreement or disagreement on ideological meaning, nor how communication can be seen as a vehicle for (positively) changing those subject positions.

3

++

Reception and hermeneutics: the
search for ideology

++

Two representatives of contemporary phenomenological aesthetic
theory that have found widespread use in American departments of
English are Wolfgang Iser's "phenomenology of reading" and Hans
Robert Jauss's *Rezeptionsaesthetik*. Both theories were developed in the
1960s and early 1970s in reaction to Husserlian phenomenological
theory (or, more specifically, to the work of Roman Ingarden and
Hans-Georg Gadamer, two of Husserl's followers). Ingarden worked
most closely with Husserl's philosophy, and as a result his theory pays
closest attention to the way in which individual human subjects come
to cognition of aesthetic objects, and pays a great deal less attention
to the ways in which those subjects are situated historically or socially.
Iser's work, in *The act of reading* and *The implied reader*, shows a similar
de-emphasis on the role of social history in the act of reading or
interpreting a text. While the role of language in the construction of
intersubjective relations is the key to Ingarden's and (even more so)
Iser's work, neither carries this notion to its logical endpoint, that is to
see how the various complex intersubjective human relations might be
seen to form a larger social construct.

   Gadamer's work also takes as its point of departure Husserl's larger
phenomenological project, but goes beyond it by suggesting that
Husserl's transcendental ego was inadequate to a theory of linguistically mediated understanding or of cultural interpretation generally.
He incorporates into Husserl's work the idea that individual human
subjects come into a unique relationship with an aesthetic artefact, and
notes that the relationship is of a different order from ordinary
experience. Further, he notes that the language of a linguistic aesthetic
construct distinguishes it from both ordinary experience and from
"everyday" linguistic constructs. From that point, though, Gadamer
understands the linguistic construct (both aesthetic and everyday) as
a *historically situated* artefact, and understands the interpreter or reader
of such an artefact as likewise historically situated. Jauss, in *Towards an*

aesthetics of reception, begins to lay out the specific interrelationships between historically situated work and interpreter.

One can begin to see why the work of Ingarden and Iser on the one hand, and that of Gadamer and Jauss on the other, is interesting in a discussion of how Bakhtin's work falls between phenomenological and historical theories. The more truly phenomenological pair (Ingarden and Iser) begin from Husserl's work and remain in the paradigm insofar as they also posit a realm of essences universal to the transcendental ego and see the interrelationship between work and interpreter as one that is compromised by the vagaries of history. Gadamer and Jauss, contrary to Husserl, though in every sense still working within the phenomenological paradigm, *begin* from the theorization of a messy and biassing history. Bakhtin was acutely aware that a philosophical aesthetics had to begin from a broader theory of human cognition, and only from that point could one understand the place of aesthetics within that general theory of understanding. Nevertheless – particularly in "The problem of content" – Bakhtin notes that human understanding does not take place in a void but in a world of other humans, and the communication that takes place in that world severely affects the nature of understanding. Though a phenomenological aesthetics is certainly important, it is not enough.

What is most interesting in this inquiry, though, is not how Bakhtin's work in philosophy generally and philosophical aesthetics specifically compares to the work of Ingarden and Iser or Gadamer and Jauss; more interesting is that, in trying to theorize a phenomenology that is at once a theory of the individual relationship to verbal aesthetic constructs and a theory of broad social construction, Bakhtin often succumbs to the same theoretical blind spots that infect reception theory and hermeneutics. In addition, the results of succumbing to these blind spots call into question whether Bakhtin's theories can be seen as superior to those of Iser and Jauss, or even whether Bakhtin's notions of human aesthetic understanding and, later on, his notion of human social relations and history, can be reconciled at all to form a coherent, useful critical or cultural theory.

I

It was the Structuralists who made Roman Ingarden's project accessible to readers in the West. In its evolution from the Formalism which preceded it, Structuralism had to come to terms with how the work of art functioned with specific relation to the so-called everyday world. F. W. Galan suggests that, in maintaining some distance between the aesthetic and the everyday, Structuralism gained a certain advantage as a theory, especially over what was being generated in West Germany at the time as "reception aesthetics": the former did not have to suggest whether one realm was predominant over the other, and in questions of interpretation of works of art, it was the Structuralists – as opposed to the common reader–who would be the arbiters of meaning (see especially Galan, *Historic structures* 45–64). Yet despite any advantage it gained in retaining this separation, Structuralism presents a grave contradiction – as does the work of Ingarden, on which it is partly based – to its own stated project, namely how to reunite cognition of the aesthetic object with everyday cognitive events.

Ingarden's *The cognition of the literary work of art* introduced an explicit concern with the reader and his or her subjective apprehension of the work in aesthetic analysis. Earlier in his career, Ingarden's concern was primarily theoretical, and his interests in the nature of the aesthetic object came out of his broader concerns, originating with Husserl, with philosophy and the nature of human cognition. For Ingarden, the work of art presented an ideal case "of an object whose pure intentionality was beyond any doubt and on the basis of which one could study the essential structures of the mode of existence of the purely intentional object without being subject to suggestions stemming from considerations of real objectivities" (*Cognition* lxii-lxiii). According to a later formulation, the literary work is at once a purely intentional and heteronomous object: it is neither determinate (that is, possessed of a distinct form, different from every other, a point derived from Husserl), nor autonomous (that is, independent of the existence of any other object or some perceiving subject for its own existence), qualities which both real and ideal objects possess. Rather, the work depends entirely upon the act of consciousness for its existence, and its determinateness relies completely upon this outside subject.

There are, according to Ingarden, four layers of "intentional strata" that comprise a literary work. These are the phonetic formations, word meanings at the level of sentences made present in the work's structure, represented objects ("intentional objectivities projected by units of meaning") and "schematized aspects through which the represented objects manifest themselves" (quoted in Galan, *Historic structures* 73). These strata comprise a work's structural skeleton which must be completed by the perceiving subject. In particular, within this skeleton are numerous gaps or "spots of indeterminacy" that the reader must fill according to his or her aesthetic experience. In contrast to real objects, which are *"unequivocally, universally* (i.e., in *every* respect) determined"* (Ingarden, *The literary work of art* 246), objects represented by literary works exhibit "points" or "places" of indeterminacy. "We find such a place wherever it is impossible, on the basis of the sentences in the work, to say whether a certain object or objective situation has a certain attribute" (*Cognition* 50).

An example of how this theory works also points to one of its principal weaknesses in drawing a connection between the (literary) work of art and the historically real world. Ingarden's objects have infinite numbers of inherent determinants (those things which make an object what it is), and there is no human act of understanding that can take account of every determinant of some objects. Objects of *literary works*, however, because they are intentionally projected from meaning units and aspects (that is, someone means for the units of determinants to make a certain kind of sense), must therefore also retain some degree of determinacy. A book's cover may be of a certain size or color, but since it is wholly determined, it must have a particular size and a particular color. "The woman opened the red book" is a sentence in which a reader is confronted by any number of indeterminacies: we do not know, for instance, who the woman is, whether she opens the book from the front or the back (or, for that matter, which end of the book is its beginning depending on whether it is written, say, in Arabic or English), what the book's size (or subject) is, and so on. Given this limited amount of information, the reader just does not know. Real readers of real books have the missing determinants at their disposal, but the reader of the above sentence does not. Certainly there are ways to reduce indeterminacy such as exists in this sentence, but one cannot eliminate all indeterminacy, so in theory all literary works – and, in fact, all verbal objects, aesthetic or otherwise – contain infinite numbers of indeterminate sites.

However, Ingarden's distinction of determinateness versus indeterminacy – like Iser's later formulation, as we will shortly see – is fraught with problems. If subjects are able to produce any number of different readings or interpretations of aesthetic objects, and yet those objects are distinct, by dint of their intentionality, from real objects, then those readings – which take place at the level of everyday human social interaction – would seem to be at least once removed from the objects under discussion. By allowing an aesthetic object to be variously composed of determinate and indeterminate spots, Ingarden's theory proposes that "indeterminacies" are foregrounded upon determinate objectivities within that object. Stumbling upon the same problem the Formalists had also encountered, the work is no less an object than a poem is an objectified or "estranged" one. And like language for the Formalists, the work is by nature distinct from the world of real objects as a result of its indeterminateness. Readers may concretize works based on their previous aesthetic experience, and these experiences are comprised differently from those one experiences in a world of non-aesthetic objects, since the subject is attempting to determine some "indeterminacy" that has been *intended*. As a result, these experiences cannot be concretized with reference to the subject's "everyday" experiences. The work cannot be "translated" into real terms, and though it may bear some resemblance to the historically real, it can have no effect.

Moreover, because of the way concretizations are "made," each individual, depending on her mood, her current situation, where she happens to be during her reading and so on, reads quite differently from any other individual, given that she has had different aesthetic experiences (that is, has determined works differently) from any other individual. Since decisions about reading (aesthetic "receptions") are made differently from decisions made about "everyday" receptions of autonomous objects, two receivers of the same work cannot make a transition from the reception of some aesthetic object to agreement upon those receptions in terms of the everyday. Because individuals make decisions about works of art precisely as *individual subjects*, any real social interaction based upon those decisions is impossible, because aesthetic effect cannot have real historical effect. In a way, the problem is similar to Husserl's, in that any conversation between subjects about aesthetic reception jeopardizes that reception by opening it up to the messy world of brute material fact and historical (read "biassed") side-taking. Reading literature cannot make a human subject *do* something, nor can it have the effect of getting a number of its readers to agree on meaning, let alone on an action that may be taken as a result.

What one is left with in Ingarden's conception of human understanding, based as it is on the "concretization" of literary works of art, is an impasse between actual aesthetic understanding – in Bakhtin's terms, consummation – and the negotiation of that understanding between various subjects. Moreover, the language of a work is understood as having some reference to or intention toward an objective state of affairs or definite object, but that language is *understood* aesthetically. The language that might comprise any negotiation of the meaning or "concretization" of such an aesthetic construct will also be autonomous and independent since it will make reference back again to those determinate objects or states of affairs. There is no transition, in other words, from the phenomenology of the text to the phenomenology of understanding and back again. Or, to put this into Bakhtin's context, there is no way to understand the way "discourse in art" functions in terms of "discourse in life," or, more precisely, no way to understand the way in which aesthetic acts of consummation lead to cognitive–ethical action.

Wolfgang Iser's model of reading is based largely on Roman Ingarden's, particularly on *The cognition of the literary work of art*, but differs from it in that Iser attempts to make a more direct connection between the aesthetic "phenomenology of reading" and cognitive understanding in one's lived life. He does this by beginning with the same premise Ingarden began with: readers or interpreters "concretize" the intentional object according to various different levels of perception. Iser's concern is mainly with the individual relation between a single reader and a single text – both the theoretical *The act of reading* and the practical application of that theory in *The implied reader* are discussions focused mainly on the ways individual readers concretize individual texts. Nevertheless, Iser, more than Ingarden, also begins to focus on the ways, depending on the "background understanding" of works a subject has previously received, "concretizations" can differ from subject to subject and in fact from initial understanding to a later understanding of the same work in a single subject. The crucial difference here is that Iser is more acutely aware that there must be a way for literary works explicitly to affect the lived experience of a subject, and so he attempts to theorize a way for this to occur in the act of reading. The importance of this shift for the language philosophy of Mikhail Bakhtin is that it mirrors a similar shift (or, more precisely, an ambivalence) in his work between the way individual subjects construct meanings – and selves – and the way individuals communicate meaning and negotiate a broader social understanding. Iser – like Bakhtin in "Author and hero" – is highly concerned with what goes on between the author and subsequent reader of a given text and the language that comprises it, but leaves out larger questions of how language is largely determined by real social interaction.

From the beginning of his work, Iser was most interested in the conditions under which a text had significance for a reader (see Miller, *Aspects of narrative* 1–45). Iser begins to lay out his model of reading upon what initially appears to be a stable text, one that doesn't vary in structure from reader to reader, or from initial reading to subsequent rereadings. Rather, Iser stresses the importance of the creative role of the reader, and it is this – not the text itself – that changes from reading to reading (see Miller, *Aspects of narrative* 2–3). Iser's procedure is hermeneutic: meaning is gathered not from the text, but from a complex interaction between text and reader. *The act of reading* provides a detailed description of what occurs during the reading process, and Iser there focuses on two interrelated areas that had confounded phenomenologies from Husserl through Ingarden: the intersection between text and "social reality," and the interaction between text and reader.

Iser argues that "literature supplies those possibilities which have been excluded by the prevalent [thought] system" of the work's historical period.[1] It does so by causing the reader to formulate those possibilities for himself; the text is not seen as fulfilling those possibilities for him. The author "extracts" social and historical norms, as well as references to literature of his past, from their original contexts and puts them together to form the "repertoire of the text" (*AR* 69). In the novel, for example, these norms are distributed among the characters and narrators of the text as well as the "implied reader" and aspects of the plot, and this system of perspectives outlines the author's view without actually saying so explicitly, and also forms the

---

1 Wolfgang Iser, *The act of reading* (Baltimore: The Johns Hopkins University Press, 1978), 73. All further references that appear in the text will be abbreviated *AR*. Iser's book of practical criticism, *The implied reader: Patterns of communication in prose fiction from Bunyan to Beckett* (Baltimore: The Johns Hopkins University Press, 1974), is considered a "companion volume" to *AR*. References to *The implied reader* that hereafter appear in the text will be abbreviated *IR*.

"potential" structure (like Ingarden) for the reader to realize. This reader occupies the "shifting vantage points that are geared to a prestructured activity and to fit the diverse perspectives into a gradually evolving pattern" that forms the "configurative meaning" of the text (*AR* 115). By presenting familiar norms in unfamiliar arrangements, the literary text points up the deficiencies of those norms and manipulates the reader into formulating a reaction to these deficiencies.

The formulation of these reactions is what Iser calls "consistency-building," which term implies the problem it entails vis-à-vis Bakhtin: a reader, in finding inconsistencies in his reading of a text, must construct a way to make consistency out of inconsistency, or to smooth out contradictions. The reader groups together

all the different aspects of a text to form the consistency that the reader will always be in search of ... This "gestalt" must inevitably be colored by our own characteristic selection process. For it is not given by the text itself; it arises from the meeting between the written text and the individual mind of the reader with its own particular history of experience, its own consciousness, its own outlook. (*IR* 284)

The act of reading does not focus so much on the individual creation of the reader as it does on the intersubjective nature of the time-flow of reading and the perspectives that guide consistency-building and restrict the range of configurative meanings.

Iser's text is the guidepost by which meaning is hierarchized, the "given structures" leading the way. Since reading is an interactive process, it is the reader who constantly responds to the meanings *she* produces in understanding a text. Consistency-building and image-making are the continual reading activities guided by the text; the configurative meaning must be assembled by the reader, who is then in turn affected by what she has assembled. This literary effect results in a restructuring of the reader's experience, something that occurs most frequently in reading texts most of whose norms the reader already shares. In these cases, the deficiencies of the text force the reader to locate and "correct" them through the "norms" that allow her to structure her own reality or experience. Iser thus asserts that reading literature allows for "an experience which entails the reader constituting [her]self by constituting a reality hitherto unfamiliar" (*AR* 151). Literature changes its readers; aesthetic understanding changes subjects.

I want here to schematize two of the three domains through which Iser explores the ways in which literature does in fact change subjects; in examining them in depth, I want to suggest Bakhtin's (corresponding) potential intervention into these domains, and the possible results. The first domain (1) involves the text's potential for manipulating the production of meaning. (This is close to Ingarden's text-as-skeleton of schematized aspects actualized by a reader.) Second (2), Iser examines the *process* involved in reading, especially the "mental images" that build a cohesive aesthetic object during a reading. The third of these, the way in which literature has a communicative function (or, more precisely, the way in which aesthetic verbal constructs have a relationship to acts of communication as they occur historically), I will leave aside, since its central problem – how to conceive history in aesthetic analysis – is taken up by Jauss in his *Rezeptionsaesthetik*, and it is in relation to Jauss that Bakhtin's attempt to historicize aesthetics can be seen most clearly.

(1)   Both Iser and Bakhtin claim that the negotiation of language – both through the reading of texts and in day-to-day activity – functions to form the self at least in part. Iser's notion of the self is complicated because it takes place only in terms of its relation to the cognition of literary artefacts. To be fair to Iser, his work in *The act of reading* and *The implied reader* is explicitly concerned only with such aesthetic phenomena, and does not address broader philosophical concerns. Had he wished in those books to broaden his scope or emphasis, he might well have taken on such larger topics as the constitution of subjects; as it stands, it is reasonable to suggest that these broader considerations rest with the work of his predecessors, Ingarden and Husserl.

That Iser did not address the broader question nevertheless does not enable us to ignore the fact that a problem exists: the self forms the text, at least in the sense that a self orders perspectives "found" in a text; and at the same time the text forms the self. How does this work? It sounds a little like a circular chicken-and-egg argument in which nothing gets decided. Iser attempts to resolve the problem by positing a "bifurcation of the subject" which occurs during the reading process. When a reader appropriates an alien experience foregrounded in a text, she simultaneously backgrounds her own previous experiences. In assimilating this other experience, she alienates part of her self. "The division, then, is not between subject and object [as Poulet might suggest] but between [the] subject and [her]self" (*AR* 155). By reading this other experience, we come to recognize hitherto unrecognized parts of our own consciousness, and so reading becomes a therapeutic process.

One also needs to ask how the subject is constructed in the first place, and how this subject (who presumably picks a book off the shelf, opens it and begins reading) creates what Iser calls the "implied reader." This latter is a construct different from the real reader and which is "implied" by the language of a text. With this construct, Iser attempts to account for a reader's presence without having to deal with empirical readers. And yet the implied reader presents problems of its own: any text-structured "implied reader" is in effect simply another language-construct of the text itself. Iser's construction of a language-effect stresses the way in which aesthetic objects are *intentional*, but more to the point, the implied reader suggests that someone – the author, presumably – constructed ("consummated") the language of the text. The presence of this author cannot be ignored, since, aside from the subject or subjects reading a given text, there also exists the subject who, as a conscious, language-using being, is intimately involved in the transaction that comprises reading. Iser attempts, by creating an implied reader on the side of the actual reader, to avoid seeing the text as the product of a subject, and this in a sense doubles the problem. Now instead of having to consider how *one* subject is constructed and figures in the reading process, he has to deal with *two*. Iser eliminates the agency of the reading subject – a messy problem – in favor of the (much neater) prospect of placing meaning (the "implied" reader) in the text itself.

As I have suggested, the implied reader also operates on the assumption of merging the reader and the text into a single textual construct. Yet Iser characterizes the "construct," a "merging" of "subject and object" which absolves differences, as "an effect to be experienced" (*AR* 10). Putting this another way, by identifying the implied reader, the reading subject will be able to build a consistent text with which he can then rearrange his lived experience. The suggestion is that there exists in a text a single identifiable implied reader, and all one has to do is successfully figure out who or what this is in order to make sense out of (initially) alien experiences. Moreover, any reader in any historical site is able to do this. "The pragmatic historical dimension of reading is controlled in Iser's view by the stability through time of the cognitive structures of the reader. Iser's

'reader' is a Husserlian pure consciousness, a Transcendental Ego"
(Sprinker, *Imaginary relations* 41n.). Iser has here sacrificed a real reader
completely in favor of keeping a consistent aesthetic process;
moreover, he has avoided having to posit the way in which the
apparatus of consciousness changes through time by finding an
identifiable textual construct that remains immutable. Iser has thus
eliminated any chance of real, historical aberrations or contradictions
interfering with his procedure.

What you get when you read a book is closure. Iser's model of
reading is comprised of "repertoires" and textual "strategies" – the
ordering of material in a text – by way of a "wandering viewpoint,"
which is designed to describe what actually happens to a reader as she
"journeys" through the language of that text. Iser calls this journey a
"dialectic of protension and retention" (*AR* 112). These terms are
derived from Husserl and refer to the "modified expectations" and
"transformed memories" that inform the reading process. During such
a process, a reader evaluates the events in a text by comparing them
to her expectations for the (text's) future, and against a background of
(textual) events from past reading. If something occurs that the reader
hasn't expected, then she is forced to reformulate expectations
according to that disrupting event, and to reattribute significance to it
based on this new "schedule of events." The wandering viewpoint
"permits the reader to travel through the text ... unfolding the
multiplicity of interconnecting perspectives which are offset whenever
there is a switch from one to another" (*AR* 118). In a number of ways,
this process of "reattribution" and "reassessment" sounds a great deal
like Bakhtin's answerability: one assesses the validity of one's current
situation based on previously interiorized language and experience,
and if the two don't match then one has to reassess the current
situation. (For Bakhtin, the two will *never* match.) But we need to
investigate further: since Iser's phenomenology of reading is based
upon how one reads the language of a text in order to come to some
understanding of that text and in turn one's own situation, how does
a change of language actually work in such an assessment/
reassessment? Moreover, as I have suggested, the Bakhtinian process
of negotiation of meaning and of the self does not end, because the
cognition of the self and the understanding of the other's relation to
the self will never match. The suggestion Iser supplies is that, if the
reader is trying to build consistency, the end product must be some
gestalt or finished whole. If Iser wants to make literature a "living

event" (*AR* 127–8) by making and then breaking expectations through the images a text provides, then his finished product would seem to counter his stated project.

(2)   The concept of "image-making" appears in the last section of *The act of reading*. Iser's final move in that book is to examine the way reading a text is like a model of communication. He likens reading to a face-to-face dialogue in which two equal partners reach a degree of understanding; yet in reading, there is an "asymmetry between text and reader." This asymmetry arises, first, because the reader cannot test whether her understanding of a text is "correct," and second, because there is no regulative context between text and reader to establish intent, and so the context has to be constructed by the reader from textual "clues." Nevertheless, the text *does* exert some control over the communicative process by way of "blanks" in the text. These blanks are places where the "story" breaks off and another segment begins. The break often presents a locus of indeterminacy that must be, in Iser's words, "resolved" by the reader's ideation in order to complete the gestalt of the text's meaning.

However, Iser does not say precisely how to identify blanks in a text. He attempts to resolve the indeterminacy in *The implied reader*, where he performs readings of various blanks in literary works. In his discussion of *Vanity fair*, for example, Iser calls attention to Thackeray's strategy of breaking up the plot, and giving different sections of the story to different narrators, each of which is reliable in differing degrees; as well as the way in which Thackeray describes incidents "indirectly." Thus

simple situations are taken apart for the reader and split up into different facets. [The reader] is free to work his way through each one and to choose whichever he thinks most appropriate, but whether this decision favors [one or another of the "images" Thackeray has provided], there will always remain an element of doubt over the relationship under discussion.   (*IR* 117)

But these blanks seem to be conceptual, invisible at the level of the sentence or utterance. Iser seems to be speaking in terms of "ideation," of the way certain images in texts are formed, and the way one reads blanks or disparities between the gaps in ideation or conceptualization of a text.

Given that there exist indeterminacies in texts, and given that each reader brings a different background of aesthetic experience to such texts, it would seem likely that there would be the potential for all kinds of different (and probably some very far-fetched) readings of any given text. But this is something Iser would want to foreclose: his aim is to read texts in such a way as to gain some "gestalt meaning" from them. Like Ingarden, he proposes that texts possess a "skeleton," and if one reads a text correctly, one can flesh it out. All the reader has to do is follow the text: "Although the reader must participate in the assembly of meaning by realizing the structure inherent in the text, it must not be forgotten that he stands outside the text. His position must therefore be manipulated by the text if his viewpoint is to be *properly* guided" (*AR* 152; my emphasis).[2] But by explicitly placing the reader outside of a text, rather than in some relationship with it, to decode some meaning that the "implied reader" function in the text has determined for that outside reader, he ignores the possibility that subjects have at their disposal radically different "tools" with which to read. More problematic is the notion that an author constructs his "implied reader" in such a univocal way that it will draw out these "proper" readings.

Iser appears to be trying to do away with language's "ideological content," both in the language of the text as well as in the "background language" or background of previous aesthetic experiences of the reading subject. Biases need to be eliminated:

The more committed the reader is to an ideological position, the less inclined he will be to accept the basic theme-and-horizon structure of comprehension which regulates the text–reader interaction. He will not allow his norms to become a theme, because as such they are automatically open to the critical view inherent in the virtualized positions that form the background. And if he *is* induced to participate in the events of the text, only to find that he is then supposed to adopt a negative attitude toward values he does not wish to question, the result will often be open rejection of the book and its author.
(*AR* 202)

Rejecting a book or its author is something we have all done – we do not like his or her particular position on some subject or another, or we do not like the particular characterization in a book (or we just do not like the writer's prose), and we put it down, or we finish the book and reject it either as worthwhile or pleasing. The reason we do so is because language is the currency with which all business is transacted,

2 In *Interpretive conventions*, Stephen Mailloux discusses Iser's tendency to advocate a "valid" interpretation of a text, and that tendency in relation to Iser's wide acceptance into the American academy, an academy which is still largely influenced by New Critical "close readings" and "humanistic values." See especially 52–6.

and it carries with it to our encounter with this book or utterance all the meanings it has carried previously. No reader can read disinterestedly – at least not in the way Iser would like us to. Certainly Iser is right to propose that literature situates its readers in some sense differently from "everyday" experiences; but to suggest that it can do so in all senses, or that if it does, it should not, is insupportable.

Before I proceed to Iser's third domain for exploring the relationship of subjects through aesthetic phenomena, I want to go back to the first two in order to suggest how Bakhtin might be seen to intervene in Iser's method. By leaving the third domain to the end, I want to suggest that it is this domain that presents the most acute problems for both Iser and Bakhtin as they attempt to negotiate a phenomenological model of reading and subject-creation.

The similarities between Bakhtin and Iser should by now be apparent: both stress the importance of the interaction between text and reader, and both stress the two "nodes" of interaction (but to differing degrees), between the social structure of which the text is a product, and the text's "consumer." The biggest difference, of course, is that Bakhtin is more interested in the complex relation between both nodes of interaction than he is in examining those nodes as separate entities. Iser also assumes a stable text, and in doing so he also assumes a "givenness" to its structure apart from social considerations, something Bakhtin does not do. Thus the (aesthetic) verbal construct ceases to be a "social text," as it is for Bakhtin, and the constructive relationship between reader and text becomes more difficult to explain. Moreover, this lack of textual "stability" makes necessary for Bakhtin a constant negotiation of the meaning of a text or utterance, as well as of the very restrictions that would produce stability at all. Consummated aesthetic wholes are always non-coincident with themselves; if this non-coincidence is distinct enough, then the "ground rules," as it were, for their consummation have also to be reestablished along with the utterance. The problem this presents for Bakhtin – as we will see – is that it allows a broad range of "allowable" meanings for utterances and texts: one could say that almost anything goes.

As the negotiation of language changes the text, so it also changes reading and speaking subjects. What is strikingly familiar in the model Iser so far provides is the consistency-building and image-making capacity of literature. For Bakhtin, a speaking or reading subject interiorizes the language of a text (or of some other to whom she is speaking) by "searching" through a background of already spoken language and matching it up with what has been spoken in the current situation. If the contexts are similar, and if there is a "common sign-experience," then the interlocutors are able to reach similar understandings of that situation. If the backgrounds are different, then there must occur negotiation. Moreover, it is also remarkable that Iser refers to the reader as "constituting [her]self," a process Bakhtin asserts occurs in all language situations. The main difference, however, is that Bakhtin is not so much interested in finding a self-same consistency in all texts and experiences of texts, but rather in finding value that inevitably arises out of the necessary *in*consistency that comes from reading. Of all the difficulties that will come up with regard to Bakhtin's project, this one will prove the most problematic.

At this point, we should return to the corresponding domains of exploring literature to see how Bakhtin's phenomenology figures into Iser's.

(1) In Iser's conception of the way a text's meaning is produced by the subject, "alien" experience is matched up against a subject's already perceived background, resulting in a "bifurcation of the subject" whereby the reader recognizes hitherto unrecognized parts of his own consciousness. This does at first glance seem similar to the way in which aesthetic experience takes place through the interiorization of language. In aesthetic consummation, as we have seen, the subject recognizes in the utterance that which could only be seen if he were in a position *outside* of himself, as viewed by some other. But the difference lies in what each theorist foregrounds: for Iser, it is *experience*. That is, Iser suggests that the understanding one acquires when one reads a text is the understanding of some represented experience (or person, or event, or object) provided by the author. We are able to conceive of a world we did not know existed. Yet Iser ignores the distinction between the event and the *linguistically represented* event: the text is in a very real sense the utterance of some subject (the author) which must be negotiated not as an object but as the result of the aesthetic consummation by some subject who has in turn taken cognitive–ethical action and produced an utterance or collection of utterances. Iser's reading "compares" the world of the reader and the world of the text, and when those worlds are unlike, the

reader "recognizes" the possibility (or perhaps the impossibility) of that textual world, and assimilates it into her background. Bakhtin's "text" or utterance is the cognitive–ethical result of an aesthetic event which is itself the result of intersubjective negotiation between a self and some other, which in at least some sense serves to re-author the subject himself. Iser's reading is a kind of therapeutic comparison of content; for Bakhtin, the therapeutic nature of reading derives from the creation and reorientation of selves. Moreover, Bakhtin's phenomenology of experience takes place in all language transactions; Iser's is grounded specifically within the aesthetic, with no possibility of translation from the aesthetic realm to the everyday.

Neither the "comparison of contents" (Iser) nor the constant reorientation of selves (Bakhtin) solves the problem of the *agency* of the subject involved in a language exchange. How, if language in both cases is at least partially formative of the self, does the self in turn have the ability to "choose" or "recognize" other experiences heretofore unexperienced? Or, to put this another way, how does a subject recognize something (either an experience or an ideological sign) that is not in his language or experiential background? Iser claims that the imagination "experiences" previously *unimaginable* experiences. The language that comprises the "images" in literature can spark *new* imaginary power. This is a determinately aesthetic process, that results from the reading of a formally invariant text. Bakhtinian agency is built in the interiorization process. What characterizes the uniqueness of human sentience is the capacity of humans for sign-production. We interiorize signs as they are spoken in particular contexts, and we reutter them in similar (but by definition distinct) contexts; because these situations are distinct, the reuttering of a sign that we have heard before will also necessarily have meaning that is different from its original meaning. Different contexts force subjects to "project" the non-coincident signs already interiorized differently, in effect forcing the subject to "create" a new utterance. Signs do not create new imaginative experience, but they can force speaking or listening subjects to consummate situations differently and as a result utter newly contextualized language. Bakhtin's conception of agency can change, it would seem, one's lived experience by changing one's language. The difficulty with Bakhtin's solution to Iser's problem is that such change in subject positions is a lengthy process. If, for example, one wishes to change one's understanding of "poverty" or "working poor," the reorientation of linguistic meaning may take place over several years, as the subject who reads (or experiences and reutters) such language also is able to judge how this understanding changes depending upon the situations of the "others" who also hear or utter such language. But even the change that might take place at the level of language experience does not guarantee that one's material (lived) situation to those terms – and the "others" by whom the subject consummates the context of the language – will change coincidentally. It *can*; but this is a slow process, built by the relation of many non-coincident selves (see Rhadakrishnan, *Theory in an uneven world*). We will see how this process works in more detail in succeeding chapters. Suffice it to say at present that one's lived relation does *not* radically change, if it changes at all – as in Iser's conception of the self – through the act of reading.

And yet this change was the reason Iser saw the need to construct an "implied reader" in the first place. In that conception, the implied reader was a textual construction that was to lead the actual reading subject into relations of expectation and disappointment or con-firmation of those expectations in a "reading interaction." We have seen the problem with this construction. For Bakhtin, there also takes place an interaction that might be called, similar to Iser's model of reading, a "merging," but not of an object (that is, the text's "meaning") with some other object (that is, a construction of that text, such as an implied reader). Instead, reading is the work of a subject to match the language she has already interiorized with what she can define in the text as "speech genres," which are utterances from various contexts placed into a single construction for some current verbal context. These "speech genres" are in turn consummated aesthetic moments produced by the author and can be considered cognitive–ethical evidence of that author's verbal background. The text is evidence of yet another subject whose acts of answerability are being "consummated" by the reading subject, so in effect reading a text, aesthetic or otherwise, is an intersubjective act which should be considered as such when it is analyzed. Bakhtin's reader thus must find places at which she is being "addressed" (as in, for example, Fielding's addresses to his "dear reader," which Iser points to repeatedly as evidence for the implied reader), and from there also locate contexts in which she seems to be implicated by finding language that matches her own language background. Then all of this must be used in the double movement of consummation to constitute the aesthetic whole of the text as well as the newly configured reading subject herself.

This "merging of subjectivities," however, presents a problem for a Bakhtinian textual analysis. Since a text is not completed (in Iser's sense) — because there are no fixed meanings in a text around which indeterminacies hover to be finished — then, when a subject finishes a book and closes its cover, the aesthetic consummation may have ended, but any cognitive–ethical acts that result from that consummation begin. The language-event of reading does not end when the subject finishes the book, but rather continues in dialogue: once a language-act is completed, it becomes interiorized and acts as a springboard for yet another aesthetic event to be consummated either by that same subject or by some other. What do you do, using Bakhtinian terms, when a person finishes a book, reaches some idea of its "meaning" or "significance," and then goes on to live his life only to find that the language from that text, now interiorized, comes back in his own utterances? Moreover, not only does it "come back" when this subject goes on with his (at least partially) aesthetic consummations in everyday life, but the language of the text, in its various contexts, works to *change* that subject's lived relations. It is not as simple as saying that once one has read Pynchon one sees conspiracies lurking behind every corner. Nor can one simply say that, having "interiorized" Pynchon's consummated aesthetic event, one's ethical action will have to account for the possibility that such "conspiracies" might exist. But it is fair to say that one cannot have read Pynchon without reaching some new understanding of the way language functions in different (aesthetic) contexts, and further, that the reading subject is *differently situated* after reading Pynchon, if not obviously so. Again, Iser's implied reader is a tool whereby reading subjects supposedly become "drawn into" a text so that they may, after "completing" that text, live their lives differently. Yet, because it is also a construct of the text — and because Iser does not go far enough in positing a historical subject responsible for placing that construct into the text — there is no way to see how that affective relationship works. Bakhtin, on the other hand, suggests explicitly that the text is the result of a historical author, but by making the aesthetic/cognitive–ethical result such a long and drawn-out affair, it is not easy to see how it effectively changes people through the reading process.

(2) We have seen some initial problems in the way that Iser defines the "indeterminacies" or gaps in his text. Here I want to raise that problem as it is conceived by Stanley Fish, because I think the

same criticism can, at this point, be brought against Bakhtin. Fish early on noted Iser's indeterminacy problem in "Why no one's afraid of Wolfgang Iser," suggesting that the "textual segments" that define the gaps in the text, while "simply identifiable" as words (chapter headings, in the case to which Fish refers), are not

"pointable-to" apart from some other interpretive perspective ... Even to see [such a feature] as a chapter heading is already to have assigned it an interpretation according to a system of intelligibility in which chapter headings are things that it is possible to see ... Perception is never innocent of assumptions, and the assumptions within which it occurs will be responsible for the contours of what is perceived.   (78)

Iser sees these gaps because he assumes they are there to begin with. Any reader who follows along will also see them.

Bakhtin makes similar assumptions. In later essays Bakhtin pinpoints various speech genres – he does this also in his work on Rabelais, Dostoevsky, and the history of the novel – and theorizes that readers can "pick out" certain micro-utterances that belong in specific social contexts (such as the marketplace, the doctor's office, and so on). Moreover, the "gaps" between the various genres (or micro-utterances) are the places at which "dialogization" occurs. These gaps are also assumed to be "pointable-to." One can raise the objection here that one has to agree with Bakhtin's theory in order to see his gaps as well.

The difference between Iser and Bakhtin here, using Fish's terminology, is that these gaps in Bakhtin's theory are "visible" but they are never "given." If I am able to recognize a particular speech genre in an utterance, I can choose to use its context if I believe that the "other" involved in the aesthetic act (or, in a simpler case, the resulting conversation that has that act as its object) will also understand that context. The difference is that the other might just as well *not* see it in the same context that I do. In fact, not only is the context of such a speech genre open to negotiation, but – if my interlocutor does not agree that such a genre exists in an utterance – the existence of it is also open to negotiation. It all depends on what kind of language the subjects in question have interiorized.

In theory at least (and as I have seen in practice in several first-year and second-year college literature courses), all kinds of different readings can be made of the same utterance or literary work, depending upon the subjects' background language-experiences. The context to which individual subjects might point for their individual readings is indeed boundless. Moreover, because context *is* boundless – since the aesthetic act takes place in a constant dialectic of consummation and cognitive–ethical act – individual subjects can constantly point to some previous context as their reason for having consummated a moment in the way they did, a context to which the other or interlocutor in such a situation does not have access. In other words, there is always the historical/ideological baggage that becomes interiorized along with a language-situation that has to be accounted for. Iser cannot find a suitable way to account for it; Bakhtin accounts for it by suggesting that it is ideological material that must be negotiated along with the "meaning" of the text.

But how does one tell whether one "meaning" is better than another? If everything is on the table for negotiation, any reading could result, and any reading is as valid as any other. It is true that within "smaller circles" – circles of national languages, classes, regions, religions (that is, within culturally defined groups) – language contexts are similar, and readings of texts or understandings of utterances are likely to be similar (Bakhtin/Voloshinov, *Marxism and the philosophy of language* 20–21). But this does not mean that variance will not occur within such groups, or that variance between such groups will not be significant. Further, it does not resolve the difference between how someone like Stanley Fish reads a novel and how Edward Said reads the same novel, not to mention how one can tell which reading is superior. The Bakhtinian view of how agreement is reached is that if various people's background-languages are sufficiently similar, then these people will come to agreement (most of the time) on how various texts or utterances should be "consummated." What is needed is some way to provide access to the social forces at work that affect the way subjects interiorize language and which determine what language is available for interiorization. Iser, like Ingarden before him, has presumed two kinds of realms, into which one alternately moves back and forth when reading. One has an object – the literary work – and a subject who reads that work according to its repertoire (a textually derived set of norms which operate by deviating slightly from day-to-day norms). Yet the ideological world of the author, in which one can presumably ask, "Where did this person acquire his or her language? How did this person understand the world in order to write this?" and the ideological world of the reader, in which one can presumably ask,

"Where did I get the language with which to engage this text and this author? and what kind of world do I live in that I can read it in this way?" are bracketed. Iser, in effect, ignores that the very norms that he uses as guideposts in his text are historically determined:

[S]ocial or intersubjective models describe the reading process whose *exact details* are relatively unaffected by broader economic and political conditions *once the process is in motion*. That is, the institutional conventions governing reading may be grossly determined by ... larger social structures; but once the conventions are in place, those extrainstitutional forces do not affect the specific dynamics of interpretation in reading.

(Mailloux, *Interpretive conventions* 41)

But the text itself is "*part of the world*, (even though the process it sets in motion [may] not [be])" (Fish, *Is there a text?* 75). Iser wants to claim that what a person says in everyday life is assessed as to how close it comes to some given material fact, but "for the literary text there can be no such 'facts'; instead we have a sequence of schemata which have the function of stimulating the reader himself into establishing 'the facts'" (*AR* 141). Iser wants to claim, in other words, that the difference between the aesthetic and the world is the former's mediated nature. But as Fish points out – and, we will see, as Bakhtin suggested before him:

mediated access to the world is the only access we have; in face-to-face situations or in the act of reading a novel, the properties of objects, persons, and situations emerge as a consequence of acts of construction that follow ... from a prestructured understanding of the shapes any meaningful item could possibly have.   (*Is there a text?* 80)

What is needed, then, is a way to judge whether one particular mediation is more "accurate" (or, if not accurate, suitable) than another. For this, one needs a way to define the nature of the mediation: the way historical mediation affects the reception and interpretation of a text.

II

The reintroduction of history and an analysis of how it affects the way an individual subject receives or consummates aesthetic objects was the aim of Hans Robert Jauss's *Rezeptionsaesthetik*. Here I want briefly to outline Jauss's theory by describing four principal problems with which it deals; to discuss the problematics in relation to the work of

Jauss's predecessor, Hans-Georg Gadamer; and to suggest ways in which the problems of integrating historical analysis into a phenomenology of reception affect Bakhtin's phenomenological project. What I will suggest, finally, is that Bakhtin – limited at least so far in his conception of how language functions socially and historically (though, as we will see shortly, he works to remedy this shortcoming) – is so limited because of his assumptions about how aesthetic events are consummated, and by a (potential) failure to distinguish between the mediated nature of history and the material construction of that mediation.

(1) Jauss's theory of reception begins with a notion of history and of historical succession. His project wishes to connect the aesthetic work to its function in the current social world – much like Iser's – and, in so doing, contribute to the progress of general history as "the ongoing totalization of the past through the aesthetic experience."[3] "[T]he process of reception becomes describable in the expansion of a semiotic system that accomplishes itself between the development and the correction of a system" (*TAR* 23). In other words, the literary artefact – though not understandable in the context of its initial creation and reception – can be understood by reading its subsequent receptions, up to and including its current reception and "horizon of expectation." This latter is defined as

the definable frame of reference of the reader's expectations: this frame of reference for each work develops in the historical moment of its appearance from a previous understanding of the genre, from the forms and themes of already familiar works, and from the contrasts between poetic and practical language.   (11)

History, as envisioned here, is a process which – though it has no *telos* which might be identified in the future – nevertheless valorizes the present moment, through which works are understood. History up until that moment is a "correctible" or "alterable" system, alterable precisely by those works that are seen to be understood through it (see Sprinker, *Imaginary relations* 97–103).

Jauss's idea of history is in part the result of Gadamer's "question and answer" model on which the former bases his work. According to this model, when a reader encounters a text, she enters into a kind of

3 Hans Robert Jauss, *Towards an aesthetics of reception* (Minneapolis: University of Minnesota Press, 1977), 20. All further references that appear in the text will be abbreviated *TAR*.

conversation with the past in which the give-and-take, the questioning and answering involved in an openness to this "other," leads to understanding. By constantly posing and reposing questions from age to age, *Rezeptionsaesthetik* assumes that the last question is that by which a work's "meaning" can be "answered," by answering a series of questions that have been posed since the work's writing. The valorization of the present moment – from which history can be seen as a long sequence of questions and answers – rests on two assumptions, both of which need to be questioned. First, Jauss (along with Gadamer) does not assume that history is overdetermined. His historical series depends on history being a kind of unified continuum, the moments of which are not composed of contradictory ideologies or systems of thought and belief. Second, Jauss assumes (as does Gadamer) that the aesthetic object, though not objectified in von Ranke's sense, is nevertheless determinate: it has *a* meaning that is approachable through the continuum of history as conceived above. This foreclosure of meaning in a sense formalizes the process of reading. Rather than allowing for contradictory ideological elements that may appear in a work, and opting instead for a "smoothed-over" definition of meaning, Jauss also potentially eliminates the possibility that the very method with which he is working – and the rules by which it operates – is itself ideologically defined and likewise subject to negotiation (in Bakhtin's sense). Moreover, this negotiation of the rules by which hermeneutics operates takes place at the same time and at the same level as the negotiation of meaning.

(2) At the end of "Literary history as a challenge to literary theory," the essay that begins *Towards an aesthetics of reception*, and in the essay that follows, "History of art and pragmatic history," Jauss begins to construct what in his view is an alternative way to think of literary history based on his ideas about horizons of expectation. The cornerstone of Jauss's model of reading is a hermeneutic in which certain aesthetic objects are discernible to individual reading subjects. More specifically, Jauss's model posits a relationship between subject and object (a reader and an identifiable text). In order to do so, Jauss reintroduces, from Gadamer's *Truth and method*, the idea of the subjective, in which the experience of the interpreter is called upon (as opposed to suggesting that the interpreter is ideologically neutral) during the reading and interpreting of a work. The writing of literary history is a "fusion of horizons" of the current reader or interpreter

and those that have come before (rather than the objectivist description of those horizons as being unique and unrelated). Jauss thus builds obsolescence into the writing of literary history: at one moment, one reads and interprets a work; in the succeeding moment or moments, another interpreter, drawing upon your interpretation, comes up with another, different interpretation of the same work. No literary history is immune from such a scheme.

This appears similar to the model Bakhtin proposes, in which literary genres come to be accepted into the "canon" of literature: observers or readers of a particular work interpret it according to their own background language and consummate it accordingly. Readers and writers of a given time have particular languages (speech genres within a national language) with which they inscribe their "own" language (in various "dialogic" or "monologic" contexts) in a work (see "From the prehistory of novelistic discourse" 61–5). Various readers, using the speech genres they have at their disposal, "author" individual works according to their own language-contexts. Each reader forms her own "horizon" from which she reads or judges verbal aesthetic constructs.

The real difference between Bakhtin's and Jauss's notions of how works are actually read by human subjects lies in the latter's concept of societies. Jauss believes that, in reading a work, readers receive it initially "within the objectifiable system of expectations that arises for each work in the historical moment of its appearance" (*TAR* 22). The notion of "systems of objectifiable expectations" is difficult since those systems are also socially determined along with the texts that must be judged in relation to them. Jauss posits a variability in the understanding of historical subjects: they have different understanding depending upon their historical situatedness, and also depending upon the various previous "concretizations" of a work and upon the general history at the time of those concretizations. Two terms are held constant here: the general history of the time, and the objectified previous concretizations. What is most problematic for Jauss is that, by holding these terms constant and suggesting that it is the prejudices of the readers that create "horizons" against which works will be read, history – the term which is most important for Jauss's conception of literary analysis and reception – is a monologic, monolithic term.

(3) Jauss, like Iser and those that preceded them, wanted to stress,

and find a way to analyze, the "socially *formative* function of literature" (*TAR* 40). Literary events have an effect upon the lives of the people that read them, as Jauss illustrates in his example of *Madame Bovary*: Flaubert was accused of propagating immorality, at least partially because his innovative use of the "style direct libre" was misunderstood. The significance of the artistic device in this case is that it enabled a questioning of social mores:

Since the new artistic device broke through an old novelistic convention – the moralistic judgment of the represented characters that is always unequivocal and confirmed in the description – the novel was able to radicalize or to raise new questions of lived praxis, which during the proceedings caused the original occasion for the accusation – alleged lasciviousness – to recede wholly into the background. (*TAR* 43)

Yet literary language and historical events are distinct categories of events, between which there needs to be a connection, one Jauss asserts but seems not to be able to show. Stephen Mailloux points to the fact that the connection between life and art is language (*Interpretive conventions* 169), the same connection Bakhtin shows most vividly in *Marxism and the philosophy of language* and *The formal method*. Literary language is the most complexly ideological language: it is language where authors must not only consummate aesthetic moments, but must contextualize those consummations explicitly in the language of a text. Yet Jauss cannot do the same. Whereas Bakhtin notes that the difference between "discourse in life" and "discourse in art" is a matter of the degree of contextualized language in a text or utterance, Jauss maintains that the difference is one *in kind*. Jauss characterizes a literary event as taking place within a system of objectively determined, aesthetically established norms, which itself is situated within another system, namely history; and characterizes general history as causal (*TAR* 22). If both the aesthetic object and the historical system in which it exists are objectively determined, there is no possible way in which a reader can have anything to do with the relationship between the aesthetic object and historical knowledge. As de Man suggested in his introduction to Jauss's work, a hermeneutics of reading and a hermeneutics of experience may not be compatible (*The resistance to theory*, 64–5, 67).

(4)   Jauss tries to resolve the above difficulties by trying to engage a concept of ideology that at once is instrumental in producing both

literary texts and everyday language artefacts and everyday human experience. In "History of art and pragmatic history," Jauss calls literary history a kind of system:

Literature ... is a kind of grammar or syntax, with relatively fixed relations of its own: the arrangement of the traditional and uncanonized genres; modes of expression, kinds of style, and rhetorical figures; contrasted with this arrangement is the much more variable realm of semantics: the literary subjects, archetypes, symbols, and metaphors. (*TAR* 38)

The problem here, though, is that literary history is so narrowly defined that literary texts fall outside the domain of other social things. How does one characterize literary history in relation to a more general history? How does one "place the 'literary series' and the 'non-literary series' in a relation that encompasses the relationship between literature and history without forcing literature, at the expense of its characters as art, into a function of mere copying or commentary" (*TAR* 18)?

Jauss responds that the difference between literature and history consists in the following:

Literary works differ from purely historical documents precisely because they do more than simply document a particular time, and remain "speaking" to the extent that they attempt to resolve problems of form or content, and so extend far beyond the silent relics of the past. (*TAR* 69)

Yet literature itself also seems to have a documentary character. The fact that all human relations (at least for Bakhtin) inescapably reside in the realm of language suggests that the difference between historical documents and so-called literary ones is not as great as Jauss would have it.

The "way in" to the problematic relation of art to life in Jauss's *Rezeptionsaesthetik* begins with a distinction made by Mailloux in *Interpretive conventions*. Between "traditional accounts of production [of literary works] and its impact on reception," both elements that are taken up in Jauss's study, "stands its interpretation by readers and critics" (169). For Mailloux, Jauss's method is two-fold: the first task is to identify the author's view of history (or, more specifically, text production) through a reconstruction of the history of reception of a given work. The second task is to assess the current critical reception of that work, by "re-adjusting" the reception history according to current understanding. In a more schematic outline, there are two analyses: (a) that of text-production (based on the author's view of history, author→text); and (b) accounts of reception (text→critic/ reader). Mailloux explains that an intervening third step, the conception of the interpretive act itself, is ignored by Jauss. Most critical is that, according to Bakhtin, these three tasks occur simultaneously and complexly. The most important aspect, however, is the *social* definition of language itself, something elided both by Mailloux and Jauss.

One can begin to see the difference between Jauss's and Bakhtin's methods in Jauss's reaction to Marxism. In the "Literary history as challenge" essay, Jauss singles out Lukacs and Lucien Goldmann for their conceptions of what he sees as "reflectionist" theories of language-artefacts. He sees them as advocating art as a simple passive reflection of the external world. On the other hand, he does recognize that Marxism is not a monolithic or dogmatic system, as it is sensitive to issues of reception and effect. Framed in Bakhtin's terms, the problem is the following: Jauss insists that art is created by historical human subjects; and that the creation of works is something done in history, but in an important sense separate from that world. He also stresses the importance of the assessment of reception of the work once it has been created. But there is no connection between these two principles: Humans understand ideologically, and then they "read" the language-artefact; but they do not *read* ideologically on Jauss's account. What is missing – as I have suggested – is the connection between language and ideology: any verbal aesthetic construct is created from the language of other contexts (that is, other inter-subjective aesthetic consummations), and so any reception of a work is also necessarily yet another intersubjective consummation. Selves, for Jauss, and reactions to the world are social creations, but works are still somehow objective. Jauss rails against Marxism's one-sided reliance on theories of (authorial) production, but goes on in equally one-sided fashion to stress that the *reader* in fact produces the text's meaning without understanding sufficiently the role of social language for either author or reader.

Jauss begins laying out his theory of reception on a basis that suggests a dialectical movement between the process of production and the process of reception. In this way, he moves between what could be considered the poles of a formal phenomenology of the text and Marxism, much as I will argue Bakhtin does. His aim is to build an analysis of the way an author of a work produces out of the everyday material of the world around him; and to build an analysis of how readers of such a work "re-create" it according to their own assessment of the everyday material of their world. He hopes to have united history and aesthetics:

The aesthetic implication lies in the fact that the first reception of a work by the reader includes a test of its aesthetic value in comparison with works already read. The obvious historical implication of this is that the understanding of the first reader will be sustained and enriched in a chain of receptions from generation to generation; in this way the historical significance of a work will be decided and its aesthetic value made evident.
(*TAR* 20)

Substitute the terms "language" and "ideology" for "aesthetics" and "history" to see a bit more clearly what Jauss is attempting to do: language is placed in a text in a particular way in order to "refract" the world; receivers of that work, situated ideologically, read according to expectations generated by works they have read before. In Bakhtinian terms, the author consummates a moment or situation and writes it in language that is by definition ideological material, and a reading subject in turn consummates that language for herself (with relation to some non-coincident self) from within her own ideologically situated position. For Jauss we have an author writing language that is ideological, but once it gets put on the page it becomes an object; the reader "judges" the work according to her own ideological placement (that is, what she has read before), but gathers only information about the text *as aesthetic object*. In a sense we have a reversal of the Husserlian position: there, works could be perceived aesthetically, not ideologically, but any communication between subjects with reference to that work was necessarily "dirtied" by ideology; here, works are perceived with reference to ideology, but after the moment of ideological reference, the object is "completed" aesthetically.

Jauss tries to integrate the dialectical movement between ideological and aesthetic evaluation in the "horizon of expectations," which Robert Holub calls an "intersubjective system or structure of expectations, a 'system of references' or a mind-set that a hypothetical individual might bring to any text" (*Reception theory* 58). We will see, in relation to Gadamer, the specific problem hermeneutics has in defining the subject involved in such a system. Jauss tries to objectify his horizon, which brings up two additional questions: how does one perform an empirical procedure (which Jauss tries to do in the later essays in *Towards an aesthetics of reception*) when one posits the transcendental nature of a "horizon." Further, if the horizon is in fact transcendent, how, if one is ideologically situated, does one move from one's position to the horizon in order to make literary judgments?

Let us take Robert Holub's definition of "horizon of expectations" as a "'system of references' ... a hypothetical individual might bring to any text." If one takes into consideration only the interaction between various readers of a given work (and one has to understand that certain readers have read certain works, and so have different ideas of what comprises the different genres, and as a result each will have a different "horizon of expectations"), then "intersubjective" is a felicitous term for what goes on in the interpretation of texts. Even if one considers (as is, I think, Jauss's purpose) the different responses from age to age of a particular work, and looks at the written record of the differences in response (consummation) between such ages, then the term is still useful. But Bakhtin's conception of intersubjectivity is rather different. A work is *not* objectifiable. Certainly a book is a material production of ink on paper, (usually) between two bound covers to be sold or loaned, yet what specifically comprises the work is languages/ideologies. In defining things in terms of language, one also has to account for the persons who utter that language; the language-orientation of those persons (the way language has been contextualized and consummated); the person for whom the utterance is intended (and that person's "contextual baggage"); as well as those for whom the utterance is not intended but who nevertheless hear the utterance and are implicated in it. I am suggesting in all this that Jauss's intersubjectivity is one-sided in favor of the "consumption" of the work. Different people with distinct material and temporal situations consume works differently. But there isn't any ideological accounting for the language of the text, insofar as how it got there and what ideological sign-orientations are contextualized in it. Jauss considers language more like signals than complex signs:

The psychic process in the reception of a text is, in the primary horizon of aesthetic experience, by no means only an arbitrary series of subjective impressions, but rather the carrying out of *specific instructions* in a process of *directed perception*, which can be comprehended according to its constitutive motivations and *triggering signals*, and which also can be described by a textual linguistics.   (*TAR* 23; my emphasis)

As in Iser's phenomenology of the text, all a reading subject has to do is "follow the directions" he finds in the text. Language is only ideological insofar as readers instinctively "know" how to read, provided the signposts.

A second problem that accompanies Jauss's so-called intersubjective method is the way the method itself works. Jauss suggests that the procedure involved in an aesthetics of reception is an empirical one, which would seem to contradict his often-stated intention of finding a *transcendent* aesthetic construct. As in "History of art and pragmatic history" (particularly in his analysis of Baudelaire), Jauss's procedure is largely a semiotic analysis, in which he reads the intertextuality of signs that have been placed in the language of a work and then goes on to discuss their "meaning." This semiotic analysis is intersubjective only insofar as it analyzes the way different readings coexist, and insofar as it examines what this coexistence brings to the reading of a work. What it does not do is to suggest the way in which the language was the act of some language-using subject (that is, the author), and that the author's relation to the language she uses is just as important to the reading of any work as that of the reading subject. "De-ideologizing" the language of the written text freezes any reading of it and effectively takes it out of history. And finally, in bracketing the reader's historical situatedness during the moment one reads (or in Bakhtin's terms, consummates) a text (or utterance), one falls into the analysis of system without a corresponding analysis of the system's origins, which runs completely counter to Bakhtin's stated beginnings, where he castigated contemporary literary scholarship (that is, Formalism) for not having worked out the philosophical grounding of its system.

III

What lies at the heart of many of the inconsistencies in Jauss's work is Gadamer's hermeneutic project, and it is in relation to this earlier and broader work that, finally, we can begin to say where Bakhtin's phenomenological work fits, and how it can be seen to solve – or if not solve, intervene in – those problems. In the "story" above, Iser's and Ingarden's work is most closely related to the original phenomenological project set down by Husserl; Jauss's explicitly works against that project's ignorance of the historical situatedness of reading subjects. Bakhtin's work, in some sense pivoting upon the notion of historical situatedness as Gadamer's does, turns at this point from its beginnings in phenomenology toward a more social theory of ideology and language.

Gadamer's work, like Ingarden's, began with Husserlian phenomenology, but the former's project developed from the notion that the transcendental ego elaborated by Husserl was inadequate to a theory of linguistically mediated cultural phenomena. What should be asked of this starting point – as it should be asked now in retrospect of Iser and Ingarden as well as of Jauss and Bakhtin – is whether a theory that understands human cognition as historically situated (and thus incapable itself of assessing the validity of its claims) is adequate to an analysis of aesthetic artefacts that are likewise situated, and of the cultural and historical material out of which those artefacts come. Both Ingarden and Iser began with the idea, contrary to Husserl, that it is necessary to account for what happens after the moment of aesthetic response to a verbal construct, not only because humans can and do discuss those constructs, but because the constructs also have a communicative function that is by definition *inter*subjective. But in positing an objectified construct that could only be partially completed, and by ignoring the very mediatedness of human cognition, neither Ingarden nor Iser could adequately explain the communicative or aesthetic function of verbal aesthetic artefacts. Jauss's project, like Gadamer's before him, began by thinking of human cultural artefacts as being created and received in historical contexts. But, as we will see, Gadamer's notion of what history is, and how the historical situatedness of contemporary interpreters is formed, jeopardizes his project and lies at the root of the problems of his followers; moreover, these notions can also be found to be at work (at least in some sense) in the project of another phenomenologist of language, Bakhtin.

For the purposes of exploring the difficulties in Gadamer's project in relation to Bakhtin's, I rely on what John Brenkman has set up as three "theoretical – or ... ideological – commitment[s]" in which Gadamer is invested:

(1) The cultural tradition is a *universe of meaning* in the strong sense that meaningfulness of transmitted texts is determined by the tradition as a whole just as the tradition as a whole is a unity comprised of the meaning of the texts transmitted within it.   (2) The tradition derives its authoritativeness in the present from the power of transmitted texts to carry meaning forward in time without reference to or dependence upon the social context in which they were originally produced.   (3) The tradition is renewed and reappropriated in every age through the application of an

interpretively secured understanding which renders the tradition the sole and unified source of meaning for that age.

Each of these principles is actualized through a corresponding set of procedures, as follows:

(1) Interpretations are regulated by the postulate of the unity of part/whole relations ...   (2) The social genesis of the text is methodically bracketed on the grounds that the internal coherence of the text and its meanings can be separated from their original context.   (3) The sociocultural context of contemporary reception is also methodically bracketed.[4]

I want to explore each of these suppositions as they contain Gadamer's (and to a great extent, Jauss's) project, and as they can be seen to define (to a greater or lesser extent) the genesis of Bakhtin's project from a phenomenology of utterance and subject to a historical or ideological phenomenology of culture. I will discuss the second and third of these presuppositions and come back to the first, since it is that first which founds the second two, and which is the block on which Bakhtin will stumble.

The commitment to bracket the social genesis of the text (2) has already been discussed at some length in relation to Jauss's *Rezeptionsaesthetik*, namely that it effectively pulls the rug out from under his own claim that it is precisely the historical situatedness of that text and its subsequent reception that guides one's interpretation of it. Gadamer's explicit aim is the same: "The real meaning of a text ... does not depend on the contingencies of the author and whom he originally wrote for. It is certainly not identical with them, for it is always partly determined by the historical situation of the interpreter and hence by the objective course of history" (Gadamer, *Truth and method* 263). Gadamer wishes to expand the cultural value of aesthetic interpretation by insisting that such interpretations understand their activity as fully within and productive of contemporary culture. At the same time, the contemporary force of aesthetic experiences signals that the work's claim to validity reaches beyond its original context. Gadamer here moves from granting that works reach beyond their original site to suggesting that such works only retain in a limited way their historical origin and thus go beyond *any* historical confinement, and likewise suggests that the work offers absolute contempor-

---

4 In John Brenkman, *Culture and domination* (Ithaca: Cornell University Press, 1987), 30. Further references cited in the text will be abbreviated *CD*.

aneousness with the present historical context. Brenkman has got it
right, I think, when he states that these assertions cut short "another
possible line of inquiry – one which would entertain the possibility
that the opposition between an artwork's historical inherence in a past
society and its expressive power in the present is an open, complex
relation, rather than assuming that 'historical confinement' and
'contemporaneousness' are mutually exclusive" (*CD* 33). The work
that can be done if one does not accept Gadamer's claim that works are
either confined or contemporary takes the form of an analysis of how
the formal and communicative structures of a work mark its inherence
in a set of social practices; how at the same time it might break these
contexts; how this break becomes readable by contemporary readers;
and how the continuities (and discontinuities) between the artwork's
genesis and our reception of it are experienced aesthetically.

It is precisely these kinds of analyses that Bakhtin suggests are the
"proper work" for literary scholarship in both *Marxism and the
philosophy of language* and *The formal method*. Since language is
ideological material, and since the utterances found in books (or in any
verbal constructs) are cognitive–ethical results of (successful or
relatively unsuccessful) aesthetic consummation, what we do when we
come into contact with language is to assess its formal and
communicative structure to find in what ways the author has
consummated the situation (or character) that is "in" the text. For
examples of this, one has only to look at the sections in "Discourse in
the novel" where Bakhtin analyzes the different speech genres in
Dickens's novels, for instance, in which he is able to locate distinct
speech genres that he guesses belong to diverse cultural and political
groups in nineteenth-century England. What a reader does, when
coming into contact with such language, is to search her own language
background to find if there are any cultural equivalents for such genres
in her own experience, and how they have been structured. Finally, she
begins to analyze how they are structured differently in her own
experience from how Dickens has structured them, and how that
conflict of experience becomes consummated aesthetically. We will
see how this kind of ideological analysis works in more detail in the
following chapters. What must be said here is that this kind of analysis
marks a departure for Bakhtin from one that is purely interested in the
relationships between an individual reading subject and the language
she experiences in a text to one that must necessarily inquire into the
previous construction of the language, not only of the text but of the

reader's own conscious understanding. As I have tried to suggest in my discussions of Iser and of Jauss, this is a logical transformation in the mode of inquiry, one that – because of these latter's stated aversion to ideological "interference" – they resist. It is hardly possible to define the aesthetic object as a human linguistic construct and fail to inquire into just how it was constructed and of what its material building blocks (that is, language and utterance) came to be made. To some extent, Bakhtin's work in *Marxism and the philosophy of language* and *The formal method* lays the groundwork for such material inquiries into the ideological construction of language. What actually follows from these works – in *The dialogic imagination* essays, the Rabelais and Dostoevsky books and some other essays – is less an inquiry into how the construction of the novel and other aesthetic (and non-aesthetic) forms is relatively determined by the exchange of cultural material, and more a close study of how this material becomes evident in verbal aesthetic constructs. In other words, Bakhtin's beginnings with a phenomenological model of aesthetic understanding in some ways limit the project he lays out in the "Marxist" texts. How this occurs we shall see later.

The second result of Gadamer's commitment to foreclosing the ideological genesis of the text is his valorization of classical texts and the classical tradition. He indicts historicism for denying the process whereby its objects of inquiry emerge within a culturally evolved field of inquiry in the first place, and suggests that it is the classical work, which "resists historical criticism because of its historical dominion," that "precedes all historical reflection and continues through it" (*Truth and method* 255). This is because the "classical norm ... [brings] awareness of ... something past, unattainable yet present. Thus there culminates in the classical a general character of historical being, preservation among the ruins of time" (256–7). Gadamer assumes that the (Western) retrospective–normative mode of cultural transmission is that on which all aesthetic theories of valorization should be based and which should not (and cannot) be fundamentally challenged (cited in Brenkman, *CD* 36).

This fundamentally misunderstands the nature of "tradition." Gadamer insists that it is the meanings and values that appear continuous and unified across the whole of tradition – that these classical works retain their cultural and historical determinateness for all ages – and are valid and binding for contemporary reading subjects. But it is those very subjects, or their counterparts, who have constructed this "tradition" in the first place. Thus Gadamer's notion that it is classical works of art that should be seen as models for the way hermeneutics function is made questionable because what appears "classical" to us now might not be later on. Tradition is a dynamic concatenation of cultural forces, the particular interpretive commitments of which are themselves inseparable from (and in fact validate) the methodological procedures in which they are elaborated.

In some sense, this blindness in Gadamer's project is at once avoided and stumbled upon in Bakhtin's notion of historical progression. Bakhtin acknowledges that tradition – though he seldom calls it that – is the product of implicit and explicit agreements between subjects over what is most often written and uttered. Speech genres, for example, come to be generic through their use over time, and what began as a "dialogic" force of language gradually becomes "monologic," in that it loses its original meaning and becomes a kind of commonplace of language for one or another social group. It is precisely this notion of how language expands and contracts with use over time that leads him to stretch the "tradition" (at least the novelistic tradition) from its common borders in the seventeenth century back through Greek antiquity: language constantly "reinvigorates" itself as it is used by various cultures and segments of cultures; when it becomes "monologic," speakers have no qualms about de-regularizing its use or ignoring it altogether (*The dialogic imagination* 366–422). And yet this very realignment of the tradition is in some ways the result of Bakhtin's own commitment to dialogism that, some have argued, stems from his growing resentment of Stalinism in post-revolutionary Russia. This commitment ignores, for example, the construction of a "monologic tradition" – precisely an extra-linguistic, brutally material monologization that takes place alongside linguistic "persuasion" – in the Soviet Union, the symptoms of which included the exile of writers like Solzhenitsyn, the banning of Western pornography and contemporary music, to mention only two. That is, in realigning his tradition, Bakhtin will ignore that his very own ideological commitments are in part formative of his theory, and is blind to the way brute material force plays a part (and in some sense undermines) his philosophy of language.

Gadamer initially grants that interpretations are affected by two vectors of determination: on the one hand, the effective mode of preservation–transmission of the tradition in question; and on the other, the "historical situation of the interpreter and hence ... the totality of the objective course of history" (*Truth and method* 263). Gadamer here devoids the "historical situation of the interpreter" of any specificity (3), failing to show how "our age" is marked by gender, class, race, or any concrete historical or ideological commitments.

Everyone knows that curious impotence of our judgment where the distance in time has not given us sure criteria. Thus the judgment of contemporary works of art is desperately uncertain for the scientific consciousness. Obviously we approach such creations with the prejudices we are not in control of, presuppositions that have too great an influence over us for us to know about them; these can give to contemporary creations an extra resonance that does not correspond to their true content and their true significance. Only when all their relations to the present time have faded away can their real nature appear, so that the understanding of what is said in them can claim to be authoritative and universal. (*Truth and method* 265)

One has here the same kind of resistance to ideological interest in the reading process (here with relation to contemporary works) as Iser attempted to eliminate in his reading theory and Jauss did in his.

Bakhtin operates out of an opposite assumption, namely that the present historical moment – like all historical moments – is necessarily contradictory. In "From the prehistory of novelistic discourse," Bakhtin emphasizes the possible occurrences of various contradictory genres and national languages, as well as the opposite "pulls" by the forces of monologism and its corresponding force – authoritarianism – and of dialogism and its corresponding force – carnivalization. What must be noted here is that these forces not only operate historically on utterances or verbal aesthetic constructs from "classical" periods, but that they operate as well in contemporary works; further, the reading subjects who encounter those works, contemporary or classical, are likewise under the pull of the forces of monologism and dialogism. That is, they have at their disposal the ability to consummate a work as relatively "monologic" or "dialogic" depending upon the way various ideological material has been interiorized and reuttered by them in the past. The context of language-signs in any text entails answerability, the consummation according to some non-identical "other" whose vision must be (at least partially) identified. Thus, any reading of contemporary works and the utterances that comprise them cannot objectify the text (as Jauss's "horizon of expectations" attempted to do), and cannot form a unified "horizon," in which a work's meaning or impact has a definable effect. Specific effects are defined moment by moment, but more importantly, from reader to reader. If some horizon is to be identified, it must take into account the varying number of distinct subject-positions of a culture (if a culture can be identified as a grouping of subject-positions), and account also for what will inevitably be disagreement among these positions, and contradictions within them.

I am suggesting that the kind of univocal notion of the receiving culture Gadamer suggests – and with which Jauss works – might better be supplanted by one of "conjectural moments" of individual subjects consummating and coming to agreement (or disagreement) on texts or utterances based upon the language contexts they have previously experienced and interiorized. In a sense, then, literary history – which Jauss and Gadamer wished to revise – would become less a continuum of distinct but unified horizons (a unity which Jauss himself tried to get around), but instead an amalgam of distinct moments, moments which, nevertheless, have some kind of authorial relationship to one another through consummation. At this point I should add – and I will explore the implications of this later with relation to historical materialism – that the Bakhtinian "alternative" may be more consistently grounded in a philosophy of human relations, but it still does not resolve the problem of how subjects are able, with their limited repertoire of language and experience, to judge what utterances fit a genre and which do not, or further, what interpretations of a text or utterance are more right than others. If criteria, as socially defined, are always under negotiation at the very moment the interpretations on which they rely are as well, then agreement might or might not ever be reached, and any corresponding social change (since we are talking about negotiating the constitution of selves in many respects) will also be slow and contested.

Finally (1), Gadamer takes as axiomatic

the hermeneutical rule that we must understand the whole in terms of the detail and the detail in terms of the whole ... The anticipation of meaning in which the whole is envisaged becomes explicit understanding in that the parts, that are determined by the whole, themselves also determine this whole ... It is also necessary for this expected meaning to be adjusted if the text calls for it. This means, then, that the expectation changes and that the text acquires the unity of a meaning from another expected meaning. Thus the movement of understanding is constantly from the whole to the part and back to the whole. Our task is to extend in concentric circles the unity of the understood meaning. The harmony of all the details with the whole is the criterion of correct understanding. The failure to achieve this harmony means that understanding has failed. (*Truth and method* 258–9)

We have already discussed the problems inherent in finding "understood," "correct" or "harmonious" knowledge of aesthetic constructs as regards Jauss's use of those terms. Gadamer concedes that an interpreter might only arrive at an approximate completion of the unifying understanding of a text, or in fact might discover a disjunction of part and whole, at which point the interpreter experiences the unintelligibility of the text and seeks "to discover in what way it can be remedied" (*Truth and method* 261). As with Iser's contention that a text, if the author has placed into it a disjunction, should be "remedied" by the reader and be supplied with some kind of overarching totality of meaning, Gadamer suggests that textual disjunctions, while part of the aesthetic whole, are there to be "fixed." In a way this is the same kind of blindness he experiences when he discusses the "horizon" of the reading public. Simply stated, if language-using subjects are not grouped together in harmonious wholes by dint of their different language experience, then language constructs "uttered" by such subjects will also tend to exhibit contradictory ideological material according to their different language experiences. Bakhtin takes this as a first principle: humans are radically exotopic in relation to one another, and language is the material with which they will engage in (necessarily unfinished) relations with one another's exteriority. Texts are not there to be made whole; subjects, on the other hand, are by nature not completed, though aesthetic consummation approximates this kind of completion. It follows that utterances are a means by which humans are able to "consummate" distinct moments of their lived lives through the "other," and it is principally through the *disjunctions* that such relationships bear the most fruit.

But what of this "consummated whole" that Bakhtin suggests it is possible to achieve in works of art and is approximable in lived human relationships? If we mean here by consummated wholes only aesthetic verbal constructs, then surely it is so, in Gadamer's sense, that artistic works *are indeed* unified in their meaning, specifically in their meaning for the author. In a sense, this is similar to the unresolvable difficulty with which Husserl tried to deal by positing the transcendental ego: aesthetic understanding is unified in human cognition, but it goes all awry when it experiences the chaotic reality of lived human experience. So, in one sense, it is true that, for Gadamer (and for Jauss), works are consummated wholes that, unfortunately for the stated aims of their theories, will not be replicable in the understanding of a reading subject.

However, in his theory of authorship, Bakhtin suggests that not only works are consummated but that lived life in its constituent moments is also consummated (though to a different degree than aesthetic artefacts themselves). It is not simply a matter of an author "consummating" a work, which will then be perceived by a reader; rather, human subjects consummate wholes differently and must then negotiate the disjunctions (cognitive–ethically), and in turn recon-summate the consequent moments, and so on. The disjunctions that occur in Bakhtin's (dialectical) phenomenology of consummation and ethical action can never be "remedied," but must necessarily be read, since human subjectivity is defined by the disjunction, and com-munication is defined by the "reading."

But, as I have said, all of this negotiation does not solve the problem of what happens when subjects disagree over the validity of the interpretations of texts or, more specifically, how one decides whose meaning will hold dominance over another's. If language is dependent (at *least* in part) upon the experience of the subjects who use it; and if the communication (in the broadest sense of "coming into contact") between humans is (at least in part) dependent upon language; and if language, as Bakhtin has it, is ideological material; then the way language has to do with the way social wholes function in relation to one another must be inspected more closely. Habermas, here objecting to Gadamer's hermeneutics, puts it this way:

It makes good sense to conceive of language as a kind of metainstitution on which all social institutions are dependent; for social action is constituted only in ordinary language communication. But this metainstitution of language as tradition is evidently dependent in turn on social processes that are not reducible to normative relationships. Language is *also* a medium of domination and social power; it serves to legitimate relations of organized force. Insofar as the legitimations do not articulate the power relations whose institutionalization they make possible, insofar as these relations merely manifest themselves in the legitimations, language is *also* ideological.

(Habermas, "A review of Gadamer's *Truth and method*" 360)

Once again, it is John Brenkman who pinpoints the problem: Gadamer conceives ideology as a kind of "misinterpretation of the world" whereas, for Habermas, it is "the dogmatism of *life-practices*," humans' lived relations to their material surroundings. Gadamer states that

there is no societal reality, with all its concrete forces, that does not bring itself to representation as a consciousness that is linguistically articulated. Reality does not happen "behind the back" of language; it happens rather behind the back of those who live in the subjective opinion that they have understood "the world" (or can no longer understand it); that is, reality happens precisely within language. (*CD* 35)

Gadamer fails to see that reality in fact does not happen within language, though our cognition of reality does. What happens between the two — reality and cognition of it — is most important: cultural traditions are plural and often conflicting, not univocal or monological; conflicting interpretations, and in fact competing cultural constructions, are ideologically charged conflicts; and those conflicts are by definition internal to aesthetic constructs. In the transition from a rather. narrowly defined phenomenological inquiry to a more broadly construed theory of language and ideology, Bakhtin recognizes these mediated realities more clearly than either his predecessors, concerned with "pure phenomenology," or his contemporaries, concerned with "historical hermeneutics." But the way Bakhtin understands how ideological material functions in verbal (aesthetic) constructs in some ways mirrors Gadamer's — he comes close to agreeing that all reality takes place at the level of language, and as a result cannot find a way to gain access to extra-linguistic forces that are as important to the formation of the subject and play a role in the construction of the very language which is so central to Bakhtin's theory. Interpretations are socially critical or socially uncritical according to the commitments they develop with regard to the symbolic and social struggles that take place at the level of language, which are, according to Brenkman, struggles "between the legitimation and the contestation of domination" (*CD* 55). But unless there is access to something outside symbolic and social struggles, there will be no guarantee that the contestation of domination will have any real effect.

4

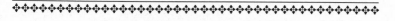

The Marxist texts

In *Marxism and the philosophy of language* and *The formal method in literary scholarship*, Bakhtin shifts his attention from the relationship of the self and the other in the process of understanding utterances and texts, and takes up instead the problem of how humans use language to construct history and the ways in which the construction of that history might provide a vehicle for social movement and change. What marks these texts from earlier ones is Bakhtin's discussion of language as ideological material. Rather than seeing language interiorized simply as language – that is, as a medium of social exchange – in these two texts (as well as in parts of *The dialogic imagination* and in the Dostoevsky and Rabelais books), Bakhtin understands language as a material object that is as much formative of as it is formed by human subjects, and takes part in the transformation' of the world in the same way as tools of production. Particularly in *Marxism and the philosophy of language* and *The formal method*, this explicit acknowledgment that language is ideological material allows Bakhtin to understand not only how language is used to construct selves, but also how it constructs collections of selves into social groups, and how the linguistic commerce between those groups is formative of social reality and produces social change.

The difficulty in reconciling Bakhtin's account of language and ideology lies in his adherence to earlier phenomenological models of subjects. Though materialism allows Bakhtin to "do things with words" (that is, to begin understanding language as productive of social change), nevertheless the notion that language is a medium in which humans are "trapped" and outside of which there is no understanding at all stops short of a historical materialist account of language and social change. Since there is no way to understand how readings or interpretations of cognitive activity are better or worse than competing readings or interpretations, then Bakhtinian theory is left with no way of saying whether a change in the composition of one's social orientation or understanding of it makes more or less sense than one's previous understanding. In other words, Bakhtin's materialism does not seem able to provide an extra-ideological or scientific understanding of ideology.

That *Marxism and the philosophy of language* and *The formal method* bear the names of authors other than Bakhtin does not seem reason enough to remove these books from the Bakhtin canon. It is absolutely certain that none of the books that bear Bakhtin's name alone discuss materialist theory to the same extent that these two books (and a third, *Freudianism*) do. It is also certain, as Allon White and others have suggested, that Bakhtin's work as a whole (even including the two works under discussion here) does not provide an adequate materialist theory of language.[1] Finally, there does not seem to be much evidence in his work to support the notion that Bakhtin read much Marx or of any other materialist theory, and Katerina Clark and Michael Holquist go so far as to suggest that Bakhtin was hostile to many of the ideas of Russian Communism, at least in the form that it took during the years of Stalin's rule (*Mikhail Bakhtin* 132–42).

The most significant evidence for not discounting the claims that Bakhtin's work is at least in some respects fellow-travelling with the work of historical materialism lies in his heavy reliance on the social aspect of language and language's central part in the composition of social reality. In terms of the Marxist project of mapping ideological relations through language artefacts, the two projects seem quite close, as we will see. The historical materialist view that language is a product of social relations, and that the study of such products can yield information about those social relations which produced them, closely parallels Bakhtin's view in *Marxism and the philosophy of language* that "signs are conditioned above all by the social organization of the participants involved and also by the immediate conditions of their interaction" (21).[2]

There are, however, important differences between the two concepts of language as well. The most important of these is that, for Bakhtin, though (in the "Marxist" writings) the "economic base" is said to play a part in the conditions of human interaction, those economic conditions are assumed (or largely ignored), and are not

---

1 See Allon White's "The struggle over Bakhtin: A fraternal reply to Robert Young," *Cultural Critique* 12 (Fall 1988).

2 Subsequent references to *Marxism and the philosophy of language* will appear in the text abbreviated *MPL*; references to *The formal method* will be abbreviated *FM*.

significantly factored into the equation of human understanding. Moreover, ideology is subtly different in the two accountings of materialism. Bakhtin's ideology is determined and determining; contemporary materialism contends that ideology is a product of the real conditions of existence and is determined in the last instance by the economy, though also determinant of the social whole. This difference will prove important in Bakhtin's accounting for social change. Finally, Marxism claims scientificity, in that it is able, by way of theory, to dislocate and decenter ideological formations and artefacts in such a way as to disclose the object of knowledge (that is, the operation of the material conditions of existence). Yet Bakhtin places the purview of science *inside* the study of ideologies, implying that scientific knowledge is not possible because it is always bound up with ideological coloring.[3] In this chapter I will briefly examine the connections between Bakhtin's materialist conceptions of ideology in *Marxism* and *The formal method*, and discuss their general relations to the earlier phenomenological essays (that is, "The Problem of content" and "Author and hero"). We will see there a hesitance to "go all the way" with materialism, a hesitance brought on at least partially by Bakhtin's adherence to what might broadly be called "individualist" conceptions of human understanding.

Bakhtin/Medvedev lays out in the very first paragraph of *The formal method* the most basic premise of the study of literature, one which Bakhtin works out in all subsequent work.

Literary scholarship is *one branch* of the study of ideologies. On the basis of the single principle it uses to understand its object, and the single method it uses to study it, the study of ideologies embraces all areas of man's ideological creativity. (3; my emphasis)

All human activity is evaluated in terms of how those who take part in it understand that activity. Humans understand ideological activity while they are *in* ideology: one cannot study literature, a branch of ideology, without studying other ideological activities; and that very study is also ideologically determined. Bakhtin suggests that it is

---

3 In *Problems of Dostoevsky's poetics*, Bakhtin draws attention to the possibility of an Einsteinian concept of the world – a "new scientific" concept – in which "indefinite quantities" and relations are taken into account (16). He connects this to a world-view which he calls a "complex *artistic model of the world*," which is neither definitive nor closed. The point is that ideological knowledge should not be seen to operate scientifically, but rather that so-called scientific knowledge operates in a complex (that is, ideologically multivalent) fashion.

obviously impermissible for a Marxist to draw conclusions about the social reality of a given time based on novels written during that time; it is necessary to "study the language of other ideologies on the basis of more direct documents" and not on their "refraction" in literary works (*FM* 21, 20). But as Bakhtin suggests, though it is "absurd to imagine scientific intercourse as constitutive to ... the scientific meeting or conference," it is nevertheless a fact that the mutual orientation of people – such as that in the scientific community – "defines each act of cognition, and the more complex, differentiated, and organized this orientation is, the deeper and more important is the resulting comprehension" (*FM* 13). All knowledge is formed ideologically, and all subsequent study of that knowledge is also the result of ideological understanding. So, as literary study is one area of human activity governed by linguistic relations, then part of that study must be an attempt to discern the ideological placement and composition of the subjects involved in those linguistic relations. It is ideological study – Bakhtin/Medvedev calls it the "general definition of ideological superstructures, their function in the whole of social life, the relationship to the economic base, and some of their inter-relationships" – to which language studies subordinate themselves (*FM* 3). And, as I have suggested, it is precisely for ignoring considerations of the social nature of language that Bakhtin/Medvedev takes the early Formalists to task:

If the poetic construction had been placed in a complex, many-sided relationship with science, with rhetoric, with the fields of real practical life, instead of being declared the bare converse of a fabricated practical language, then formalism as we know it would not have existed. (*FM* 98)

Bakhtin works out the social connection of language early in the first chapter of *Marxism and the philosophy of language*. "[T]here is no such thing as experience outside of embodiment in signs ... [T]he location of the organizing and formative center [of the embodiment of signs] is not within (i.e., not in the material of inner signs)" – such as the inner word Vygotsky theorizes – "but outside. It is not experience that organizes expression, but the other way around – *expression organizes experience*" (*MPL* 85). Bakhtin/Voloshinov then goes on to explain the interaction through which experience is organized by expression in terms very similar to those he uses in describing the largely phenomenological process in "Author and hero." Utterances are constructed between two socially organized persons. If an addressee is absent, then one is presupposed in the person of a "normal representative of the social group to which the speaker belongs" (*MPL* 85). Such a presupposition requires surmising social organization, with the suggestion that one needs to extrapolate "*who* that addressee might be: a fellow member or not of the same social group, of higher or lower standing, someone connected with the speaker by close social ties or not" (*MPL* 85). In other words, the speaker must ascertain the language background of the "other" before returning to organize his own verbal material in order to make himself understood to that other. A word "is precisely *the product of the reciprocal relationship between speaker and listener, addresser and addressee* … I give myself verbal shape from another's point of view, ultimately, from the point of view of the community to which I belong" (*MPL* 86).

Bakhtin/Voloshinov here is at pains to describe the process of communication as one that takes place not only within a particular context – as in a greeting, or in the reading of a book or newspaper, or watching a movie or seeing an advertisement. More generally, the act of communication is similar to the consummation of an event in aesthetic activity: the current context is never closed, but has connected to it complex linguistic relationships that have been interiorized both by the speaker and the addressee. One needs to discover how these relationships have been constructed beyond the immediate context of speaker and listener. As I have shown, this can never be done definitively, and more likely than not the extrapolation of the other's position will have to be negotiated because it will necessarily be impossible to complete. "Each individual act in the creation of ideology" – and, leaving aside for the moment Bakhtin/ Voloshinov/Medvedev's definition of ideology, one could say that ideological creation functions in the same way as Bakhtin's earlier notion of aesthetic activity – "is an inseparable part of social intercourse, one of its dependent components, and therefore cannot be studied apart from the whole social process that gives it meaning" (*FM* 7).

Studying the artistic construct "apart from the whole social process that gives it meaning" was precisely the way the Formalists operated. It was only later in their evolution – one that came about at least in part through pressure from such "Marxist" theorists as Bakhtin, Medvedev, and Voloshinov – that Formalism added to their considerations of the "fabric" of the work of literature such things as the "state of the world cotton market" (Mukarovsky, *Structure, sign and function* 140). Bakhtin/Medvedev insisted that the difficulties the Formalists had in integrating the operation of the social world – and, I would add, the difficulty phenomenological theorists had with the same integration – stem from ignoring the social constructedness of aesthetic artefacts, and the ways in which these constructs are ideologically situated real (palpable) constructions. Definitions of ideological systems formulated by West European scholarship – and here Bakhtin/Medvedev has in mind neo-Kantian philosophy and early Husserlian thinking – "are atomized into insipid and positivistic empirical data which are lost in a wilderness of senseless detail," or else "these definitions are estranged from all empiricism and locked into a self-contained idealist kingdom of 'pure ideas,' 'pure values,' and 'transcendental forms,' and therefore rendered completely helpless before the concrete ideological phenomenon, which is always material and historical" (*FM* 4). Bakhtin/Medvedev sees these attempts as a desire "to make ends meet in abstract thought about the world," in a sense to build an epistemology that would unite phenomena in the human mind, and from which a "theory of everything" could be developed. Instead of this kind of thinking – a phenomenology of pure cognition – we need "to comphrehend the concrete facts of life and history in all their variability and diversity," to construct an open-ended social theory of multivalence. Ideological creation does not take place inside the human understanding, but "it in fact unfolds externally, for the eye, the ear, the hand. It is not within us, but between us" (*FM* 8). Ideal concretizations (Ingarden), proper concretions and ideological horizons (Gadamer) or autonomous artistic incarnations of a work (Mukarovsky), all remove the work from the real world of conflicting ideologies.

By characterizing language (and the linguistic work of art) as such an ideological phenomenon, one opens a completely different sphere of theoretical inquiry, one that scholars working with Bakhtin sometimes overlook. Humans interact with one another by taking into account their social surroundings, including the other to whom the speaker wishes to communicate. It is assumed that one's perception of the social surrounding (the "situation") both of oneself (the speaker) and of the other (the interlocutor) and the context can never be complete because one can never "be" the other to whom one is talking and can never "see" all that is taking place at a given time. "Whatever a word's meaning, it establishes a relationship between individuals of a more or less wide social environment, a relationship which is objectively expressed in the combined reactions of people:

reactions in words, gestures, acts, and so on" (*FM* 8). Ideological understanding – like aesthetic consummation – reflects the "ideological purview, i.e., other nonartistic, ideological formations (ethical, epistemological, etc.) ... Reflecting something external to themselves, literary works are at the same time in themselves valuable and unique phenomena of the ideological environment" (*FM* 18).

There are two types of reflections that take place in literature, and in order to undertake a materialist inquiry into the ideological "reflections" – or the constructedness of aesthetic consummation – one should analyze them separately:

(1)   the reflection of the ideological environment in the content of literature; [and]
(2)   the reflection of the economic base that is common to all ideologies. Literature, like the other independent superstructures [that is, ideologies], reflects the base.

This double reflection, this double orientation of literature in reality, makes the methodology and concrete methods of literary study extremely complex and difficult.   (*FM* 18)

The task of literary scholars, for Bakhtin/Medvedev, is neither that of finding the "ideal" hermeneutic interpretation (reading a work's "unmediated content") or the division and cataloguing of a work's devices. Rather, art is intimately related to life, but it is a refraction of it, and it is the understanding of the different ways in which this double reflection occurs that must be undertaken, *not*, notably, an investigation of the object of reflection: it is easy to make the (erroneous) assumption that Bakhtin is looking for this object, since he seems to want to catalogue "speech genres" in novels and·other works, genres that, as I have suggested, are "pointable-to" (*Problems of Dostoevsky's poetics* 199).

The task of (1) above would be to analyze the "situations" of speakers in a verbal relationship – what each can perceive from her position, what language each has at her disposal to make that position "present" to the other, how each of these speakers perceives the other and projects the other's capacity for understanding. This is the kind of work Bakhtin/Voloshinov does in the third section of *Marxism and the philosophy of language* where he closely analyzes "reported speech" in various utterances. The task of (2) would be something like an attempt at translating these different "orientations" into information about the historical situation, by also investigating other non-aesthetic verbal constructs to see how they reveal different ideological orientations.

This is what Bakhtin/Medvedev call the proper subject of Marxist science of literary scholarship. It is significant to note that, in all of Bakhtin's work — though he calls for it — task (2) is never accomplished, that is, Bakhtin never investigates the different ideological orientations that exist in verbal constructs other than the aesthetic ones he investigates (though judging from the more broadly construed phenomenological theory laid out in "Author and hero," such an investigation is possible in non-aesthetic constructs, as aesthetic consummation takes place in all verbal interchanges to some degree).

The larger problem with task (2), however, is that an investigation of primary material presents the same difficulties as an investigation of aesthetic material. It is not permissible for a Marxist "to draw direct conclusions about the social reality of a given epoch from secondary ideological reflections in literature, as quasi sociologists have done and continue to do, being ready to project any structural element of the artistic work ... directly into real life" (*FM* 21). Rather, he must "study the language of other ideologies on the basis of more direct documents and not on the basis of their secondary refraction in the structure of the literary work" (*FM* 20). He must recognize that the "whole unity [of literature] and the individual works which are its elements cannot be understood outside the unity of ideological life. And this last unity, whether it is taken as a whole or as separate elements, cannot be studied outside the unified socioeconomic laws of development" (*FM* 27). And yet the documents a Marxist literary historian investigates to understand the unified socioeconomic laws of development or the "other ideologies" are themselves comprised of language that is negotiated and ideologically implicated in the same way that aesthetic language is. By having earlier proposed that all human cognitive activity takes place inside language, and that linguistic activity also has as an inseparable element, aesthetic consummation, then the documents and other non-aesthetic verbal evidence that must be investigated in order to see how the "economic base ... common to all ideologies" is reflected have the same boundless context as any utterance. For Bakhtin/Medvedev, in a sense the scientific inquiry that takes place in the investigation of the reflection of the economic base is also a sociological inquiry and, though this problematizes the inquiry, it does not make it impossible. "Science need not cease being science to become a social phenomenon" (*FM* 29). One might put this differently and say that simply because it is a social phenomenon does not mean it is not science. This may be true but, as I have said, Bakhtin does not undertake this inquiry. Nor do I think, if he stuck with the phenomenological categories he sets up in "Author and hero," he could without acknowledging that scientific inquiry includes some element of consummation and therefore entails the same potential boundlessness of negotiation. This problem will come back to plague Bakhtin again and again.

As for the analysis of social content in works of literature (that is, task [1] above), there are two specific problems that have to be addressed:

(1) problems of the characteristic features and forms of organized ideological material as meaningful material; [and]
(2) problems of the characteristics and forms of the social intercourse by which this meaning is realized.   (*FM* 9)

These tasks Bakhtin does address specifically. The second task is addressed in a philosophical way in "Author and hero," and "The problem of content," where he outlines the intersubjective mechanics of verbal and verbal aesthetic constructs and situations. The first task – the investigation into the organization of ideological material in language – is addressed generally in *Marxism and the philosophy of language* and more narrowly in almost all of Bakhtin's works on literature (*Rabelais and his world*, *Problems of Dostoevsky's poetics*, the texts on dialogism and on speech genres). It is specifically to *Marxism* that I will now turn.

Bakhtin/Medvedev, in *The formal method*, defines language as one of several ideological constructs – first by placing literary constructs within the realm of language, and then by placing language into relation with various other ideological constructs by which humans are able to create information about one another and their world. In *Marxism and the philosophy of language*, however, Bakhtin shifts the relation of ideological constructions and language. Bakhtin/Voloshinov suggests that the task of Marxist literary theory is especially difficult because, at the time of writing, 1929, "Marxist literature as yet contains no conclusive and commonly accepted definitions as to the specific nature of the reality of ideological phenomena" (*MPL* xiii). In a note, he goes on to say that "as far as questions connected with the material of ideological creativity and the conditions of ideological communication are concerned, those questions, as secondary matters for the overall theory of historical materialism, did not receive concrete or conclusive resolution," nor have they, I might add, today. Ideology here is defined in terms of language: certainly all human constructs – including social constructs, relations and objects shared between people – are ideological, because of the "shared idea." However, language is the only medium through which humans understand those relations or objects. Bakhtin/Voloshinov uses the example of the hammer.

A tool by itself is devoid of any special meaning; it commands only some designated function – to serve this or that purpose in production. The tool serves that purpose as the particular, given thing that it is, without reflecting or standing for anything else. However, a tool also may be converted into an ideological sign. Such, for instance, is the hammer and sickle insignia of the Soviet Union. In this case, hammer and sickle possess a purely ideological meaning. (*MPL* 10)

It should be added, then, that a hammer – after such a linguistic "web" of meaning has been constructed – from that point on "possesses" the ideological meaning at the same time that it remains an object of production. I may see or use a hammer, but when I wish to communicate something about the hammer, or I understand (or "consummate," in Bakhtin's terms) this hammer so that I can talk about it or represent it verbally or aesthetically, then the ideological content of that hammer – including its use in the insignia of the Soviet Union – is part of the context of that understanding. Though the tool does not become a sign, nor the sign a tool, the two are inseparable in human understanding.

In the first several pages of *Marxism*, a sign is defined as the "image" of a "perceived object" (*MPL* 9). Every physical object that can be perceived must be perceived by some subject. The object-as-object (the hammer, for example) does not exist for the subject, but rather the subject – as she stands in front of, or beside, or takes possession of, the hammer – has a particular vantage point from which to perceive the object. From the vantage point, the perceiver produces a sign, and that sign, "without ceasing to become a part of material reality" – given that the produced sign is real to the subject, and any interlocutor for whom it is intended – "to some degree, reflects and refracts another reality" (*MPL* 9).

Bakhtin/Voloshinov goes on to explain that

[U]nderstanding itself can come about only within some kind of semiotic material (e.g., inner speech), that sign bears upon sign, that *consciousness itself can arise and become a viable fact only in the material embodiment of signs*. The understanding of a sign is, after all, an act of already known signs; in other words, understanding is a response to a sign with signs. And this chain of ideological creativity and understanding, moving from sign to sign and then to a new sign, is perfectly consistent and continuous ... And nowhere is there a break in the chain, nowhere does the chain plunge into inner being, nonmaterial in nature and unembodied in signs.

(*MPL* 9)

Humans only come to an understanding of the world through the creation of signs. Language is not simply one way in which ideological "data" become articulated: in this view, which might be called crudely scientific, language articulates ideological relations, but economic, political, and historical data can be articulated outside of ideological material. In a Bakhtinian conception, all ideological constructs are conceived in language, including the scientific (see *FM* 7). We do not come to understand the world of objects and people, but rather we know the world of the *signs* for "objects" and "people." Though it is possible to come into contact with the unmediated objects, it is not possible to understand them without recourse to forming signs of them.

The next move in *Marxism* is to throw out the model of language as the interaction between two speakers based on the notorious view presented in Saussure's *Course* (95). Instead, all kinds of communications are going on at the same time between different sets of interlocutors. Furthermore, the communication that is going on in "our" set of interlocutors depends on how language is understood in those other communicative models: "An interlocking organic unity joins the form of communication (for example, on-the-job communication of the strictly technical kind), the form of the utterance (the concise, businesslike statement)," and the subjects of the utterance, what Bakhtin calls the "theme" (*MPL* 20–21). If I have heard a conversation, for example, in which the sign "bat" is understood as a small mammal with wings, and I use this understanding of a sign in another conversation with someone else who looks for signs of contusions after I tell him that I had a bat fly into my face the other night while I was out walking, then something somewhere in the conversation has gone wrong. This "misunderstanding," what Bakhtin elsewhere calls an "excess of seeing," must be negotiated in order for the two of us somehow to share in a similar construction of the sign in question. This goes to show that one can only use the language (signs) one has previously understood in a particular *context*, and that a synchronic model of language – a norm-based model that is understood by one speaker in one particular place and time – is a fiction (*MPL* 66). This kind of infinite potential for variation puts a burden on speakers of language: no one is free from language. In one individual's use of the production of signs based on the use of signs that the person understands going on around her, she is constantly aware of the various *other* uses of language that go on around her, and must take them into account. One's ideological orientation in the world-as-object is different from everyone else's. Therefore, communication between interlocutors about that world is necessarily incomplete, as we have seen with relation to "Author and hero," and the negotiation that results from this incompleteness produces linguistic change. As Bakhtin/Voloshinov puts it in *Marxism*, "*social intercourse is generated* (stemming from the basis); *in it verbal communication and interaction are generated; and in the latter, forms of speech performances are generated; finally, this generative process is reflected in the change of language forms* (96; Bakhtin's/Voloshinov's emphasis).

The Formalists proceeded from assigning a special function to poetic language to a theory of evolution based on the novelty and subsequent repeated use of particular poetic forms. Once the novelty of a poetic form or genre wears off, some new "estranging effect" must be found to reinvigorate poetic language. Bakhtin/Voloshinov maintains that there is no distinction between "types" of language, and that all language forms are negotiated, depending upon the contexts in which they are used and produced. Language has the potential to be constantly reinvigorated, because language never gets used in the same way more than once, since situations are constantly in flux. Further, if language remains "monologic" in a succession of new contexts – if it is "uttered as received" – Bakhtin suggests that it will become "generic," after which variation is inevitable ("The problem of speech genres," in *Speech genres and other late essays* 65–6). This is a close relative of the Formalist theory of evolution, but its significant difference is that "estrangement" takes place constantly and at all levels of language.

The result of constantly changing contexts in language/sign production, as Bakhtin/Voloshinov would have it, is a constantly changing social arena. "The behavioral genre fits everywhere into the channel of social intercourse assigned to it and functions as an ideological reflection of its type, structure, goal, and social composition" (*MPL* 97). One's very social situation is in turn changed, based upon the difference in real social position, since that real social condition is possible only in and through language to begin with. Changing a word's (or the use of a sign's) context in the "negotiation" results in a change in the (social) relation of speaker and interlocutor and that in turn changes the very social condition which has been made real in already produced signs. The suggestion is that not only language constantly changes in production, but that the social reality which it comprises is changing as well. Language is not algorithmic; its so-called norms are negotiated every time it is produced.

And yet there are problems with this notion of language as productive of social change. We will see this more clearly with relation to more recent developments in historical materialist theory, but for the time being, one can begin to see how difficult it is to conceive of social change as produced linguistically according to Bakhtin's theory because of some contradictions within *Marxism and the philosophy of language* itself.

In what could be considered a direct confrontation with Bakhtin's neo-Kantian predecessor, Hermann Cohen, Bakhtin/Voloshinov notes that "The idealistic philosophy of culture and psychologistic cultural studies locate ideology in the consciousness," and in a note he proposes Cassirer's revision of neo-Kantianism, in which elements of consciousness bear a symbolic function, and in which the represented elements of consciousness are comprehensible in relation to a greater whole (*MPL* 11). This is wholly compatible with Bakhtin's own neo-Kantian revision in "Author and hero," in which the elements of a consummated work are comprehensible only in relation to the whole, and in which the relation of subjects brings together elements of consciousness otherwise impossible to unite. Moreover, this semiotic material is precisely *material*, and not simply a function of consciousness. And yet this devotion to neo-Kantianism throws a wrench into Bakhtin/Voloshinov's version of materialism: he goes on to say that idealistic philosophy overlooks the fact "that understanding itself can come about only within some kind of semiotic material (e.g., inner speech), that sign bears upon sign, that *consciousness itself can arise and become a viable fact only in the material embodiment of signs.*" And yet "The understanding of a sign is, after all, an act of reference between the sign apprehended and other, already known signs; in other words, understanding is a response to a sign with other signs" (*MPL* 11). The result of this passage − given that all human understanding takes place through the production of signs, and that signs always carry with them the previous contexts (though always partially understood) of language situations – is an inescapable world of signs. Humans are first and always inside ideology, and there does not seem, in this version of things, to be any way out of it. This is not a real problem if all we are talking about is how subjects read and interpret texts: cognitive–ethical action as regards the language of a text consummated aesthetically (that is, reading), takes place with relation to the subject and her characters as represented in the language of a text; any negotiation of the meaning or function of that text with some other subject may or may not be felicitous, but in the end the stakes are fairly low. It does not really much matter who is right. But consider the current climate in academia: the conservative right holds that cultural studies and pluralism are a threat to the canon of great works, and that a bow in the direction of pluralism will eventually fragment culture beyond recognition and dispossess Anglo-Europeans of their heritage. Those on the liberal left hold that cultural studies and pluralism have been a long time coming in an educational institution that has long ignored the achievements of women, homosexuals, and people of color (among others), and that attempts to quiet debate on this subject is tantamount to Eurocentric racism. If "understanding is a response to a sign with signs," and if we can consider the divergence in readings current in academe as a divergence in ideological representations of culture and its canon, then "moving from sign to sign and then to a new sign" (or moving from ideological representation to another and yet to another) is by definition an endless process, and nowhere is there recourse to deciding which representation makes more sense than another. The stakes in the debate currently running in academe *are* high – who teaches what to whom, and as a result of that transmission of information, whose version of reality holds sway and determines the others' versions – but at this point in Bakhtin's/Voloshinov's theorizing there is no way to resolve the disjunction of ideologies save through negotiation. And if we take Bakhtin's notion of negotiation to mean not face-to-face, around-the-table negotiation but the linguistic negotiation of language through interiorization and reutterance, then it does not seem likely that a resolution can be found soon, nor does it guarantee that linguistic negotiation will not have its place taken by legislation or some other (possibly more heavy-handed) kind of extra-linguistic force.

In a sense, this is precisely a problem of the place of extra-linguistic elements in the philosophy of language. For the phenomenological Bakhtin, any aspect of human consciousness – including the response to extra-linguistic phenomena – takes place by way of the production of signs. Moreover, the various productions that take place between interlocutors – be they face to face in conversation or be they temporally far-removed, as in a subject recollecting something she read on the editorial page a week ago – affect one another, and can produce change in the ideological situation of one or the other or both interlocutors. The question, though, is whether this kind of linguistic exchange can affect the material conditions (and, "further down," if you will, the economic base), and if so, can that change be said to be for the better. I quote a longish passage from *Marxism* that suggests Bakhtin's/Voloshinov's partial response.

It is essential above all to determine the *meaning of any, given ideological change in the context of ideology appropriate to it*, seeing that every domain of ideology is a unified whole which reacts with its entire constitution to a change in the basis. Therefore, any explanation must preserve *all the qualitative differences* between interacting domains and must trace all the various stages through which a change travels. Only on this condition will analysis result, not in a mere outward conjunction of two adventitious facts belonging to a different level of things, but in the process of the actual dialectical generation of society, a process which emerges from the basis and comes to completion in the superstructures. (*MPL* 18)

There is a slide in reasoning in this passage that is symptomatic of the uncertainty of how social change takes place. Domains of ideology – in this passage Bakhtin/Voloshinov refers to large social groups who share, in some sense, ideological representations – interact as a unified whole, and change as changes in the basis occur. More importantly (as suggested by the second sentence of the passage), changes take place *between* the ideological domains, and it is the task of the historical materialist critic to "trace all the various stages through which a change travels."

One can read this sentence to mean that the interactions between various ideological representations should be traced *in the realm of ideology*. But one can also read the phrase "all the various stages" to mean that ideological changes have an effect *on the basis* as well. Granted, this reading of Bakhtin/Voloshinov is not explicitly supported by the rest of *Marxism*, but if one assumes that reading and interpreting texts, or that negotiating utterances by analyzing the linguistic contexts and the ideological material that inheres in those contexts, can produce change in the subjects who negotiate them; and further, if those subjects understand language as ideological material that mediates their lived relation to the material conditions of existence, then a change in that relation resulting from reading should also have some effect on those material conditions. While not equating base with those material conditions, it appears that there must be an affective relationship between the two. The question for Bakhtin/ Voloshinov is how one theorizes this kind of relationship. The last sentence in the passage quoted above suggests that Bakhtin/ Voloshinov slides back to the causal relationship of basis and superstructure, closing off the possibility of a two-way relationship. Further on in his discussion of the characterization of "superfluous men" in Russian literature, he suggests again that "even if it is true that 'superfluous men' did appear in literature in connection with the breakdown of the economic structure of the gentry," it did not occur mechanistically. The suggestion again is that, though the base does not simply touch off ideological changes that are represented in the language of a text, it is a one-way relationship. There is no way to make a change except through ideological change.

The questions above will appear again and again in historical materialism: how does one go from changes in one's mediated relation to the material conditions of existence to an actual change in those conditions, and in turn how does that affect the economic base, if at all? That Bakhtin/Voloshinov begins his theory of the subject by positing that all humans exist first and always in language, and further that language is ideological material, stalls him in his attempt to pass further into a discussion of the relationship of the basis and the various superstructures represented linguistically. In fact, moving far from what I have characterized as a potentially explosive open-ended passage, Bakhtin/Voloshinov suggests two pages later that "*A typology of [linguistic forms and types of verbal communication as they arise from the social situation of their speakers]* is one of the urgent tasks of Marxism" (*MPL* 20). This is a far cry from the claim that one of Marxism's most urgent tasks is to discuss the relations of the base and superstructure, and a much more modest one. It is no indictment of Bakhtin to suggest that the task of inquiring into the nature of the relationship between base and superstructure – and whether that relationship, as represented in literary and other non-aesthetic verbal artefacts, is mechanistically causal or complex – was beyond the scope of his project. The fact that Bakhtin laid out the epistemological groundwork of a philosophy of language so that he could systematically work through a theory of literary and non-literary language is borne out by his work on Dostoevsky, Rabelais, the novel, and the earlier work on the relationship of the author and hero – as well as by the later portions of *Marxism and the philosophy of language* and *The formal method*, which are devoted almost exclusively to discussing the typologies of various speech genres (which is cited as evidence that Bakhtin at least had a hand in writing these texts).

The fact remains that even in the purely literary texts there is the consideration of the materialism of language, at the very least in Bakhtin's continued insistence on the social constructedness and potential for authoritarian repression of language, and in his defining language as ideological material. In doing so, Bakhtin suggests that the material conditions of existence – the world as we know it – exist only through their ideological construction in signs. Though this does not mean to suggest that the material world outside of language does not exist – in fact, it is the material world out of which and for which signs are created – nevertheless, without these signs, the material world would not *consciously* exist: humans would not be able to generate sense-data of it. The material world is constantly mediated through sign-production. The suggestion is that one cannot conceive of ideology *without* language. And yet this suggestion also implies that, since humans are always already embedded in a world of language, that a science of the text – a way to theorize extra-ideologically – is also always in ideology. That is, extra-ideological theorization is impossible: you cannot get past language.

5

❖❖❖

Science and ideology

❖❖❖

Though, as I tried to suggest in the previous chapter, there are a number of reasons for suggesting that the work of Mikhail Bakhtin is at least in some ways reconcilable to that of certain versions of historical materialism, there are still enough differences between the work of a Bakhtin and, say, an Althusser, to ask just how reconcilable they are. The primary reason for "claiming" Bakhtin for Marxism is the notable Marxist "content" of three works which, at least potentially, bear his name: *Marxism and the philosophy of language*, *The formal method in literary scholarship*, and *Freudianism: A critical sketch* (which will not be under discussion here). But it is not just in these texts that Bakhtin suggests the power of subjects to construct their social reality through the construction of language, thus granting "dialogization" a kind of emancipatory power. In sections of the books on Rabelais, Dostoevsky, and in *The dialogic imagination* there is also evidence that Bakhtin began shifting his emphasis away from the ways in which individual subjects constructed relations through the construction of language, and toward a theory of how language works to shape ideology and human social reality.

Yet this shift, as I tried to suggest with relation to *Marxism* and *The formal method*, is a troublesome one, particularly because Bakhtin in many ways refuses to give up the phenomenological claims that mark his early work. Humans undoubtedly have the power to shape and reshape their social makeup each time they hear, interiorize and then reutter language. And, in connection with subjects' contact with other subjects, the ability to change one's individual makeup implies – and Bakhtin works out the way in which it does so – a larger theory of the construction of society in and through language. But because humans are first and always beings who are defined by their use of language – and because they cannot escape from this embeddedness into considering how social or natural phenomena function extra-ideologically – there is some question as to whether a change in a subject's social position can change the material conditions of that subject's existence. Current theories of historical materialism, on the other hand, claim that because of the scientificity of the study of ideologies, they are able to consider extra-ideological material.

In this chapter, I want to consider the historical materialist claims for a scientific theory of ideologies, and to set Bakhtin's watered-down materialism against it to see how it fares. It must be noted at the outset that historical materialism's claim to function as a science will not go unquestioned here, though the most forceful rebuttal of its scientificity – in the form of Fish's and Rorty's pragmatisms – will come in for critique in the next chapter. It also should be said here that, in the same way that Bakhtin's version of language and its relation to subject-formation was not strictly phenomenological and did not match up exactly with other similar theories, so his materialism and notion of societal change will also not match up with the versions of historical materialism here considered. It is close enough, as I have said, however, to warrant comparison.

The problematic relationship between Bakhtin and historical materialism has several aspects. For Bakhtin (in the Marxist writings), the "economic base" is said to play a part in the conditions of human interaction, and yet those economic conditions are assumed (or ignored), and are not significantly factored into the equation of human perception. Moreover, ideology for Bakhtin is subtly different from ideology for more orthodox historical materialists: for Bakhtin, ideology is determined and determining; for historical materialism, ideology stems from the real conditions of production, and so is determined in the last instance by the economy. Finally, Marxism claims scientificity, in that it is able, by way of theory, to dislocate and decenter ideological formations and artefacts in such a way as to disclose the real object of knowledge (that is, the operation of the material conditions of production). Yet Bakhtin clearly places the purview of science *inside* the study of ideologies, implying that the scientific object of knowledge (material conditions of production) are likewise always affected – even in their theoretical "disclosure" – by ideological considerations (that is, anomalies and the "play" or dialogization of language).

I want to consider these problems by way of two related questions. The first of these involves the problem of Bakhtin's social language theory and how it can (or cannot) include a theory of "social movement" (or revolution). This question really has two parts: how

are subjects constituted socially; and how can one say at once that
language can play a part in changing a subject's orientation in the
social world, presumably for the better, when that very language in
turn becomes "monologized" and can be used as a tool for
authoritarianism.[1] The second principal question is how, given the
way Mikhail Bakhtin views language and ideology as being
determined and determining of human consciousness, Bakhtin's theory
can be reconciled with the Marxist claim to scientificity beyond the
realm of the ideological. Simply, does Bakhtin undermine the Marxists,
or do the Marxists undermine the project of Bakhtin, when it comes
to theorizing the relation between science and ideology?

I

Ken Hirschkop, a historical materialist as well as a scholar of the work
of Mikhail Bakhtin, in a sense took issue with Bakhtin for not allowing
in his language theory for the kind of social change necessary for
"liberation" or social upheaval, and that dialogism and intersubjectivity do not allow for any other change than renegotiation of
contexts, which leaves out the possibility of radical, social change
(Hirschkop, "Bakhtin, discourse and democracy" 92–111). "Bakhtin,"
he argues,

> allows that subjects may be collective or continuous through history. [The
> problem] is that Bakhtin defines social context purely in terms of a multiplicity
> of consciousnesses. In all his varied formulations of the social relations which
> determine style, the relations are entirely intersubjective. Discourse is
> dialogical in the sense that within it the ideological imperatives of at least two
> consciousnesses intersect. But the social situation is thereby reduced to the
> interplay between the speaking subject and alien subjects. (97)

Hirschkop, in effect, reduces dialogue to a kind of "meeting place" of
contexts, the process of which will determine a new linguistic context,

---

1 I am thinking here of the way Bakhtin speaks of the power of the carnivalization of language
in *Rabelais and his world*: "Rabelais' images have a certain undestroyable unofficial nature. No
dogma, no authoritarianism, no narrow-minded seriousness can coexist with Rabelaisian
images [of carnival]; these images are opposed to all that is finished and polished, to all
pomposity, to every ready-made solution in the sphere of thought and world outlook" (3).
As a transformative phenomenon, he suggests that the "[carnivalesque, or non-official]
image reflects a phenomenon in transformation, an as yet unfinished metamorphosis, of
death and birth, growth and becoming" (24). Bakhtin notes, though, that the genre of
carnival (much like the genre of the novel at certain times) becomes a monologized formula,
used in "chamber carnivals." "It became," in the Renaissance, "as it were, an individual
carnival, marked by a vivid sense of isolation" (37).

and so on and so on. Historical forces, in other words, are exterior to
the process of dialogism, which is purely a function of language. What
Bakhtin – in Hirschkop's view – leaves out is the potential repression
of dialogism, which tends to stifle the "meeting" that can take place
through dialogue; nor can he explain the ways in which monologue,
far from being a kind of "tired" form of language, can become a tool
of authority.[2] According to Hirschkop, this tendency is relegated to a
history that is outside the purview of language study.

I do not want to discount Hirschkop's critique of Bakhtin here, since
in the end I want to endorse his claim – that language for Bakhtin
supercedes the "process of history." Yet, in his characterization of
history, Hirschkop ignores the kind of "institutionalization" that goes
on constantly in language. In *The dialogic imagination*, not to mention
the Dostoevsky and Rabelais books, one of the main components of
any language-genre (be it in written language – novels, say – or in
spoken micro-genres) is its tendency toward institutionalization and
monologization. "The [finished monologic utterance] is set toward
being perceived in the context of current scientific life or current
literary affairs, i.e., it is perceived in the generative process of that
particular ideological domain of which it is an integral part" (*MPL* 72).
This kind of world-view is finished, closed off. It not only can be
imposed – as Bakhtin says of "official language" in the Rabelais book
as well as in "From the prehistory of novelistic discourse" – but it can
also evolve (as in micro-genres, just as "Nice day, isn't it?" is part of
the micro-genre "talking about the weather": it is finished, closed off,
it has a pre-given meaning, and yet it is a part of the discourse that
goes on around it, be it monologic or dialogic). What aggravates
Hirschkop is that this conceptualization of the dialogic and its relation
to the monologic does not do what he wants it to (or what he believes
Bakhtin claimed for it): namely, to be a tool that can be used in the
emancipation of people from monologism (or, politically, authoritarianism).

I think Hirschkop is right on this count, though he misconstrues
Bakhtin's intentions in arguing that Bakhtin saw dialogue as an

---

2 Hirschkop has made a similar argument in his "Response to the Bakhtin forum" in *Bakhtin:
Essays and dialogues on his work*, ed. Gary Saul Morson (University of Chicago Press, 1986).
In this essay, Hirschkop claims that the liberal tendency in literary studies is to construe
"dialogism" as a harmonious process in language, the impulse of which is to smooth over
ideological discrepancies and inequities which appear in works in favor of a kind of "forum
of differences" in which everything comes out right in the end.

explicitly political liberating device. Dialogism and monologism are not only literary tendencies, but tendencies in thought and language. More precisely, they are ideological tendencies: depending upon the language-background a speaker has at his or her disposal, utterances (and the sign-relations "embedded" in them) can be either interiorized and then dialogized, or interiorized "as already defined," that is, monologically. Certainly, political institutions tend to monologize utterances as "already given," yet this tendency cannot prevent dialogizing of these same monologic utterances. All language carries with it all its sign-baggage: all the different contexts in which it has been used and all the different sign-orientations in which it has been implicated. And while all the sign-orientations that are implicated in any utterance do not guarantee that they will be "deployed" by a speaker, they do carry with them the potential for dialogization.

Monologism is thus not a process of historical forces that lies outside the purview of language and ideological study. Rather, all language – as an incarnation of human consciousness and communication – contains both the impulse to "re-orient" an utterance as well as the impulse to interiorize it more or less "as is." Hirschkop's reading of Bakhtin's characterization of the novel as a disruptive tendency in the nineteenth-century literary world – and as symptomatic of a particular moment in history – oversimplifies Bakhtin's intent. It is not the novel *as genre* that he is talking about, but a novelistic tendency, a tendency that is current at *every* moment in history (as one can see in Bakhtin's painstaking chronology in "Discourse in the novel" as well as in "From the prehistory of novelistic discourse"). Moreover, at the very moment of the novelistic impulse, there exists an opposite impulse to read and use language monologically, in a sense to make the dialogic into a kind of genre. This is the reason why scholars who wish to use Bakhtin's conception of the novel as a new way to characterize genre will inevitably fail: the novel is an anti-genre, an amalgam of various different, dialogized components of monologized literary genres (see Morson and Emerson, *Mikhail Bakhtin*; Van Buuren, "Quelques aspects du dialogisme"). Since history, then, is the very process of these two conflicting tendencies, rather than an external force that has a counteractive effect on dialogism, social change (that is, a change in human consciousness by way of the process of authorship of utterance) is painstakingly slow, and never unidirectional.

Hirschkop contends that "cultural oppression becomes explicable only as the prevention of social connection. The resultant idealist politics should fatally overestimate the power of the natural form of social interaction – dialogism – and underestimate the power of monologism, whose hegemonic mode of domination it cannot comprehend" ("Bakhtin, discourse and democracy" 106). In fact, oppression is a "social connection" based upon a monologic mode of relation rather than a dialogic one, yet one in which the potential for dialogism is present. Monologism is as much a part of social language theory as is dialogism.

If social change only takes place in this slow, because locally determined, way, then the historical materialist idea of revolutionary social change is put in question. In Bakhtin's/Voloshinov's discussion of "quasi-direct discourse" near the end of *Marxism and the philosophy of language*, one begins to glimpse the sweep of the movement in language-generated social interaction as not unified or directional, but rather as one of "social shifts" and "alterations," one of "continuous generation and change" (157). This suggests – when taken along with the drawn-out process of answerability and the fits and starts of the generation of novelistic discourse – that any political "revolution" for Bakhtin will be a long way off, and may be short-lived before shifts take place to quell it. I will come back to this point, since the idea of revolutionary versus gradual, non-unidirectional change bears on the problem of a "theoretical vanguard" that stands outside the social whole. Specifically, Althusser's idea of Marxism as a science – which requires scientific modes of discourse that are by definition subjectless – seems to preclude the possibility of social movement (that is, movement of subjects in the process of history). More directly related to my immediate concern here is the characterization of the social self in Marxist theory and its relation to Bakhtin's conception of the self: in what ways do the different constitutions of the self contribute to different conceptions of social change?

For Althusserian Marxism, history is a process without a subject.[3] History and society are not created by individual (or collective) subjects;

3 In Louis Althusser and Etienne Balibar, *Reading capital* (London: New Left Books, 1970), 271. All further citations in the text will be abbreviated, where necessary, *RC*. *For Marx* (London: New Left Books, 1969) will be abbreviated *For M*; *Lenin and philosophy* (London: Monthly Review Press, 1971) will be abbreviated, where necessary, *LP*.

the structure of the relations of production determines the *places* and *functions* occupied and adopted by the agents of production, who are never anything more than the occupants of these places, insofar as they are the "supports" (*Trager*) of these functions. The true "subjects" (in the sense of constitutive subjects of the process) are therefore not these occupants or functionaries, are not "concrete individuals, "real men" – but *the definition and distribution of these places and functions. The true "subjects" are these definers and distributors: the relations of production* (and political and ideological social relations). But since these are "relations," they cannot be thought within the category *subject*.

(*RC* 180)

For Marx, Gregory Elliott notes (in *Althusser: The detour of theory*), Althusser argued that the relations of production involve the distribution and means of production as well as the relations between "men" (social agents) distributed to antagonistic social classes. If one interprets these relations as purely intersubjective human relations, then one is making a "remarkable presupposition: that the 'actors' of history are the authors of its text, the subjects of its production" (*RC* 139).

For Althusser, the term "intersubjective" signifies a relation that is determining for its subjects: the contact between subjects – communication, conceptualization – determines these subjects' ideological perceptions and relations. In other words, if one takes intersubjective ideological conceptions to determine one's relations to the material conditions of existence, one is ignoring that the material conditions of existence were there long before the subject perceived them. Clearly, for Althusser, intersubjective relations can determine information about material conditions, but they cannot determine their nature or their existence. The ideological relation to the mode of production and the mode of production itself are analytically distinct.

Yet, for Bakhtin, the mode of production – a concept that he did not address explicitly, but one nevertheless he related to the economic "base" – was also a product of intersubjective human relations. In a sense, the difference between the positions of Althusser and Bakhtin on the primacy of intersubjective relations amounts to a distinction in degrees of determinacy. In the very first pages of both *Marxism and the philosophy of language* (9) and *The formal method* (3), Bakhtin characterizes ideological study as subsuming studies of economy, religion, ethics, and so on. This does not mean that he would disagree with Althusser that the material conditions of existence were there prior to human consciousness of them. What it does mean is that

Althusser (and other orthodox Marxists) believes that intersubjective relations are always determined in the last instance by the economy, one of the elements or levels of the mode of production.

Bakhtin would counter that the very concept of "mode of production" is determined intersubjectively. For Althusser, the chronological order goes something like: material conditions exist, humans then come into existence within the material world, the mode of production is initiated (in which the ideological understanding – including intersubjective relations of communication – of all that has come before comes into existence). Though the superstructure is *relatively* autonomous from the base, it is nevertheless that which in fact determines the *way* it is set into motion. It then, in turn, affects the base, which revises the operation of the superstructure, and so on. Intersubjective relations are *determined* in the last instance by the material forces of the economy. Yet, seemingly for Bakhtin, though material forces no doubt exist, what determines that we know about them at all are intersubjective human relations. For Bakhtin, what is determinate in the last instance is language. For example, I can feel pain outside of intersubjective (ideological) human relations; but the only way that I *know* that I feel something called "pain" (the *concept* of pain) is inside the authorial process of sign-negotiation. Whatever it is that I feel or hear, it is felt or heard always and primarily intersubjectively and ideologically. For Bakhtin, pain is certainly determined by material forces; but the subject who feels pain, in authorial (sign-)relation with other subjects in coming to an understanding of this pain, is both determined by the relation (the subject comes to recognize the sensation as what she has known in other contexts as "pain"), and determines it (the subject determines whether this pain is like any other she has experienced, the degree of its significance, her interiorization of the sign-relation and how she can subsequently utter it in a future context, and so on).

Finally, these relations are never complete – no sign-relation is ever truly closed, defined – or felicitous, since any intersubjective (sign-) relation can take place dialogically or monologically. The primary difference between Althusser here and Bakhtin is that Althusser believes that subjects do not determine themselves (but believe because of ideological relations that they do), but rather they are determined by material forces; while Bakhtin believes that subjects both determine *and are determined* by their relation in language.

Althusserian historical materialism goes a long way toward solving the dilemma of how ideologies are related to the infrastructure, and the ways in which the relationship is structured with its recuperation of the term "overdetermination;" moreover, overdetermined contradiction is one way of understanding how Bakhtin sees the complex interrelation of ideologies in the superstructure. What the concept does not solve, though, is the way in which ideologies are related to the base, either for Marxism or for Bakhtin. Althusser's analysis of contradiction begins with a discussion of how the Revolution occurred in Russia, particularly when Russia was the *least* likely candidate for such a revolution. Althusser contends that because Russia was the *weakest link* in the "imperialist chain" (*For M* 98) – because the historical contradictions that accrued and were exacerbated in the state were the most pronounced of any other state's – it was in fact the *most* likely candidate for revolution. This is so because "it was at the same time *the most backward and the most advanced nation*, a gigantic contradiction which its divided ruling classes could neither avoid nor solve" (97). The *objective conditions* of a Russian revolution were there, and the collectivity of subjects living within those objective conditions had to make "a decisive assault on this weak link" (98).

The contradictions in Russian society on the eve of the Revolution – or, in fact in any society – "derive from the relations of production, which are, of course, one of the terms of the contradiction, but at the same time its *conditions of existence*; from the superstructures, instances which derive from it, but have their own consistency and effectivity; from the international conjuncture itself, which intervenes as a determination with a specific role to play" (*For M* 100). These contradictions fuse into a revolutionary rupture, but "the 'contradiction' is inseparable from the total structure of the social body in which it is found, inseparable from its formal *conditions* of existence, and even from the *instances* it governs; it is radically *affected by them*, determining, but also determined in one and the same movement, and determined by the various *levels* and *instances* of the social formation it animates; it might be called *overdetermined in its principle*" (100–101).

It is here that we get the Marxist dictum that ideologies (and ideological structures and institutions) are determined by the economy in the last instance. The material conditions of existence in some sense generate the data which humans process ideologically; moreover, humans, in their relations with one another (which, taking our cue from Bakhtin, we realize occur first and always linguistically, or in terms of the generation of signs), have an effect on the social composition of their own selves and the construction of other subjects with whom they come into contact. Althusser cites Engels's letter to Bloch to underline the relative autonomy of ideology: "The economic situation is the basis, but," he goes on,

> the various elements of the superstructure – the political forms of the class struggle and its results: to wit constitutions established by the victorious classes after a successful battle, etc., juridical forms, and then even the reflexes of all these actual struggles in the brains of the participants, political, juristic, philosophical theories, religious views and their further development into systems of dogmas – also exercise their influence upon the course of the historical struggles, and in many cases preponderate in determining their form.
> (*For M* 112)

In other words, depending upon the overdetermined nature of the contradictions within a given social structure – in Bakhtinian terms, depending upon the ways in which authorial relations are characterized (either dialogically, monologically, or in some combination) and depending upon what form ideological institutions take based upon those authorial relations among individuals and segments of society – there are times at which the superstructures predominate in the determination of the composition of the social whole over the economy.

It has been established, then, that in historical materialism the superstructures are a determining factor in the composition of social wholes as much as the base is, though the base is determinate in the last instance. There is some question, though, whether there is a two-way relationship between the base and the superstructure: that is, is it possible for the constantly changing social whole to affect the mode of production and the economic base? Althusser suggests that this is possible, since humans in Russia in the early twentieth century seized the moment of rupture and began significantly to change the economic forces of production in the Soviet Union. But how does this two-way relationship work? Althusser suggests that this "remains to be elaborated" (*For M* 113); Bakhtin suggests the same and then goes on to ignore the problem altogether. This indeterminacy – a solution to which has been attempted by various historical materialists, including those I will discuss below – is a sore point in historical materialism (and those who would claim Bakhtin for historical materialism), since the ways in which humans change their social composition, and more importantly, their material conditions of existence, must be elaborated for a useful theory of social change.

The second major question that needs to be asked – and this is one that *is* answered by Bakhtin, as I have suggested – is how, if a relationship between base and superstructure has not been articulated, does one theorize social and economic change? Althusser suggests that one must think in terms of *survivals*, since past material realities exist in present reality, and will have an effect. Contradiction and overdetermination suggest – as the complexities of ideological linguistic relation do for Bakhtin – "(1) that a revolution in the structure does not ipso facto modify the existing superstructures and particularly the ideologies at one blow (as it would if the economic was the sole determinant factor), for they have sufficient of their own consistency to survive beyond their immediate life context, even to recreate, to 'secrete' substitute conditions of existence temporarily;" and "(2) that the new society produced by the Revolution may itself ensure the survival, that is, the reactivation of older elements through both the forms of its new superstructures and specific (national and international) 'circumstances'" (*For M* 115-16). In other words, as Bakhtin suggests in "From the prehistory of novelistic discourse" and elsewhere, social change occurs slowly, and there is no guarantee that authoritarian forces will not suppress the dialogic forces that will inevitably be present.

This has several implications both for Marxism and for Bakhtin (all of which will be followed up here and in the next chapter). First, going back to the problem of how humans effect change in their historical (real-world) situation by way of intersubjective relations – or, for Marxism, by way of relation of the economic base (within the mode of production) to the ideological superstructures (that is, the imaginary relation to them) – the above again suggests that the traditional base/superstructure model will not work without some serious elaboration of their relation. In other words, humans, through intersubjective relations, can indeed effect a change not only on their ideological placement (that is, their orientation within ideology), but also their condition in the material world (more specifically, their status within the mode of production). How this occurs is something of a question both for Bakhtin and for Marxism, though – as I have tried to suggest – there is some real question as to how seriously Bakhtin might have taken the traditional Marxist notion that it is the economy that is ultimately determinant. Bakhtin asserts at the beginning of *Marxism and the philosophy of language* that material objects or processes cannot "become a sign." He uses the example of bread: "bread and wine become religious symbols in the Christian sacrament of communion. But the consumer good, as such, is not at all a sign. Consumer goods, just as tools, may be combined with ideological signs, but the distinct conceptual dividing line between them is not erased by the combination ... Thus side by side with the natural phenomena, with the equipment of technology, and with articles for consumption, there exists a special world – the world of signs" (*MPL* 10). Yet, in "Discourse in life, discourse in art," though Bakhtin makes a similar claim for "processes in nature," the only persons capable of performing analyses of such processes are "physicists and chemists with the help of the specific methods of their fields" (95). Later on we discover that the only way those methods can be set up is by way of certain "genres" of intersubjective communication (112–16; "Speech genres" 80–83).

Since all human relations (either with other humans, or in isolation during the act of negotiating sign-relations in the presence of objects of natural phenomena) are intersubjective, then the idea of the function of the economic base, determinant in the last instance, is still determined intersubjectively (that is, ideologically). That is, the economy may indeed function in the way that we think that it functions, and in the way that we have intersubjectively determined; whether it does in fact function – extra-ideologically – in this way at all has yet to be determined, since our concepts of "economy" and so on are always ideologically colored. (I will have more to say about this Bakhtinian "contingency clause" in the next chapter.) What all this goes to show, I think, is that for historical materialism, the problem of the base's relation to the superstructure poses problems for processes of historical change; for Bakhtin, it is not so much of a problem (or at least not the same type of problem). There must be some kind of real connection between "natural" and "ideological" spheres over and above the structure Althusser envisions.

One way to begin to see real connections between historical materialist definitions of the subject (as well as the relations between ideology and its determination of the social whole) and a Bakhtinian definition of the subject – in order to see a way out of the difficult relationship between base and superstructure – is by way of Michel Pecheux's analysis of language construction. In particular, Pecheux's discussion of the "subject form" of discourse is interesting in its relation to Bakhtin's assertion that all human activity (both in relation to humans and "natural phenomena") is intersubjective. In *Language, semantics, and ideology*,[4] Pecheux takes aim at the "ideology that supplies the evidentness with which 'everyone knows' what a soldier is [for example], or a worker, a boss, a factory, a strike, etc., the evidentness that makes a word or an utterance 'mean what it says' and thereby masks in the 'transparency of language' what I shall call *the material character of the meaning* of words and utterances" (111). This is similar to the assertion Bakhtin makes that all human utterances (all human sign-relations, relationships of authorship) carry with them all the background signs (and ideological formations) that have been uttered previously. Both for Bakhtin and for Pecheux, utterance is a *material* thing, something real and historical. (In *The formal method*, Bakhtin suggests that "All the products of ideological creation ... are material things, part of the practical reality that surrounds man" [7].) Interdiscourse is for Pecheux this "complex whole" of discursive formations which always "before, elsewhere, and independently" speaks.

What is peculiar about the "subject form" of discourse is that in it the subject identifies himself as the perceiver or originator of a given utterance (thereby ignoring the "interdiscourse" that is embedded in utterances that the subject has interiorized, or that the subject utters himself). In a sense, what the subject is doing is identifying himself with "himself," or what Bakhtin (in defining a subject's apprehension of an experience or utterance) calls the "I-experience" (*MPL* 88).[5] The subject's apprehension of interdiscourse in effect serves to prevent that subject from falling into the trap of making identities in his own language. Upon "receiving" an utterance, the subject can do one of two things (note the similarities to the options that Bakhtin affords his subjects): the subject can identify himself as the originator of the response to that utterance (in a sense, he will orient his response without first authoring his self through an analysis of the interlocutor's

4 Michel Pecheux, *Language, semantics, and ideology* (New York: Saint Martin's Press, 1975, 1982). All further references that appear in the text will be abbreviated *LSI*, where necessary.
5 In *Marxism and the philosophy of language*, Bakhtin talks about the way people ideologically interpret material processes, such as hunger. In what might be interpreted as one of the more "Marxist" sections of the work, Bakhtin discusses collectivities in terms of "I-experiences" (in which a person feels himself isolated, socially and therefore verbally) and "we-experiences" (in which a person feels himself a member of a collectivity, and therefore a member of a larger "community of authorship"). What I wish to emphasize here is the degree of "verbal isolation" that takes place in the "I-experience," an isolation of verbal or linguistic experience that is similar to a monologic verbal experience, in which it is closed off, pre-determined, with emphasis on the "already encountered," rather than the "re-orientation" of ideological "interdiscourse."

position and orientation); or the subject can orient himself in such a way as to perceive the background (interdiscourse, the complex ideological formations in the utterance) language – to "author himself" according to this *re*orientation – thereby breaking out of the subject-relation. The breaking away from this subject-relation is in a sense a recognition that the "I" is *not* "I," that there is not a direct identity between an utterance and the speaker of that utterance.

For Marxism, too, ideology is a *representation* of the "imaginary" relation, and for that reason is also an objective reality, a material practice which, according to Elliott, can be apprehended but not surpassed. *Theoretical* ideology is a kind of knowledge, but, according to Althusser, it is a "recognition" rather than a "cognition." In recognition, "the formulation of a *problem* is merely the theoretical expression of the conditions which allow a *solution* already produced outside the process of knowledge ... to *recognize itself* in an artificial problem manufactured to serve it both as theoretical mirror and as a practical justification" (*For M* 231). In the words of Alain Badiou, "ideology ... is a process of *repetition*."[6]

Pecheux's debunking of the process of the "subject-form" of discourse provides an alternative to making the kind of "self-identification" that identifies utterances as having been generated solely by the subject. Recognizing that all utterances – that is, all material sign-relations (by definition in ideology) – are produced by some subject's "point of view" will not enable a person somehow to get outside of ideology. (That person will still, at some level, make the identity that "I" somehow am originating this utterance, that this point of view is "my" point of view and mine only.) Nevertheless, the subject is able to perceive – for the first time – that he is inside ideology, that he has a place inside it. The disruption of the subject-form is similar to the dialogic double movement of authorship: though it cannot allow a speaking (or perceiving) subject to glimpse at her material conditions without mediation through language, it nevertheless allows that subject to perceive the dialogic potential (the fecund language/ideological background) in any authorial relation and guarantees at least the possibility for dialogization.

To make clear this "Bakhtinian identity relation" and the way it

6 Quoted in Gregory Elliott, *Althusser: The detour of theory* (London: Verso, 1987), 100. The Badiou quotation comes from "Le (re)commencement du matérialisme dialectique," *Critique* 240 (1967), 49.

relates to the monologic and dialogic tendencies, I quote at length a section from the Clark and Holquist biography, in which this identity relation is discussed in terms of the *Art and answerability* texts:

The pronoun *I* marks the axial point between the pre-existing, repeatable system of language and my unique, unrepeatable existence as a particular human being; "language is so organized that it permits each speaker *to appropriate* to himself an entire language by designating himself as 'I.'"
(*Mikhail Bakhtin* 90; quotation is from Emile Benveniste, *Problems in general linguistics* 226)

"This is what Bakhtin means in describing consciousness as being always on the border: it is on the border ... between the centrifugal forces of subjectivity [that is, dialogism], which are chaotic and particular, and the centripetal forces of system [that is, monologism], which are rule driven and abstract ..." (Clark and Holquist, *Mikhail Bakhtin* 91–2). Finally, all language relations take place within this personal pronoun's domain: consciousness of self, the single important ingredient of language relation, is only possible if experienced in contrast. So, to greater or lesser degrees, the identity of self (I am I) or resistance to it determines the degree to which a person is able to see the materiality of language, and to orient himself differently in it.

Returning to Pecheux, he notes that there are three "modalities," possible ways by which to break out of the "subject-form" of discourse. "The *first modality* consists of a superimposition (a covering) of *the subject of enunciation and the universal subject* such that the subject's 'taking up a position' realises his subjection in the form of the 'freely consented to' ..." (*LSI* 156–7). In effect, a subject in this modality recognizes the interdiscourse as having been determined prior to his having encountered it, and simply recognizes this determination "'in complete freedom'". In literary terms, Bakhtin recognized this form of utterance in the works of Tolstoy, in which characters "are portrayed as ... fixed and finalized image[s] of reality" (*Problems of Dostoevsky's poetics* 79), a kind of predetermined feature of the materiality of discourse. It is language already spoken; when it is uttered, it is in turn spoken in its previously spoken form. For Bakhtin, this is a form of monologism, of self-identity. And in this form, the speaking subject does not realize his placement within the "background" language (in Pecheux's and Althusser's terms, the subject does not recognize his placement in ideology).

"The *second modality* characterises the discourse of the 'bad subject,' in which the *subject of enunciation* 'turns against' *the universal subject* by 'taking up a position' which now consists of a *separation"* from the "evidentness of the terrain" (*LSI* 157). The subject in this modality counteridentifies with the discursive information found in the interdiscourse. This is a kind of "railing against" any exterior imposition on the subject. But again, this nevertheless isolates the subject (who identifies himself as the originator of the *exclusion* in this case, in a sense willing himself outside of ideology) by failing to acknowledge his own complicity in (and potential dialogization of) ideology. Bakhtin recognized this kind of monologic repudiation in Tolstoy's work (*Problems of Dostoevsky's poetics* 80–83). The *third modality*, according to Pecheux, is not a simple abolition of the subject-form, and for that reason this third modality represents a way for historical materialism to claim a method of analysis of the material conditions of existence while still not being able to "escape from ideology." "The operation of the 'third modality' constitutes a *working* (transformation-displacement) *of the subject form* and not just its *abolition*." In effect, this modality works ideological analysis upon ideology itself. In Bakhtinian terms, while not repudiating one's placement intersubjectively in the background of language, and while neither simply "taking as already said" any utterance (or spoken authorial relation); the subject interiorizes the interdiscourse in a discourse situation, and, in analyzing its complex ideological makeup, dialogizes it. This does not by any means allow Pecheux's (or Bakhtin's) methods for debunking self-identity to pass outside of ideology into the realm of the "real" or the realm of the "base." What they do is allow subjects to recognize their placement in the material reality of the *social* world (that is the ideological world), and work from that placement. To say that some subjects do not manage to engage in this third modality is as erroneous as saying that some subjects operate (authorially) monologically, and some dialogically. Again, this is not a matter of one or the other. Subjects to some degree or another will engage in discourse in this third modality all of the time. (The authorial relation does not work for some humans; it is what *defines* humans.) Nevertheless, depending upon the interdiscourse that is present during any series of utterances (that is, in any dialogue or authorial relation), and the degrees to which it also takes part in the first or the second of Pecheux's three modalities, any glimmer or recognition of the materiality of the ideological nature of language is as apt to lapse into those first two modalities in the same way as any dialogic utterance is apt to lapse into monologism.

All this goes to show that, for both Bakhtin and Pecheux (and to some degree, Althusser), language is the active component for the production of selves (or, if you prefer, subjects). Moreover, given the materiality of language relations, and their ability to produce changes in social relations, and given that material conditions (and so the [economic] material conditions of existence) are apprehensible only in the materiality of language – uttered ideological signs – then it would seem that the Marxist distinction of base and superstructure is highly complex and the relationship between them overdetermined. Social conditions (ideological phenomena) do in fact affect the economic base (here conceived as natural phenomena) in a fashion similar to the way in which the base affects the ideological superstructure. Going back to our starting point, this relationship is also never (uni)directional, and is never constant (for example, in tending to non-identification as opposed to identification; dialogism as opposed to monologism).

II

We have now come to what is the perennial bogey of Marxist studies: the distinction between science (which Marxism claims to be) and ideology (which Marxism claims to study). Michel Pecheux calls his third modality a scientific moment, a "subjective appropriation of knowledge." Science, in his view, is a "challenge to the subject-form of discourse," that form which keeps subjects blindly unaware of the nature of their subjectivity. Yet we have just seen that this third modality is certainly *not* a glimpse of the objective operations of the material conditions of existence. How does this square with the notion that Marxism is a science? And does the way Bakhtin looks at language and the formation of subject-relations offer any insight (or maybe a solution) to this perplexity?

I want to take a brief look at a distinction made by Roy Bhaskar in order to make a bit clearer the problem of "science" and how it is defined within the Marxist problematic. (It should be noted, however, that Bhaskar's work for a long time did not lie strictly within the bounds of historical materialism, but has relevance to all the social sciences as well, and thus is connected with the work Bakhtin has done on language.) Briefly, Bhaskar defines two dimensions of science, the "intransitive" and the "transitive." In the transitive dimension, "objects of our knowledge exist and act independently of the knowledge of which they are objects."[7] That is, natural phenomena exist and operate regardless of the human ability to identify those phenomena or to analyze the tendencies according to which they appear to operate. This then necessitates, again according to Bhaskar, the fact that "such knowledge as we actually possess always consists in historically specific social forms" (*The possibility of naturalism* 14). There needs to be some way to bridge the gap between the existence of certain natural phenomena, and the ability of humans to be able to perceive and gain some knowledge of them. For Bhaskar – as for Bakhtin – this knowledge is always socially generated.[8]

In order to gain knowledge of these intransitive elements in science, the production of such knowledge "must depend upon the employment of antecedently existing cognitive materials (which I have called the 'transitive' objects of knowledge)" (15). Science, Bhaskar continues, must be a social process, the aim of which is to produce that knowledge of mechanisms of the production of phenomena in nature, that is, the intransitive objects of inquiry. Bhaskar goes on to describe science in a three-phase schema of development: first, science identifies a phenomenon (or a range of phenomena); it constructs explanations for it and empirically tests its explanations; and this leads to the identification of the generative mechanism at work. This generative mechanism in turn becomes the phenomenon to be explained, and so on.

This seems to pose no problem for Marxism in particular, or grant inroads for a Bakhtinian solution at first glance. In fact, this kind of scientific process is very much like the one Bakhtin seems to advocate in *The formal method*, where he notes that "human consciousness does not come into contact with existence directly, but through the medium of the surrounding ideological world" (14). Science can posit certain repeatable formulations of its operation; yet, in its language and in its conceptualizations of its formulations, it is always and necessarily open to ideological analysis as well. However, there does exist a

---

7 From Roy Bhaskar, *The possibility of naturalism* (Brighton: The Harvester Press, 1979), 14. All subsequent references will be given in the text. In the most succint definition of the intransitive dimension of science, Bhaskar notes "[t]hat the analysis of experimental activity shows that the objects of scientific investigation are typically structured and intransitive, that is irreducible to patterns of events and active independently of their identification by men" (14).

8 See *Marxism and the philosophy of language*, 25–6, on the connection between "psychological" or subjective perceptions, and the social (material) nature of those perceptions.

problem when one takes a look at just what the object of knowledge for a Marxist science is: history.

History, in the terms Bhaskar uses, is an intransitive object of scientific inquiry: it is "irreducible to patterns of events and active independently of their identification by men." Or, as Althusser formulates it, history is a process without a subject. That is, history is an "intransitive" process that acts (in a sense) through the *operation* of ideology, yet is operational itself outside of any ideological misconceptions (or "biases" if you wish) of its actual operation. Yet as we have seen, though one can have "intransitive" objects of science independently of their "analysis" or transitive descriptions, there cannot be science per se without those transitive cognitive tools. And if we include the Bakhtinian notion of these "cognitive tools," that is, that any act of human cognition takes place first and always within language (the creation and negotiation of ideologemes/signs), then we have a rather more complicated view of a science of history. In this view, scientific analysis is a constantly shifting process of formulating methods of inquiry into questions that have been developed through those same methods of inquiry, all of which have been *socially* formulated. Further, the object of inquiry is equally social in its composition (history, though it may be a "process without a subject," nevertheless is a process *of* subjects, that is, it is material only insofar as it is social [see Bakhtin/Medvedev, *FM* 26–7]). What historical materialism is here left with is a process that reveals historical movement as taking place ideologically (by way of subjects), and that science is itself a part of that historical movement. The never-ending dialectic does not have the advantage of its culminating term being more significant than the two opposing terms.

What is more, if we accept that Marxist "science" operates in this way – that is, socially and ideologically – then it is subject to the vagaries of monologism and dialogism, just as Bakhtin's speech genres were. In fact, it could be maintained, I think, that "scientific discoveries" – at least in terms of historical materialist discoveries, if we stick to the Marxist self-definition of their project as scientific – are in fact a kind of "entering into genre-form" of certain structures of ideologemes. In "The problem of speech genres," Bakhtin talks about the specificity which certain "dialects" have achieved, and the subject matter which they pertain to. In a skeptic's view, the scientific categories of "working-class," "bourgeois," "liberal economy," and the like, could fall into the verbal–ideological category of such "speech genres." The historical materialist project, by complicating it in this way, is by no means invalidated; however, it *is* threatened – in a way that it would not be if in fact it did operate "more like" a science – to retreat to "institutionalization." What we are beginning to see is that, for historical materialism – given Bakhtin's method of study – science is a much more complex method of study than is traditionally thought by those like (as we will see) Richard Rorty.

Given the complication of "history" as an object of knowledge, and the problems involved in characterizing the method of analysis of that object (that is, science as a tool for analyzing the object, history), one is again faced with the problem of just how to deploy historical materialism (as a theory) for social change (praxis). Since what science can be said to accomplish is to enable subjects to have a glimpse of their subjectivity – it allows those subjects to see (but not necessarily to escape) their subjection to ideology – then one has to wonder, first, how one (or in fact *if* one) can pass outside of ideology, and second, if that passage can occur, how it occurs socially (ideologically).

Althusser's early formulation of historical materialist theory as science in effect "took the form of outright independence of the social formation and its history" (Elliott, *Althusser: The detour of theory* 109). The history of the sciences was thus disarticulated from theoretical practice and treated, instead, as a purely internal, epistemological affair of conceptual history. Elliott goes on to say of Althusser's conception of the science of history that "it was to be an account of Marxism which quite implausibly severed it, in its foundations and development, from any socio-historical connections," a problem which we saw earlier with other, non-Marxist, theories of language.[9] This distinction effectively shuts off, in other words, the possibility that historical materialism can function at once as a method of analysis of history, as well as a practical device for changing history. The first of these functions would seem perfectly operational: historical materialists could seek to understand the various relations between an economic "base" and an ideological "superstructure"; and could also seek to understand the ways in which that superstructure might affect the base in terms of its "subjectivizing" mechanisms. However, as a way to mobilize historical forces, this unbridgeable gap beteen a *theory* of

9 Gregory Elliott treats the problem with Althusser's concept of Marxism as a science of history at great length in his second chapter "A recommencement of dialectical materialism," in *Althusser: The detour of theory* (cited above), 61–114. For reasons of space and brevity, I have confined myself to discussion of only a portion of his relevant material.

history and the process of history (that is, a process that is material in its very susceptibility to ideological "blindness") would seem insurmountable.

Bakhtin seems to offer an alternative to this way of looking at the materiality of social discourse. Rather than positing a scientificity of method – as we have seen – Bakhtin instead subsumed science itself in a first move to ideology. That is, rather than set up (as Althusser did) a category of science that operates without a subject (or, at least, on a series of natural phenomena that operate outside of the human capability for conceptualizing those phenomena) and subsequently generating a social theory to understand the relationship between the two; Bakhtin set up the social theory as primary. What this effectively does is to undermine any sharp distinction (at least, as sharp as Althusser would want it) between theory and praxis, between object of knowledge and the production of knowledge of those objects. No moment of human interaction (that is, history) can be analyzed in such a way as to eliminate the subject from such an analysis, regardless of whether that analysis can, even for a moment, make the analyzing subject aware of her subjectivization (or subjection). Because even at the moment of surpassing the "subject-form" (in Pecheux's terms), the subject's blindness to the "imaginary relation" (in Althusser's), the moment of "dialogue" – the "novelistic moment" in Bakhtin's terms – the subject/analyzer nevertheless is still operating in language (that is, ideologically), and that moment is subject to the same analysis which in turn must attempt to overcome its embeddedness in ideology, and so on.

As I have said, Bakhtin's way of looking at things is an alternative, though by no means a more simple alternative. What Bakhtin offers, really, is an acknowledgment of the difficulty of analysis of human intercourse when that intercourse is always already embedded in language. What he acknowledges is the indissoluble unity of the materiality of natural phenomena and the equal materiality of its comprehension and conceptualization in language. You cannot have one without the other. In Bhaskar's terms, Bakhtin acknowledges the complement of intransitive object of knowledge and its transitive dimension by effectively bracketing the intransitive object from the equation, making it instead an (unknowable) element of the transitive dimension of the methods of inquiry.

Bakhtin's/Medvedev's discussion of the connection between "literary life" and "socioeconomic life" in *The formal method*, especially in the following passage, nearly contradicts itself: "When literature is studied in living interaction with other domains [which is what, in effect, his argument up to that point had affirmed has to occur] and in the concrete unity of socioeconomic life, it does not lose its individuality. In fact, its individuality can only be completely discovered and defined in this process of interaction" (*FM* 28). The materiality of social life (ideological-life-in-language) is material insofar as it is indissolubly connected with natural life: natural phenomena have materiality, as do humans; we only know these entities *as* humans. Humans are defined by their ability to create sign-relations. Therefore, these sign-relations, through their connection to phenomena, are also material.

This effectively changes the notion of the "scientific" moment (or in Pecheux's terms, the moment at which the subject-form of discourse is "worked" in such a way as to disclose the subject's placement in ideology). Rather than a kind of "epistemological break," the so-called scientific moment might be characterized, in Bakhtinian terms, as a "dialogic moment" at which a monologic form of sign-relations is overthrown. In social terms, it might be the moment at which a person working on an assembly line understands that the forms of discourse ("Quality of work life," "Union representative in management") being used to "include" him in the process of negotiating his life-as-subject are understood as simply another form of ideological subjection. Maybe more correctly, that assembly line worker might understand those discourse forms, which he had previously understood as "given" forms, as dialogical "re-orientations" with which he can "utter" (or author) other, different work situations and subject relations (between himself and other workers, or between himself and his bosses). Examples of how this might work in terms of literature have already been given by Bakhtin at great length in *Problems of Dostoevsky's poetics*.[10] This is the kind of "novelistic moment" of which Bakhtin speaks in "From the prehistory of novelistic discourse." It is not a given moment in history, but a tendency of all language – of all

---

10 See especially his second chapter, "The hero, the position of the author with regard to the hero, in Dostoevsky's art," and in relation to *Art and answerability*: the two provide, if nothing else, convincing evidence that Bakhtin was writing his literary works with a broader scope ("discourse in life") in mind. They also provide evidence of the ways in which language can be interiorized and reuttered dialogically by an author; "Discourse in the novel" provides examples of how language already written in a novel can be dialogized into new language-orientations by a reader.

human perceptions — toward (at one moment) dialogism, or toward (at another moment) monologism (which is the diametrically opposing, but equally prevalent and powerful tendency).

Going back once again to the problem of social movement — that is, the problem of a science of history which does not specifically provide a bridge over the gap between theory and practice, science and ideology — this suggests that a third term is necessary between what Elliott calls the "non-scientific problematic" and the "scientific problematic." The first of these is "characterized by its 'closure' — its repetitive revolution in an ideological circle" — while the second is characterized by "its 'openness' to pertinent problems and their rigorous solution, its capacity for (self-) rectification and development" (*Althusser: The detour of theory* 100). The Bakhtinian conception of "the dialogic," or that moment in which discontinuities and dis-identification of language take place to produce new language orientations is certainly "open." However, it is not tied to the idea of "development" per se. In fact, the moment of "dis-identification," or the double movement of the authorial relation, can in any number of circumstances lead to a monologic "response," if you will. One could term this lack of "development" in the positive sense a kind of "closure." But it is not characterized by closure in an ideological circle, since it is one of those moments, in Pecheux's terms, of a working of the ideological to disclose itself.

Moreover, the various dislocations — dialogic moments — or contradictions that this so-called scientific moment produces (the new language orientations) are

inseparable from the total structure of the social body in which it is found, inseparable from its formal *conditions* of existence, and even from the *instances* it governs; it is radically *affected by them*, determining and determined by the various *levels* and *instances* of the social formation it animates; it might be called *over-determined in its principle*.

(*For M* 101 [quoted in Elliott, *Althusser: The detour of theory* 148])

Because of overdetermination, no contradiction can reveal, as in Hegel's dialectic, a movement toward a *telos*. Various different kinds and degrees of contradiction (scientific "breaks") operate on one another and in different ways. Again, this seems similar to the idea, in Bakhtin, that there is no unidirectional movement that results from dialogic "moments," but rather, there exist complexities in these moments that must be analyzed "in the total structure of the social body" (that is, context) in which they take place. Social change does not take place in grand movements, or in simple scientifically determinable ways; rather, it takes place, as I mentioned earlier, slowly and locally, with great complexity, and with no guarantees of success.

This concept of overdetermined contradictions in ideology – and its relation to the notion of "science" – is a more fruitful way to think of the science/ideology problem (and, in conjunction, the problem of the "natural phenomena" – socioeconomic base – and the knowledge of it – ideologies). Rather than propose a strict distinction between science and ideology, an economic base and ideological superstructures which are, "in the last instance," determined by that base, Laclau and Mouffe propose *articulations* of the economic and the ideological.[11] The science/ideology distinction disappears in favor of the idea of articulation. This eliminates the problem of determination by the base (the economic) of the political (the ideological or political), since, if one wants to link economic and political subject positions, one constructs a discourse that articulates the two. In such an articulation, the separation between the economic and political is eliminated in favor of a relation between them. The difference between articulations depends upon the degree to which the competing demands of the economic or the political are hierarchized by the subject as well as by the situation.

The role of language – and the connection to Bakhtin – becomes clear in Rosalind Coward and John Ellis's chapter on Marxism in *Language and materialism*.[12] In that chapter, they discuss ideology in Althusser's formulation of it, and then redefine the relationship of ideology to economics and politics in terms of articulations along the lines of Laclau and Mouffe. For Coward and Ellis, there are three practices that are articulated in specific historical moments: politics, ideology, and economics. Bakhtin would agree with the authors that, of the three, ideology would be the practice on which the most emphasis should be placed in historical relations.

11 I am relying here on Robert Wess's paper, "Class, hegemony, hierarchy? – Laclau, Mouffe, and the trajectory of the Althusserian theory of ideology," given at the University of Ljubljana at a conference entitled *The politics of knowledge* in Ljubljana, Solvenia (then Yugoslavia), 16–18 June 1988.
12 Rosalind Coward and John Ellis, *Language and materialism: Developments in semiology and the theory of the subject.* (Boston: Routledge and Kegan Paul, 1977). Subsequent references that appear in the text will be abbreviated *LM*.

Coward and Ellis, however, discuss language in terms of its connection to ideology, and maintain that the analysis which Marxism ought to undertake is to elaborate "a precise notion of the status of language, in articulation with, but not subsumed to, ideology." They go on to say that there is a "persistent tendency to try and reduce language to being an element of ideology" (*LM* 78), which is motivated by the "outdated" metaphor of society as superstructure and in which politics and ideology are built on the economic base. Yet this connection strictly to ideology – to the exclusion of economics and politics – would seem to preclude language from having a role in the formation of political (which appears preposterous) or economic articulations. This seems clearly not to be the case. For Bakhtin, language plays a role in the formulation of any kind of human conceptualization. As we have noted before, even the formation of scientific categories of observation and analysis (and, one could add, the analysis of the economic tendencies) are equally ideological: all these formulations take place first at the level of authorial relations – that is, the level of language-relation – and proceed from there. For Bakhtin, it would seem more likely that the various elements in any articulation – the economic, the political, the ideological – are first and always mediated in language. Coward and Ellis state that "language is not reducible to any Marxist model of society, either to that of base and superstructure, or to that of three practices" (*LM* 80). They go on to say that language is at once determining and determinant. Both these statements would seem to hold true in a Bakhtinian model of language and the way it operates socially, as we saw earlier. What Bakhtin fails to do in his analysis – though this is less a failure than a persistence in following his own interests to the dismissal of other related topics – is to see specifically in what ways language operates in articulation with these *other* elements, namely the political and the economic.[13]

Returning to Wess's analysis of Laclau and Mouffe, the way in

---

13 Michael Holquist and Katerina Clark and others – see particularly Nina Perlina's "Bakhtin-Medvedev-Voloshinov: An apple of discourse," in *University of Ottawa quarterly* 53:1 (January–March 1983) – argue that Bakhtin did in fact take into account the political element, especially in *Rabelais and his world*, but that for reasons of censorship, the author had to submerge (dialogize) these discussions beneath otherwise literary speech genres. This point is disputable, but the larger one, that Bakhtin did take into account, at least peripherally, the political articulation is not. See especially in *Marxism and the philosophy of language*, "Discourse in life, discourse in art," and elsewhere, his discussions of rhetoric and its connection to politics.

which a subject is situated (in Althusser's terms, interpellated) by competing demands of different articulations is to hierarchize these articulations depending upon the particular situation. (In Wess's idea of articulation, in which language mediates ideology and economics, he is closer to Bakhtin than Coward and Ellis, who articulate language only with ideology.) Though the language of Laclau and Mouffe is overly facile – Wess notes that their language of articulation "allows them to think of potentially competing demands as coexisting happily" ("Class, hegemony, hierarchy?" 26) – it seems very close the Bakhtinian notion of the continuous process that any subject is involved with in the process of utterance. All the various sign-relations within any utterance (either spoken, written, or unspoken and unwritten) contain in them various articulations, each of which makes different demands upon the subject. Depending upon the subject's sign-background and the particular situation, the speaker may "dialogize" his utterance (or not dialogize at all) – he may author his sign-relation – differently in different contexts. And depending upon the degree to which the speaker does in fact dialogize, the articulation may present itself as contradictory and overdetermined, at which time that subject may be able to see himself *as located in ideology.* The degree to which that contradiction can or cannot be resolved has to do with what action (authorship) the subject pursues.

Wess contends that Laclau and Mouffe wrongly leave the subject "unable to see the historical conditions of its autonomy" (29). He goes on to claim that, through ideology – in particular the discourse Marx provided – a person is in a sense "created," and that this particular subject position – the subject's ability to see his place in the productive process, by way of Marxism – is consonant with the real conditions of existence. But the problem still remains that *the subject's view that his position is indeed consonant with real conditions of existence is still always in ideology.* And this in turn is subject to reorientation, and so on. Further, there is no guarantee that a way to hierarchize one person's articulations will work in a different situation for a different person: Bakhtin argues as much, as do Laclau and Mouffe. What we are left with is the problem we began with: how does one get outside of ideology; how does one get from ideological articulations mediated in language to an unmediated state? Bakhtin's method implies that the answer might be that you cannot, so you need to set the problem aside. For Marxism, it is *the* problem.

Given what has been said thus far, what can we say about scientific knowledge and its relation to the methods of Mikhail Bakhtin and of the historical materialists? The first conclusion one reaches is that scientific knowledge provides information about the current situation in the material world as perceived by human subjects. It further provides a systematic analysis of the kinds of perceptual tools human subjects have at their disposal for further study. On a Bakhtinian account, science cannot be used as a way to predict what kinds of phenomena can occur in the future. Althusser claims that this kind of knowledge of future historical formations can indeed be gleaned from historical materialism. For him, "the concepts of historical materialism not only provided knowledge of the present ... If properly understood and developed, they were valid for – that is, provided conceptual means of knowledge of – the past ... and the future" (Elliott, *Althusser: The detour of theory* 134).

Yet these concepts of historical materialism *as science* (more particularly for Althusser, *Marx's* concepts of historical materialism in *Capital* and other mature works) also made an epistemological claim for the scientificity of historical materialism. This claim was grounded in the fact that historical materialism did three things: (1) historical materialism was incompatible with theoretical humanism–historicism; (2) there exists a rupture between these in Marx's work; and (3) this theoretical rupture and evidence for it therefore make Marxism a science. As Elliott shows, assenting to the first two claims does not guarantee adherence to the third. "[H]istorical and conceptual discontinuity do not prove epistemological discontinuity" (138). It may just be that historical materialism is yet another theoretical ideology. And this is precisely what Mikhail Bakhtin claimed for any theory of knowledge: it, too, is embedded within a system of ideology, which is in turn articulated with politics, economics, and mediated all through by language. This is to understand that, as Pecheux says, "every 'epistemological break' is a 'continuing break,' [which in turn] means ... that the distinction between scientific [method] and ideological [method] is a political distinction and not a purely scientific distinction" (161).

Further, the fact that the kinds of contradictions in the current historical situation, by way of ideological language analysis of the phenomenological sort that Bakhtin practiced (or, by the way, the analyses of ideologies that Eagleton, Jameson, and de Man practice) can only be a local analysis. One cannot move from the particular ideological analysis to a general theory of ideologies, most simply because every context (every authorial situation, in Bakhtin's terms) is distinct. As we saw in the last chapter, this does not mean that similarities will not occur between situations; but to make the connection *as scientific connection* without understanding the problems of historical materialism as a science, is to use it, as Engels wrote to Conrad Schmidt, "'as a lever for construction after the Hegelian manner'" (quoted in Elliot, *Althusser: The detour of theory* 151).

What historical materialism is left with – and this is no small or insignificant project – is to construct narratives which "dialogize" or re-author current utterances and narrative by which human subjects are interpellated. In a sense, Bakhtin's project – as expressed in the Rabelais book, and explained by Michael Holquist – was to challenge monologic or authorized subject relations (necessarily, language relations), in which contradictions and "subject-forms" are "worked upon." What this does *not* mean is that ideological analysis of the historical materialist type can enact a "cure" of the kind Jameson suggests in *The political unconscious*. It cannot produce "the vision of a moment in which the individual subject would be somehow fully conscious of his or her determination by class and would be able to square the circle of ideological conditioning by sheer lucidity and the taking of thought" (283), since at the very moment of relative lucidity, the subject is pulled at once centripetally and centrifugally, and neither is guaranteed to become the hierarchical "articulation."

The moment of relative lucidity, the "utopian moment" for Jameson – the dialogic moment for Bakhtin – does, however, present two tendencies, one dynamic, one moribund. The first is the tendency to re-dialogize, to re-author, ideological sign-relations in language, in utterance, in order to begin to "see differently." The second, however, is to retreat to monologism – to read and author language as already authored texts. This tendency can be found no less in historical materialism than in any theoretical approach: the risk is that the dialogic will become, in a sense, "imposed" or "institutionalized," which, like the parlor carnivals during the Renaissance, were not carnivals at all, but mere recreations and "going through the motions." Jameson's caution that "the undiminished power of ideological distortion that persists even within the restored Utopian meaning of cultural artifacts [reminds us] that within the symbolic power of art and culture the will to domination perseveres intact" (299) could not be more true. There is always, at the level of language, a struggle "between hybridizations, purifications, shifts" and so on, and "the centralizing and unifying influence of the ... ideological norm" established by the authoritarian, consolidated language.[14] Emancipation, while possible, is slow and elusive. For Bakhtin, human subjects can only dialogize and continue to negotiate, not always felicitously, but constantly.

The juncture between the theories of Bakhtin and the historical materialists leads to three conclusions. The first of these is that Mikhail Bakhtin, after close consideration, did *not* offer a theory of social transformation per se. That is, nowhere in his work – though there are rhetorical flourishes in the "Marxist" volumes, *Marxism and the philosophy of language* and *The formal method* – is there a comprehensive theory of how human subjects can operate given their placement in ideology. As I suggested earlier, Bakhtin was not an orthodox Marxist in any sense – he was in fact jailed for anti-Soviet activities[15] – though he was familiar with certain historical materialist ideas. This elision is not hard to understand. One *can*, however, reconstruct the broad outlines of such a social theory of "human emancipation" from a number of his clearly non-Marxist works, especially the essays included in *Art and answerability* and *Speech genres*. These works present ideas of the interaction of human subjects, the creation of selves, and of the way humans interact in a world of different and contradictory ideologies. Bakhtin paid no attention to the economic articulation, and rather little to the political. Though these aspects of social theory interested Bakhtin only slightly, their elision is unfortunate, especially in conjunction with the work he did in the area of social interaction: they leave large gaps where historical materialist theorists are concerned.

Coming back to where we started, this would provide support to Ken Hirschkop's assertion that Bakhtin did not speak to the various articulations one would need to form a historical materialist theory of liberation. We have already seen that Bakhtin's unwillingness to concede (and probably correctly so) any way to pass outside of ideology has much to do with this failure. Without some idea of how the economic articulation operates on an intersubjective level – the

14 Mikhail Bakhtin, "From the prehistory of novelistic discourse," in *The dialogic imagination*, ed. Michael Holquist, trans. Caryl Emerson and Michael Holquist (Austin: University of Texas Press, 1981), 66, 67.

15 Bakhtin was arrested around 7 January 1929 on the charges (among several) of anti-Soviet activities and corrupting the young. See Clark and Holquist's biography, 142–5 and ff.

kind of analysis, on the ideological level, that Bakhtin provides in *Art and answerability* and the Marxist texts – his social theory is incomplete.

One advantage to having as complete an idea of ideological relations in language as Bakhtin provided is that one can place historical materialist theories – like Pecheux's, Coward and Ellis's, Althusser's, and those of others – alongside Bakhtin's to see where similarities and points of intersection exist (as I have begun to do here). As seen here, there are enough such points of intersection as to allow the construction of a Bakhtinian/historical materialist theory of language and ideology. Such work has been started already by scholars such as Stallybrass and White and R. Radhakrishnan.[16] Further, with Bakhtin's language theory – especially in works like "Discourse in life, discourse in art" and "Discouse in the novel" – and its reliance on careful study of linguistic "extra-discursive and non-rational" elements of language, historical materialism can begin to understand its own bases as a historical phenomenon, rather than as a science among others, outside of ideological determinations.

Finally, since dialogism is not something that must be "imported" from a theoretical philosophy, but is rather local and available in the very construction of language, Bakhtin's work on language provides a kind of "everyday" demystification process for ideological analysis. This process is certainly much slower than that scouted in the revolutionary theory of historical materialism, though it does provide a method – constant dialogic negotiation – by which subjects can potentially see their placement within ideology, and find some way to re-orient the language with which it is mediated in order to change their own selves.

The problem with this hopeful view of dialogism and ideological analysis of the kind Bakhtin would seem to offer is that simply to rely on the literary models he has provided (in the Dostoevsky and Rabelais books, for example) does not really suggest practical ways in which to theorize a more global view of societal change. Certainly, like the phenomenological theories that we get from Iser and Jauss, it does suggest that reading is a valuable human endeavor, and that in reading – and listening, watching, discoursing, teaching and learning, and so

---

16 See R. Radhakrishnan, *Theory in an uneven world* (London: Basil Blackwell, 1991); see also Peter Stallybrass and Allon White, *The politics and poetics of transgression* (Ithaca: Cornell University Press, 1986).

on – we undertake valuable aesthetic activity which in point of fact constructs our very subjects. But what it doesn't do is provide humans with a way to discern our placement inside the linguistic web (or, if you prefer, the ideological or *phenomenological* web) that includes not just humans but the brute material forces that ensnare them as well. How can you tell whether, in dialogizing one's self, that one isn't in the same kind of (material) predicament one was in before the dialogical moment? Historical materialism begins to provide an answer, but without a fully articulated view of the relation between brute material and ideology, the answer – like Bakhtin's – is largely incomplete. In the next chapter, I want to consider a way of thinking the contingency of the world when one gives up on the possibility of finding a way to relate ontology and epistemology, and to see whether Bakhtin's language theory isn't the same kind of theory of contingency. In a sense, we will have come full circle – from neo-Kantian epistemology to considering doing away altogether with epistemology (through certain phenomenologies), to the recuperation of epistemology in relation with ontology, and finally back to seeing what the world would be like without a hard-and-fast epistemology. What we gain from travelling this circle, by way of Bakhtin, remains the task of the conclusion of this book.

6

❖❖

Science, praxis, and change

❖❖

In the current conception of the human sciences, there exists a peculiar notion of how knowledge is possible and functions to produce a "worldview" (or, in other terms, a way of living). In this view, pluralism and multivalence are held sacrosanct, while the notion that there can be any appeal to some certainty outside of the multivalent has been overthrown. In the current political climate that exists in the world of academe, symptoms of this view include accusations of both the left and the right that Western culture (the right) and the multivalent text (the left) are in a sense just appeals to some higher certainty which is impossible to judge better or worse than any alternative, and unattainable in any case (since, if such "higher values" are no better or worse than anything else, they are not really any "higher" than anything else – it is not what we think it is). At universities, student codes of conduct draw lines between what is allowable speech (say, for example, a discussion of racism that includes epithets commonly used to denigrate women, homosexuals and people of color) and what is grounds for expulsion from the university (say, using the same kinds of epithets at a rally held by the Nation of Islam or by the B'nai B'rith). Again, it is the current view that such lines simply cannot (or should not) be drawn because the different interpretations of what is and is not acceptable are equally valid in an anti-foundationalist world.

A more difficult question than whether certain standards may be judged better than others in such a world is whether human social change is possible and, if so, whether it is progressive. If competing worldviews are simply choices among others, neither validated nor ascertainably better or worse than those others, then it is unclear why humans would want to argue so long and sometimes violently about those views. It is the case that such arguments take place. And it is also the case that certain of these views, when they finally become accepted, are said to be better than those that were held valuable before. It is, for example, widely – though by no means universally – accepted that an end to the American doctrine of "separate but equal" was a move toward justice and away from injustice. Nevertheless, at the time the Supreme Court decision that struck down the doctrine was written, few people, particularly in the white south, could see the decision in such overwhelming terms as "good" or "bad." What happened to change the perception of this, and other, decisions? How does such social change occur, and how, if at all, does it change the material conditions of existence for those affected? All of these questions must be asked with relation to Bakhtin's theory of language and social construction, since what is held as a first principle in that theory is that multivalence is the prime mover in human social affairs, and that language is the medium through which the multiplicity of human subject positions is negotiated for the act of self-construction. In other words, we have to ask, if the Bakhtinian equation begins with a multi-dimensional self – a self that is largely constructed through the interiorization of the language (and worldviews) of others – whether a change in the subject position of humans is necessarily a progressive one, and whether such change in the language-orientation of those subjects necessarily means a change in those subjects' material conditions.

In order to ask these questions, I want to inquire into the language theory of Stanley Fish, since in many ways his theories of subject-formation and social change seem similar to those of Bakhtin. Moreover, Fish's broad anti-foundationalist views stem explicitly from a more restricted language theory (or, more specifically, a theory of reading) much in the same way Bakhtin began his inquiry into the materialist condition of human existence from the question of authorship and the way in which humans "read" their linguistically defined position. I want to examine a philosophical cousin of Fish's views – Rorty's pragmatism – and to discuss that philosophy as regards Bakhtin in order to see if the two could rightly be called correlative; and to suggest both an alternative to the Fish/Rorty line as well as a corrective to Bakhtin.

I

Fish's anti-foundationalist philosophy of language begins modestly as an "affective stylistics" which he elaborates in *Is there a text in this class?*.[1] Fish explains that

I substituted the structure of the reader's experience for the formal structures of the text on the grounds that while the latter were more visible, they acquired significance only in the context of the former ... [O]ne could not point to [meaning] as one could if it were the property of the text; rather, one could observe or follow its gradual emergence in the interaction between the text, conceived of as a succession of words, and the developing response of the reader. (*Text* 22)

For Fish there are potentially as many "experiences" – texts – as there are readers of any text; and there are as many texts within one individual as there are times that the reader returns to read a particular text. Like Bakhtin, the reader accumulates "background" against which to read a text, and any time a reader returns, that background is different from the one she used before.

This background translates, for Fish, into context. Fish claims that no verbal expression on a page can be considered apart from how it enters the relationship with the reader. Furthermore, because the "ideas" that each person has to express are different each time the reader encounters a text (which Fish recognizes as language of some author), the text will be different. The possible variation in readings of texts in this view is quite high, and Fish himself acknowledges as much when he suggests that this kind of theory could lead some to believe that no agreement whatsoever could be arrived at in discussing texts.

Confronted with this multiplicity of possible readings that results from the variability of language-contexts, Fish posits a common context for the author's and reader's language (*Text* 198ff.). Fish asserts (correctly) that the truth or falsehood of a sentence depends upon the circumstances in which it is uttered. And, since any statement is always uttered in some circumstance, it is not in and of itself true or false. "All utterances are performative – produced and understood within the assumption of some socially conceived dimension of assessment" (*Text* 198). This is another way of saying that all language is social; from here Fish's theory of reading begins increasingly to stress the

---

1 Stanley Fish, *Is there a text in this class? The authority of interpretive communities* (Cambridge, MA: Harvard University Press, 1980). All further references that appear in the text will be abbreviated *Text*.

additional baggage that words carry with them, baggage that includes context, prior use, and experience, baggage that is explicitly recognized in Bakhtin's theory as well.

There are various broader implications of Fish's evolution from an "affective stylistics" to his notion of communities. One of the more important is that there is no distinction between "literary" and "ordinary" speech. If language cannot be pulled from its social context, then the only way one can know literature (as opposed to ordinary, "everyday" language) is through its context. In *Text*, Fish recounts the story of teaching a class on seventeenth-century Christian poetry. On the blackboard he had left a list of critics from his previous class on linguistics, with the names running down the blackboard. He goes on to say that he did not identify the list *as* a list to his poetry class, and so when he asked them to write some lines on what was on the blackboard, his students came up with various cryptic inter-pretations of the list as a religious poem (132ff.). Fish's claim is that "literature ... is the product of a way of reading, of a community agreement about what will count as literature" (97). Literary language in itself has no particular or special properties. It is the way that people agree to read language – shared context – that makes something literature.

At this point Fish's theory clearly resembles Bakhtin's "socio-logical" analysis of literature. Bakhtin's attention to the social dimension of language keeps him also from making a distinction between ordinary and literary language. Not only would such a distinction trivialize "poetic" utterances – by making them dependent on the everyday language over which they had been foregrounded – but it would also trivialize everyday speech-acts by making them automatic. Such distinctions fail to assume a social definition of what makes a genre, what makes literature "literary," a distinction from which, in *The formal method*, Bakhtin/Medvedev suggests the world of literary studies up to the present has yet fully to recover.

Bakhtin takes this a step further than Fish, though. Fish recognizes the importance of the social dimension of language, and thus concedes that reading takes place against a background of already interiorized language and language patterns that define the reader; however, he does not know quite what to say about this "definition" until much later in his theory (and, as we will see, what he has to say is finally inadequate). Reading is a temporal activity, and the reader who is in the act of negotiating the second part of a text is different from the same person who read the first part of it a day or two ago, but this would seem to lead to indeterminacy: you simply spawn too many readers with too many texts from a single act of reading. Fish replies thus:

Language does not have a shape independent of context, but since language is only encountered in contexts and never in the abstract, it always has shape, although it is not always the same one … What I am suggesting is that change is continually occurring in determining the meaning of a text through reading but that its consequence is *never* the absence of norms, standards, and certainties we desire, because they will be features of any situation we happen to be in.   (*Text* 268–9)

Fish tries to resolve the problem of indeterminacy with the notion of "interpretive communities."

Interpretive communities work in the following way. The reason some people believe that a collection of names left on a blackboard is a list of critics and why another group of people believe that it is a Christian poem with allegorical significance is because each set of people holds a different set of assumptions about or perceptions of the world. The reason one or another person can talk about a text as literary is because he is operating out of a similar set of assumptions about what kinds of utterance are literary (*Text* 303). Readers have certain predispositions about how a poem ought to work, and also what characters in poetic utterances should be like, what language should be used, and so on. This is similar to the way Bakhtin uses ideas of genre, and how they work into one's expectation. That is, if a "genre" is fulfilled without variance in what the reader has heard or used previously, that genre could be said to be relatively monologic. If the "genre" breaks with one's expectation, then it could be said to be relatively "dialogic." Depending upon the strength with which the reader maintains residence in his interpretive community, he will either experience the lines within the boundaries set by that community, or he will begin to refocus and shift his ideological orientation as he negotiates the voices in the text, and set up residence differently. The constant renegotiation of language has the potential to produce a different reader, in the same way that someone who is making her way through the second few hundred pages of a novel is different from the same person who read the first few hundred pages. Different language experiences lead to a new reading, a new text, and thus create the potential for reorientation within a community. If one were to substitute the word "ideology" for "community," one can see how the materialist Bakhtin manages things in a similar fashion. Bakhtin applauds Dostoevsky precisely for the way he situates the voices within his text, particularly for the way he situates them in particular ideologies, and lets those ideological voices come into conflict. The reason they come into conflict is that any utterance brings all past language experience in an utterance to bear on the situation. Dostoevsky brought into areas of contrast and conflict the aphoristic thinking of the Enlightenment and Romanticism; those areas of conflict in turn invite social value judgments to be made by readers who are themselves implicated in the text (see Stewart, "Shouts in the street" 47). Fish's communities, though, are fairly broadly constituted: one has the legal community, a literary community, the teaching community, the community of students, and of teachers, and so on. For the materialist, humans are not members of one community or another, but instead are members of innumerable communities (or, are interpellated variously by ideologies) in relation to which different kinds of language-relations operate. And, in each one of these "orientations," one is able to approach different "readings" or interpretations in different contexts, matching similar experience to similar experience, and noting the differences in "vocabularies" as well. Human subjects for Bakhtin are "inter-subjective sites," in which different and often competing ideologies or beliefs operate and work to determine knowledge.

The problems that come up with relation to Fish's "interpretive communities" are problems not simply of interpretation, but relate specifically to how the human self is constituted and how selves relate within social collectivities. We can begin to discuss these problems of social relations by beginning with Fish's act of reading. Reading is specifically a "succession of acts" that are already determined by one's position within a community, as we have seen. Stephen Mailloux, in *Interpretive conventions*, praises Fish's method because the "temporal act" gives value to responses "usually neglected in traditional holistic explications" (47). But this praise is indicative of a weakness in such a method. Fish's mapping of successive readings is much like Bakhtin's in sections of "Discourse in the novel" and "The problem of speech genres," though when Fish encounters a reading that does not at first meet with one's expectations for a particular sentence, one changes one's expectation of what might come in subsequent *sentences*. One is on the lookout for more non-standard sentences: it is only after one has generated enough information about how language functions – almost as if it is syntax rather than semantics that is paramount here – that one can use this information to change one's location in a community.

The change occurs in Bakhtin's model simultaneously. I sit here, writing these words on my word processor – an actual, semi-conscious phenomenon – and yet the terms "words," "word processor," "writing," and so on are ideologically determined, and carry with them various connotations, voices, orientations that must be accounted for in the simple act of typing on this keyboard. The act of reading is an act of self-formation. Fish's act of interpretation does not just form text through community assumptions, but rather, as Jonathan Culler realizes,

Recognition of [*vraisemblance*, which is a discourse that requires no justification because it seems to derive directly from the structure of the world] need not depend on the claim that reality is a convention produced by language. Indeed, the danger of that position is that it may be interpreted in too sweeping a fashion. Thus Julia Kristeva argues that anything expressed in a grammatical sentence becomes *vraisemblance* since language is constitutive of the world. (*Structuralist poetics* 140–41)

It is precisely this problem – how can we make decisions about how the world is constructed if our knowledge of that world is always inscribed linguistically without recourse to some extra-linguistic (that is, extra-epistemological) category – that undermines Fish's theory in the end, and it is likewise this problem, if left unresolved, that plagues Bakhtin. For the latter, we can phrase the problem in this way: what good does a theory of the construction of social reality based on the multivalence of language do us if it does not allow us to figure out which "versions" of that reality are better than others; and further, how can we change that reality in constructive ways if all we are doing is changing the *linguistic* construct? Again, I would suggest that the way to address these questions is to inquire of Fish and his philosophical counterpart, Richard Rorty, and to see what alternatives exist.

II

In his most recent incarnation, Fish's concerns have widened from discussions of reading and interpretation of texts to those of how social groupings, through which interpretations are built, are formed, and how change occurs within and between those groups. His practical project, then, is a debunking of the "essentialist" right and the "anti-foundationalist" left, a project that consists, first, in outlining what critical theory and practice is left with after the notion of Formalism has been eliminated. Fish takes as his beginning premise that "meaning [in texts] is a matter of what a speaker situated in a particular situation has in mind".[2] Intentionalists counter with an appeal to the context of the speaker and the listener: we should be able to reconstruct the speaker's intention from the context or situation in which the utterance in question has occurred. But, Fish goes on, "the context itself must be imputed – given an interpreted form – since the evidence one might cite in specifying it – the evidence of words, marks, gestures – will only be evidence, have a certain shape rather than another, if its own shape has already (and interpretively) been assumed" (*Doing* 7). This effectively counters the "foundationalist" or "objectivist" tendency in critical practice. The grist for Fish's mill here, however, is in countering the "post-Formalists" (what he variously calls "anti-foundationalists", "anti-professionalists", "subjectivists"). The post-Formalists react to the current critical situation in one of two ways. The first of these is in fear, specifically the fear that, without constraints on interpretation in criticism or the law, one will have to play an interpretive game of "anything goes," in which one interpretation is just as good as any other. This fear is countered by "theory hope," the belief that "if men and women whose acts are socially constituted and who are embedded in a world no more stable than the historical and conventional forms of thought that bring it into being ... then surely we can extrapolate from this picture a better set of methods for operating in the world we are constantly making and remaking" (*Doing* 346). The second reaction – also one of fear – is left uncountered: we live in a world of unconstrained norms, so we can only do what we can with the mess left over.

Against both of these reactions, Fish asserts that there are no *universal* constraints (that is, nothing objective, no essences) to which one can appeal, but that nevertheless there are constraints that are built into the kinds of "discourses" we can have. (The crucial difference between Bakhtin and Fish, though one not elaborated by the former, is that Bakhtin posits material constraints along with these

2 *Doing what comes naturally: Change, rhetoric and the practice of theory in literary and legal studies* (Durham, NC: Duke University Press, 1990). All further citations that appear in the text will be abbreviated *Doing*.

built-in linguistic ones.) In a discussion of Ronald Dworkin's *Law and interpretation*, Fish takes issue with a notion of constraint that relies on precedent. Judges, asserts Dworkin, cannot strike out in a new direction, since it would violate history. The judge "observes what's come before," and renders a decision constrained by that observation. Fish disagrees: what Dworkin has set up is an objective category, history, which is observable outside of any bias. Any judge will "observe" that history from a different set of assumptions: which law books are "appropriate" to the case, which cases are "arguably similar" to the one at hand. This, however, does not lead to utter relativism in Fish's estimation. A judge cannot "strike out in a new direction," by, say, "decid[ing] a case on the basis of whether or not the defendant had red hair" because that judge "would simply not be acting as a judge, because he could give no reasons for his decision that would be seen *as* reasons by competent members of the legal community" (*Doing* 93). So there *are* constraints built in to every act by the human subjects involved in those acts.

The groups of subjects which construct those "constraints" are the "interpretive communities," by which the act of judging becomes recognizable outside of objective constraints – and because of which it is different from judging a case on the basis of "red-haired-ness." "[A]s a fully situated member of an interpretive community ... you 'naturally' look at the objects of the community's concerns with eyes already informed by community imperatives, urgencies, and goals. [Any difference between one community's interpretations and another's] will be *originary*, assumed in advance and then put into operation so as to produce the formal 'evidence' of its rightness" (*Doing* 303–4). These communities are at once constitutive of their members – you are always already a member of a community – and constitutive of meaning. The judge who would have decided a case based on the color of the litigant's hair would have been operating not out of the legal community, but out of some other community. That is, that judge would have been constituted by the community before his act of judgment, and his judgment would have created an "interpretation," albeit not a legal one. In a sense – though one which, I'm certain, Stanley Fish might be a bit reticent to admit[3] – these

---

3 I say this because Fish never actually aligns himself with historical materialism. He never mentions Althusser in *Doing what comes naturally*, and though he mentions "Marxism" several times – more and more as he goes along, suggesting to me, at least, that he begins to find it more interesting – it does not appear in the index of the book.

communities operate much like the historical materialist concept of ideologies, in that what subjects ultimately recognize is that they are *always already in* ideology – by the recognition brought about by "hailing" or interpellation – but that recognition does not allow the subject to operate outside of that ideological placement. I will come back to this similarity, because it sheds light on the root problem for Fish, and also one that must be addressed apropos Bakhtin.

After outlining the way in which communities offer constraints to its members, Fish goes on to explain the way change takes place within these communities. One of the biggest problems with *Is there a text in this class?* is – as we have seen – that, in its characterization of interpretive communities, it is difficult for its members to "change their minds". Specifically, if one's interpretive strategies are always "colored" by the interests of a community, any disruption to those interests would be subsumed or "rationalized" by the very discourse of the community, thus squelching any rhetorical evidence that might be offered by some other group. Fish argues that this notion of change within communities is (erroneously) based on an idea that those groups' assumptions were "a mechanism for shutting out the world," for eliminating aberrant "evidence" for the assumptions held by a group. Rather, says Fish, communities should be seen as "engines of change" because they are mechanisms for "organizing [the world], for seeing phenomena as already related to the interests and goals that make the community what it is. The community, in other words, is always engaged in doing work, the work of transforming the landscape into material for its own project; but that project is then itself transformed by the very work it does" (*Doing* 150). This effectively allows for change within interpretive communities, but it still leaves unresolved the question of *how* those changes occur, even if one grants that those changes taking place will be mediated by the orientation of the group by which one is grasped.

Based on the above, Fish is led to the conclusion that what we think of as "theory" really has no consequences. Since what we mean by theory is a set of objective principles – based on observable phenomena – which we can then use as a guide for the way in which the world (or interpretation of it) works, then we can really have no Theory (with a capital "T") because the way we "observe" those phenomena will be from within our own (interested) communities. And, if the work of interpretive communities is to "reconstruct historical contexts," then theory (with a small "t") is an engine of *local* change because everyone's contexts are viewed differently (*Doing* 153). Theories are not "Theories" but beliefs, out of which we construct or interpret our worlds. This effectively eliminates the projects of the anti-foundationalists on the left, since they purport to construct a way to pass from mediated knowledge to an architectonic use for our consciousness of that knowledge. Because this project stems from an interested viewpoint, it is not architectonic, but rather, simply one set of beliefs among others. What we are left with, says Fish, is rhetoric: since we cannot appeal to an unmediated knowledge of things by which to settle our differences, then we are left with the act of (language-)mediation itself.

In a sense, Fish's own stated project, as, in fact, any anti-foundationalist project inevitably must – that all one can do is construct rhetorics which uncover *other*, previously unquestioned rhetorics – undermines itself. One can put this simply: all foundationalist positions are wrong because, Fish shows us, there are unstated assumptions of objectivity operating in their texts. But if what Fish tells us is true, then they are not wrong, they are wrong *for Fish*. Certainly, the kinds of unstated assumptions they are making are interesting for the sake of argument, but ultimately they are valueless (in the same way that "theory has no consequences") because any evidence Fish can marshal against them in favor of his own views will necessarily be interested, and therefore local to Fish and his particular community. It would be one thing if we could, for example, read Fish as a debunker of ideologies of the right, say, or a critic of aesthetically- or culturally-dominating ideas ("beliefs") that suppress marginal interpretations. But by Fish's own lights, this kind of cross-group change – in which interpretive communities can effect change in another interpretive community – is not possible. We can certainly change the way our own communities construct knowledge, but our views of that construction are not "translatable" to other groups. If one interpretive community effectively unmasks an ideological rift or contradiction, then that knowledge is assimilated and used as an engine of change *for that community*. (That is, it is a local change). But that knowledge is not useful for other communities, because it is not *productive* for those communities. In a sense, this renders Fish's project interesting but ultimately unpersuasive for members of communities *outside* of Fish's own because, after all, they have got their own interests and their own agendas.

Using Rortean terminology, Fish is arguing in favor of a "pure philosophy of language" over an "impure philosophy of language." The latter is an attempt to establish some kind of relationship between language and something outside of language which it "represents." Or, using Rorty's point of *Philosophy and the mirror of nature*, after overthrowing epistemology as the ground of modern philosophy, language theory was seen as a way to reestablish some of that lost ground by passing from a theory of language to a theory of what (and how) language *represents*. Pure language philosophy, on the other hand, does not make the leap from language theory to a substitute-epistemology. Language philosophy simply gives us a way to consider how language works, but does not presume to understand the way the world works outside of considerations of language.

Rorty's champions are Hilary Putnam ("impure") and Donald Davidson ("pure"). Rorty notes that it was Putnam who found that it was impossible to theorize any relationship between ("unnatural," constructed) human language and the ("natural") world because the theories – in a sense the constants that had to be held steady in order for the relationship to work – were also products of human knowledge and therefore as constructed as any notion of correspondence. Rorty puts it this way:

Putnam is saying that the attempt to get a set of nonintentional relationships (such as those offered by a causal theory of reference ...) is always vitiated by the fact that those relationships are simply further parts of the theory of the world of the present day.   (*Philosophy and the mirror of nature* 298)

If Rorty is right in assuming that philosophy needs to give up its claim to establish an epistemology (a claim that is often assented to, though not unquestioned), then the attempt to establish a relationship between the function of language and the way it represents something *better or worse* than something else must also be given up.

The result is a Davidsonian "pure" philosophy of language. Like Fish, Davidson suggests that correspondence is a relation "which has no ontological preferences – it can tie any sort of word to any sort of thing" (*Philosophy* 300). I quote Davidson – cited in Rorty – at length here because I think that he pinpoints Fish's philosophical under-pinnings:

It would be wrong to summarize by saying we have shown how communication is possible between people who have different schemes, a way that works without need of what there cannot be, namely a neutral ground, or a common coordinate system. For we have found no intelligible basis on which it can be said that schemes are different. It would be equally wrong to announce the glorious news that mankind – all speakers of language, at least – share a common scheme and ontology. For if we cannot intelligibly say that schemes are different, neither can we intelligibly say that they are one.

In giving up dependence on the concept of an uninterpreted reality, something outside all schemes and science, we do not relinquish the notion of objective truth – quite the contrary. Given the dogma of a dualism of scheme and reality, we get conceptual relativity, and truth relative to a scheme. Without the dogma, this kind of relativity goes by the board. Of course truth of sentences remains relative to language, but this is as objective as can be. In giving up the dualism of scheme and world, we do not give up the world, but reestablish unmediated touch with the familiar objects whose antics make our sentences and opinions true or false.

(cited in Rorty, *Philosophy* 310)

Pure language theory is, as Rorty puts it, a way of "coping" with the world.

At this point I must make a distinction between Fish's view of things and Bakhtin's. Fish, like Rorty, is a champion of "pure" language philosophy, which gives up the notion of a scheme/world distinction. Fish does not allow for any way to change "the world" as a category separate from our interpretive categories of it. In fact, he argues explicitly against "impure" language philosophy in the same way that Putnam does, suggesting that no impure philosophy of language that has established a relationship between scheme and world, and so no relationship should be established, thereby invalidating claims to "objective" truth outside of interpretive construction. For our purposes, Bakhtin would, on the face of things, also hold a "pure" philosophy of language insofar as his project means to determine how language is understood in literature relative to how it is understood in extra-literary situations. In other words, in explicitly overthrowing the distinction between *langue* and *parole* and the corresponding categorical distinction between "literary" and "every-day" language, his concern would seem to be purely one of relating the different language-relationships that are present in various utterances, and to see how those utterances construct human knowledge (but *not* a world independent of that knowledge).

However, on looking closer, Bakhtin's implicit adherence to materialism would suggest that he does not, in the way Davidson (and Rorty and Fish) does, eschew the possibility that there might also be recourse to an "impure" philosophy: material, extra-linguistic things might in fact be out there. Though it is the primary duty of the language scholar to determine the immediate relationships between and among different utterances and language usages, it is nevertheless not impossible for there to be some relationship between those relations of language and ontological considerations. Unlike Fish, who suggests that such a relationship is so difficult – if not impossible – to theorize as to be useless, Bakhtin does not give up the possibility of some kind of relation. More importantly, in not giving up the possibility of the relationship – let alone the possibility of theorizing it – Bakhtin likewise does not give up the possibility of theorizing a *change* in the extra-linguistic (that is, ontological) world through a change in linguistic (ideological) phenomena. Bakhtin's materialism focuses on the ideological relations in language while ignoring the possible (affective) relationships to the base – a project that Marxism has called for, in a sense making it (if one were to call it a philosophy of language at all) an "impure" philosophy – but not denying the possibility of such a relation. In a sense, Bakhtin has it both ways.

This is how Fish (and Rorty) becomes instructive for Bakhtin's materialism. If the materialist project in fact cannot claim a(n affective) relationship to "the world," but instead (in the terms of Michel Pecheux) produces the "scientific moment" by producing (ideological) knowledge of one's placement in ideology, then any change that takes place in the "scheme" does not necessarily produce a change in the "world." After all, if ideologically inscribed knowledge only lets a subject know that she is interpellated ideologically, but does not allow that knowledge to be put to some "use," then it is knowledge (like the knowledge of theory, for Fish) that has no consequences.

One reason that even small, local "theories" have no consequences for Fish in his present characterization of interpretive communities is that those communities are always very broad. One has, for Fish, the legal community, the literary community, the teaching community, the community of students, of teachers, and so on. Fish provides the example of a student in one of his classes. This student, despite fastly held beliefs about the way theory works, was persuaded by his instructor (namely, Stanley Fish) to change his mind. The student was bothered by the fact that he had changed his mind at all: he wondered how, since he had "been a member of an interpretive community, and indeed of a *literary* interpretive community" he could "move out of that community and into another" (*Doing* 145). In fact, it turns out, the movement was not from one community to another at all, but a change of belief *within* the community, the "literary interpretive community".

But Fish admits, early on, that groups are not constituted as widely as this. "[E]ach of us is a member of not one but innumerable interpretive communities in relation to which different kinds of beliefs are operating with different weight and force" (*Doing* 30). Fish goes on to enumerate a number of communities of which he is a member. "In each of these roles ... my performance flows from some deeply embedded ... sense of an enterprise, some conviction by which I am (quite literally) grasped concerning the point and purpose of being a member of the enterprise ..." (*Doing* 30–31). This would seem to suggest that human subjects are intersubjective sites, sites in which different (and often competing) ideologies (community "beliefs") operate and determine knowledge. And this in turn suggests that, in Fish's example, his student was not "on the same wavelength" as Fish – a member of the same interpretive community, interpellated by the same ideological constructions – but in fact was a member of very different (and unique) interpretive communities. I mentioned earlier that Fish's notions of interpretive communities were quite similar to the historical materialist category of ideology, in which ideologies are situated differently in different subjects, and are articulated in different discourses in different ways. I should revise that to say that Fish's interpretive communities *function in the same way* as ideologies, but they are constituted differently (at least in Fish's practice). In Fish's example, the student may have been "interpreting" what Stanley Fish was saying from an articulation of various ideological constructions, and the teacher (Fish) was interpreting his situation (and in turn uttering it) from a distinct set of articulated ideological constructions. To say that they are both operating in similar communities is a vast oversimplification, to say the least. Moreover, Fish admits as much at the beginning of *Doing what comes naturally*, making us wonder whether it is not Fish who is trying to have things both ways (as Bhaskar will say of Rorty).

Because of this characterization of interpretive communities (or ideological social constructs), Fish's notion of change suffers. Fish agrees that change does indeed occur within various interpretive communities, and this happens by way of a kind of "internalization" of viewpoints or orientations (Fish calls it "revision"). When a member of a community changes his interpretation of a particular phenomenon or series of phenomena, what really has happened is that this "extraneous" interpretation had been held all along, but there simply were no rhetorics with which it could be expressed. In other words, the person in the community whose mind has been changed has really not changed his mind at all; instead, a particular belief that had been held but not expressed is now capable of expression, and this in turn shifts that community member's remaining "belief system" (*Doing* 146–8).

Yet shortly after Fish has stated that change occurs *within* groups, he goes on to say that "when a community is provoked to change by something outside it, that something will already have been inside, in the sense that the angle of its notice – the angle from which it is related to the community's project even before it is seen – will determine its shape, not *after* it has been perceived, but *as* it is perceived" (*Doing* 147). This seems odd: either perceptions occur from without and are shaped in the process of perception, or they are always already inside the community's purview and as a result we have no conception of outside at all. One wonders how the conditions change, how what has happened has happened, what changed the situation, in what ways and by what the community was provoked, and so on. In other words, there is – as Fish states – a kind of social dynamic at work here, but one wonders just how Fish sees this happening, or if it is really important at all.

For Bakhtin, a similar difficulty exists. Since everything is always already in language, then it is difficult to conceive of anything coming from "outside" one's purview or sign-orientation; and this in turn calls into question whether social change can result either. If there is no "outside" from which other language orientations can come – even in the double movement of authorship, since the "other's" sign-orientation is also always ideologically embedded, and always "guessed," never ascertained – then how can we affect our material condition through language change?

This problem is as instructive for materialism generally as it is for Bakhtin, since what is at issue for both (though more generally for materialism, and only peripherally for Bakhtin if one takes his ignoring of the problem of extra-ideological fact as an eschewing of materialism) is the possibility of having knowledge of anything outside of ideology, and – if this kind of knowledge is impossible – how historical materialism can claim a kind of value as an agent of social change, when what change are the minds of materialists (and those that already "think" like historical materialists), and not the material conditions themselves. Fish's blind spot is evident in the way in which his communities are constructed. Specifically, they are much more complexly determined (in Marxist parlance, they are overdetermined) than he proposes. In other words, one does not operate out of one set of assumptions when one perceives or when one is in a speaking (or interpretive) situation. As in the example provided by Fish, the student isn't reacting to Fish from within *Fish's* community. Instead, the student is reacting from within the vocabularies (in Fish's terms, from within the rhetorics) of the student, the teacher, the son, the male, and so on, all at once. That Fish's rhetoric "affects" the student – that is, that it is "effective rhetoric" – does not mean necessarily that the two are speaking the same language, or are on the same (ideological) wavelength. It would seem more likely that Fish (the teacher) was speaking out of a particular articulation of ideological constructions, and using language in such a way as to provoke an affective reaction in the student, who was nevertheless listening out of a distinct articulation. To argue that language is always already *in* a particular ideological relation – to argue that it means whatever we think it means at the moment of utterance – is what Michel Pecheux calls the Munchausen effect: he likens it to the lifting up of oneself by pulling one's own hair. Linguistically, it is justifying an utterance's meaning by appealing to the fact that the utterer "meant it that way." Fish gets caught in his own trap: we change our minds by interiorizing certain languages and changing them to what we would have them mean. What Fish and historical materialism have in common is the need to justify how, given the nature of interpretive communities (ideologies) in which they have always already "called" their subject – thereby making it difficult (for historical materialism) or impossible (seemingly for Fish) for subjects to understand their "called-ness" – their project is valuable as an engine of social change. At least historical materialism, in its conception of overdetermined contradiction is able to understand more clearly the ways in which language affects change *between* these constructions, and not simply within them. Bakhtin builds his articulations of ideological baggage much like historical materialism. In Fish's example of the student changing his mind, he does not react out of a particular community (in that case, the "educational" or "institutional" community), but rather from the variously articulated vocabularies (in Fish's terms, from within the various "rhetorics") of the student, the teacher, the son, the male, the Anglo, and so on, all at once, each with their various contradictions. There are various "voices" from which the student may judge the language of the teacher. In terms of answerability, there are various "background voices" which the student may attach to Fish's language. And the student then must in turn assess (as best he can) the way in which Fish's language is aimed at him *as Fish sees him*. That Fish's rhetoric "affects" the student does not mean that they two are necessarily speaking the same language or are on the same (ideological) wavelength. It would seem more likely that Fish (as the teacher) was speaking out of a particular verbal articulation, and used language in such a way as to provoke an affective reaction (that is, an authorial relation) in the student, who was nevertheless "listening" out of a wholly distinct articulation.

This again comes back to the question of the constitution of the self. Jane Tompkins notes, in the heyday of Fish's "affective stylistics," that "As meaning comes to be defined more and more as a function of the reader's consciousness, the powers and limitations of that consciousness become an object of critical debate" (*Reader response criticism* xxiii). She notes that Fish often appeals in his texts to humility and honesty, which are notions implying a definitive concept of the subject. Fish's moral claim implies a self that is independent and free to choose among various interpretations, and yet, by his own lights, the self is itself constituted – constrained – by interpretive categories which are public and shared, and through which the "self as an independent entity vanishes."

III

In order adequately to discuss this last problem as it exists in Fish's theory, I must return to Richard Rorty on whose philosophy the former reflects approvingly.[4] Rorty claims that philosophy's recourse to a "world without mirrors" (that is, a world without an overarching epistemology) is to establish hermeneutics, or "an expression of hope that the cultural space left by the demise of epistemology will not be filled – that our culture should become one in which the demand for constraint and confrontation is no longer felt" (*Philosophy* 315). As opposed to epistemology, which proceeds from the assumption that

---

4 See Michael Sprinker's "Knowing, believing, doing: Or, how can we study literature and why should we anyway?" in the *ADE Bulletin* 98 (Spring 1991), 46–55.

all contributions to a given discourse are commensurable, hermeneutics begins from the assumption that the set of rules under which such a discussion could be settled on every point where statements seem to conflict is not always possible, and is never finally determinable. Hermeneutics is based on a model of discourse, in which interlocutors "play back and forth between guesses about how to characterize particular statements or other events, and guesses about the point of the whole equation, until gradually we feel at ease with what was hitherto strange" (*Philosophy* 319). In many ways, this sounds like the Bakhtinian notion of dialogue.

"What was hitherto strange" is "abnormal discourse." Normal discourse is discourse of whatever kind – including scientific discourse – that is conducted within an agreed-upon set of conventions about what counts as a relevant contribution. "Abnormal discourse is what happens when someone joins in the discourse who is ignorant of these conventions or who sets them aside ... The product of abnormal discourse can be anything from nonsense to intellectual revolution ... [H]ermeneutics is the study of abnormal discourse from the point of view of some normal discourse" (*Philosophy* 320). Rorty goes on to suggest that normal and abnormal discourses are modelled on Kuhn's notions of "normal" and "revolutionary" science: normal science takes place when the conditions for observation and explanation are generally agreed upon, while revolutionary science is the introduction of a new set of explanations.

One here needs to ask, on behalf of Bakhtin and materialism, of Fish and Rorty (as Roy Bhaskar has), whether the distinction between normal and abnormal discourse (and between normal and abnormal science) really obviates the existence of Bhaskar's "intransitive" objects of knowledge. That is, if on the one hand one conducts science against a background of agreed-upon principles of observation, or, on the other hand, one introduces a new paradigm with which to produce observations, neither case suggests that there is nothing upon which to agree, but – on the contrary – both suggest a need for a way to describe and observe *something* that exists ontologically. Moreover, Fish and Rorty suggest that there is no way to discern whether revolutionary science is in fact progressive, since there is nothing objective (extra-ideological or extra-linguistic) to which one can appeal in order to make such a judgment. But in response to this, Bhaskar notes that, though human explanations and interpretations of extra-ideological material may be by necessity constructed and therefore contingent, those explanations may be called progressive – by dint of their broader explanatory capacity – since the observations may be repeated and the results reproduced. In a sense, there is no need to suggest that simply because explanation of material objects and phenomena must be contingent, then the objects of that knowledge must also be called contingent. "[I]t is the nature of objects that determines their cognitive possibilities for us; it is humanity that is the contingent phenomenon in nature and knowledge that is, on a cosmic scale, so to speak, accidental" (Bhaskar, *Reclaiming reality* 25). At issue here is the possibility of describing the world in other than "hermeneutic" terms, and the possibility of changing the world by changing the "scheme." In Rorty's – and Fish's – view, there is no way to construct relations between "scheme" and "world" because no such relation will be adequate. The alternative is – as Rorty suggests – to operate scientifically when the conversation is taking place in normal discourse, and to operate hermeneutically when the conversation takes place abnormally. By throwing overboard the world/scheme distinction, there is never possible a change in the material conditions. Using Gadamer as his hero, Rorty notes that when there is no common ground on which to enter into a normal discourse, then – hermeneutically – "all we can do is to show how the other side looks from our own point of view. That is, all we can do is be hermeneutic about the opposition – trying to show how the odd or paradoxical or offensive things they say hang together with the rest of what they want to say, and how what they say looks when put in our own alternative idiom" (*Philosophy* 364–5). But restating things "in our own language" does not change the ground – impossible in Rorty's and Fish's view – on which we stand to do the talking.

For Rorty and Fish, then, freedom becomes, "through our capacity to *redescribe* [the] world (or relevant bits of it), something which is both positive and humanistically more recognizable – namely the capacity to create, and choose between, different vocabularies – that is, to speak or write 'abnormally'" (Bhaskar, *Reclaiming reality* 170). By making a new, incommensurable description of herself stick, she makes it true, according to Bhaskar. Thus she creates herself, "which is to say 'overcomes' her previous or past self" (171). Again, this sounds a great deal like Bakhtin's notion of the constant self-creation that takes place, always linguistically, through the human agency of authorship.

But this is hardly freedom, and it does not actually change anyone's material conditions. I quote Bhaskar at length:

(a) ... transformation would leave the discursive agent and her community without the linguistic resources to recognize or refer to her achievement; nor could it be literalized in the community unless there was some continuity or communality in usage [which is clearly not possible if a transformation takes place abnormally] ...   (b)   clearly the self-overcoming discourse must be abnormal [and thus incommensurable] ...   (*Reclaiming reality* 171)

Thus there is no way for any act of redescription to affect the material world in whose midst a subject stands. The resolution to this quandary rests, not with Bakhtin, but in the potential solution offered by the (latent) materialism of his position which can be squared with the Althusserian notion of overdetermination. That is, though there are any number of places to which one could point in showing the real similarities between Fish (and Rorty) and Bakhtin's philosophy of language, the biggest difference lies in the latter's refusal to ignore the possibility of materialism. In such a materialist view, it is necessary to understand that "pure language theory" of a kind is needed, to see how the ideological conflicts and contradictions work between and among utterances. More importantly, though,

there is more to coping with social reality than coping with other people. There is coping with a whole host of social entities, including institutions, traditions, networks of relations and the like – which are irreducible to people. In particular, it would be a mistake to think that we had overcome a social structure, like the economy, state or family, if we were successful in imposing our descripiton of it on the community.   (*Reclaiming reality* 175)

That is, if there is going to be some change beyond simply changing the description of one's relationship to material (that is, extra-ideological) entities – given that these exist, though for Fish and Rorty it is hard, if not impossible, to theorize them – then one has to understand that there is more at work in social relations than just intersubjective relations. Also at work are material constraints – hunger, disease, wealth or poverty, leisure or work, various economic conditions and so on – that also enter into the way humans engage with one another and construct their subjectivities (and others' subjectivities). Certainly we are not determined by such material constraints, but it does not hold true either that constraints are not imposed in one form or another. To deny this – and to suggest, with Fish and Rorty, that any redescription that looks better than the current one and that might get agreed upon given the current intellectual climate – is implicitly to allow that the recent bowing to intellectual trends is all one can hope for: go with what is hip now.

Freedom involves understanding how one's ideological surroundings are constructed in the best way one knows how, and the ability to transform – by actively transforming the ways in which those ideological surroundings work – the ways in which the material conditions affect the subject.

Fish and materialism are left with the problem of the exact means of building such a product (and Bakhtinians have an even more demanding project, since only the barest outlines of such a project exist in Bakhtin's work, though, by my best guess, such a project can be built based on the remainder of Bakhtin's writings). If change only occurs locally (that is, within communities for Fish, between unique ideological social constructions for historical materialism), then there can be no Theory conceived as an overarching model by which the practice of social change can be ordered. Moreover, since theories (again with a small "t") are always socially foregrounded and therefore necessarily incomplete (since any change that will occur because of them has to in turn lead to some further change, since one group's positive perception will always be another's negative perception), we need to find a way to see the world as changing positively rather than just changing.

Fish, quoting Paul de Man, asserts that "a deconstruction always has for its target to reveal the existence of hidden articulations and fragmentations within assumedly monadic totalities," and goes on to say that in doing so it must be careful that "a new monadic totality is not left as the legacy of the deconstructive gesture" (*Doing* 493).[5] In a sense, this is what Fish has left us: a reified vision of the mediated world which leaves us – as he says in the final words of his book – in an "oxymoronic state of constant wavering" (*Doing* 554). The necessary second step in Fish's project, after the assertion that the world is made not of objective perceptions but of rhetorical (political) constructions, is to construct our own rhetorical constructions. This is *not* to say that these rhetorics will not be "interested" or incomplete. If, as Fish asserts, the project of the artist and critic is to "remake culture" by opening up the social space to encompass other discourses, then destroying already held beliefs is just the first step in a long

---

5 It is interesting to note the strangeness of Fish's bedfellows here, theorists with whom he strictly avoided association in *Is there a text in this class?*, namely Terry Eagleton, Fredric Jameson, Paul de Man, and Jacques Derrida.

project. Fish notes Eagleton's call for a rhetorical project for historical materialism at the end of his *Literary theory: An introduction*, where he says that rhetoric saw "speaking and writing not merely as textual objects, to be aesthetically contemplated or endlessly deconstructed, but as forms of *activity* inseparable from the wider social relations between writers and readers ... and as largely untintelligible outside the social purposes and conditions in which they were embedded."[6] This can occur only if discourses are not always already pre-constructed, but only if they carry with them the "social baggage" of their "past life." The agency by which humans can do this would be useless, in a sense, because even "some momentous political event, a war, a shift in federal policy, an economic crisis, etc." would only affect those outside of, say the political community, to the "extent to which the members of the [non-political, literary] community see the event in question as one that has direct bearing on their conception of what they do ... [and if what they do] is bound up in an essential way with political issues" (*Doing* 149). That is, since politics is not part of the baggage of non-political groups, then wars, revolutions, and the like (and the "ideological baggage" sign conceptions of them carry) are "not important" to the act of interpretation. This seems patently false, for two reasons. First, there is *no* group or community unaffected by political discourse; and second, *all* discourse is first and always – by Fish's admission – rhetorical (that is, political).

Bakhtin's work provides a second step to succeed the first, that of "debunking" or uncovering the mediated nature of the perceptive world through language, that is, the construction of alternative rhetorics. As we saw, Fish doesn't believe this kind of work can be done, since we can only construct our *own* rhetorics. Nevertheless, Fish does laud the work of Bakhtin, as well as (what he calls) "antifoundationalists on the left," like Terry Eagleton, whose call to "rhetorical criticism" Fish cites. In such work, language is not an act of members of groups describing to each other what they "see" going on around them. Instead, it is an act of very distinct agents (that is, speaking subjects) enacting or constructing their ideological orienta-tions so that other agents may read those constructions and in turn insert their own orientations. What Fish seems to deny, in smoothing over the complexity of intersubjective relations, is that there do exist

6 Terry Eagleton, *Literary theory: An introduction* (Minneapolis: University of Minnesota Press, 1983), 206.

a variety of different vantage points, and that these are explicitly related to material conditions. Certainly we cannot definitively understand them (that is, we cannot, in the authorial relation, make ourselves see as the other can see), but we can act and construct utterances *in the attempt* of seeing others as they see us. We certainly are all situated in language, as Fish comes in the end to see. Yet without understanding the relative autonomy of that linguistic situation vis-à-vis the material conditions of existence and the complexity of their relation; and without being able to move between and among the various languages and vocabularies that attach themselves to the language which creates us, then reading, speaking, and active consumption of utterance do not get us anywhere. Fish's debunking process simply feeds off previous discourses unless there is the possibility of real change in material as well as ideological situatedness, through language, across ideological structures as well as within them (through the agency of authorship and the ability to construct alternative discourses). A suggestion for how this is possible will be left for the conclusion.

❖❖

Bakhtin, the problem of knowledge, and literary studies

❖❖

There are two versions of Mikhail Bakhtin current in the literary academic community, and these two versions suggest, in microcosm, divisions within that community itself. The first version is the phenomenological Bakhtin. This is the theorist whose *Art and answerability* essays suggest that the grounding for all language theory is the sharedness of linguistic material, and the creation of selves that is possible only through such sharedness. The creation of the self depends upon individuals interacting with various "others" in exchanges of linguistic material. This process is lengthy, complex, and indeterminate, since the exchange is marked by unique time and space coordinates. This boundlessness of context makes literary criticism virtually impossible (or, at the very least, it makes reading and the interpretation of texts an endless task), since any single interpretation can be agreed upon or rejected based upon the language-background of the person with whom one is conversing. According to those like Richard Rorty, Stanley Fish and (to some extent) Don Bialostosky, this richness itself makes literary criticism a worthwhile enterprise: if you do not foreclose meaning, and since the creation of texts and readings of texts is largely the work of individual readers (from within their communities), then what we do in reading, writing and interpreting texts is liberatory since it allows us to *imagine* different contexts for our lives, and place ourselves into a "lived relation" with those contexts. This change of lived relations is what Bakhtin called "authorship;" the aesthetic consummation of cognitive moments always leads to a further need for aesthetic consummation, so authorship is a continuous process of self-formation.

The second version of Bakhtin is, as I have suggested, the Marxist or materialist Bakhtin. This is the Bakhtin who, along with Pavel Medvedev and Valentin Voloshinov, concerns himself with questions of the materiality of language, the ways in which the material is constructed, and the degree to which the construction of language affects the real conditions of existence for the subjects who use it. Selves are defined in an equally lengthy and complex process: the interiorization of language material takes place at the same rate and in the same way as it does with the phenomenological Bakhtin (which is one reason why it is so tempting to try and unify the two Bakhtins into one overarching theoretical perspective), but the concerns are different (which is why such temptations are doomed to end in failure). Though it is important to try and discern the way in which the language exchange in any given situation serves to create the subjects involved in that exchange (and in fact the very situation), it is more important to try and understand the *degree* to which that language is ideological material, and the degree to which that material makes the real conditions of existence knowable. It is understood, both for the phenomenological and for the materialist Bakhtin, that the language situation is potentially boundless. But the assumption for the materialist Bakhtin is that this boundlessness of context does not mean that there is in fact no access to the real conditions of existence that are mediated by the linguistically-constructed context. This means that literary studies are valuable in that they provide access, albeit tentative access, to the conditions of existence for both authors and readers of texts. Literary studies provide not only the liberatory potential offered by the resituation of selves through a reconstruction of one's (or one's group's) context, but the analysis of texts also provides for a change *in the lived relations* to the conditions of existence, which in turn potentially provides for a change in those conditions themselves.

The academic macrocosm suggested by the Bakhtinian microcosm is the division between epistemologically based theories of language and literature, and those theories that dispense with epistemological claims. One can put this another way by suggesting that the current division in the academy can be characterized as a split between those who think that access to material conditions is possible, and those who think that questions of access are fruitless and are best left alone. These latter theorists, like Rorty and Fish, do not believe it is worthwhile to suggest that we can have access to what might be called "scientific" knowledge, because that knowledge is only attainable linguistically; and since language is such a messy and boundless thing, then so is science. Better to suggest *un*scientific ways in which humans can know, like hermeneutics, with which humans can recontextualize or reimagine their material situation without having to bang their heads against the wall of tough (and unanswerable) questions of epistemology. The fear that results from closing off epistemology is one that asks, "Well, if there is no categorically right or wrong answer, then anyone can interpret anything any way they want, and there are some pretty scary interpretations out there." And the answer to that frightened question is, "True, but that's all we have recourse to."

The former group of theorists, like Roy Bhaskar and some Althusserian Marxists, believe that such an answer is not only insufficient, but wrong. Certainly, it is true that context construction is potentially boundless, and that almost anything goes when it comes to interpretation. But this does not mean that everything that *does* go is well and good. In order to discover which interpretations are better or worse than others, one *must* ask epistemological questions, and the answers to such questions come with appeals to scientific observation. It may be, for example, that Justice Clarence Thomas interprets the American Civil Rights statutes of 1964 and 1965 as retrogressive, and that Affirmative Action programs promote the hiring of unskilled and unqualified minority workers, and that persons defined as members of minority groups, like himself, are done more harm than good by the statutes. Yet saying this does not make it so, nor does it make it right. What one has to do is to understand the language of the Civil Rights legislation as it intervenes not only in subjects' lived relations to their material conditions of existence, but how it works to change those conditions themselves, and whether the change is materially for the better or for the worse. That is, language works to change relations, but also the conditions, of subjects; and those changes are observable and testable.

The broader issues of whether it is fruitful for critical theory to consider epistemological questions are prefigured in the tension in Bakhtin's language theory, but there is another reason I bring up these issues here in a concluding chapter. By interrogating the tension in Bakhtin, one can, I think, begin to see a way to understand it as useful for critical theory, a way that is more interesting (and in some sense closer to what is actually going on in Bakhtin's work) than "unified" theories of that work suggest. One could put the question thus: if there is a tension between phenomenology and materialism (or, between hermeneutics and epistemology) in Bakhtin's work, is there a way to see the tension as a useful tool rather than an obstacle to a critical language theory? More broadly, is there a way to see the tension between hermeneutics and materialism as a way to ask questions (and to get some answers) about language, literature, and the people that use them?

As I have said, looking at Bakhtin's work in particular is helpful when trying to answer this question since he probed the issues involved with what might be called a contemporary understanding. But what is even more interesting is that an incident in Bakhtin's own career illustrates and highlights the problems above. Moreover, the incident helps explain, I think, the problem of "extra-linguistic knowledge" as it bears upon literary study and also the study of human social movement and interaction. I want to explore this incident, show how it bears on the questions of how we can know what we know, and to suggest briefly two ways in which these questions show how the tension in Bakhtin's work prefigures a theory that may work to answer them, a theory that we could call a "materialist rhetoric."

Mikhail Bakhtin was a voracious smoker. Moreover, he was a dabbler in certain religious thinking that was ostensibly treasonous. Because of his "dangerous thinking," Bakhtin was internally exiled in 1929. In the years following the Revolution, many things were hard to come by in the Soviet Union, and scarcity was even more prominent out in the provinces to which Bakhtin was exiled. Among the commodities that were not readily available to Bakhtin was cigarette rolling paper. Bakhtin had to make do with what was available.

During this exile in the later 1930s and early 1940s, Bakhtin was at work on a book on realism entitled *The novel of education and its significance in the history of realism*. Having finished a manuscript of the book, Bakhtin sent his only copy to the publishing house with which he was presumably contracted. In the early stages of the German invasion of the Soviet Union, the publishing house that had possession of his manuscript was bombed. As a result, the manuscript on realism was destroyed; Bakhtin had retained only certain preparatory materials and a prospectus of the book (Bakhtin, *Speech genres* xii–xiii; Clark and Holquist, *Mikhail Bakhtin* 270–74).

The connection between the shortage of cigarette paper and the explosion of the publishing house is this: because of the trouble Bakhtin had finding rolling papers with which to make cigarettes during the German invasion, and because he probably thought he would never be able to do anything to replace the destroyed manuscript, he began tearing up the notes he had made on the book, page by page, into little squares with which he could roll cigarettes. He began by smoking pages from the back of the manuscript, and worked his way toward the front. By the time the invasion was over – or at least by the time Bakhtin found other more suitable cigarette papers – all that was left of the notes was a small portion of the opening section, primarily about Goethe, which we know as "The *Bildungs-roman* and its significance in the history of realism (Towards a historical typology of the novel)."

This is more than just an interesting anecdote, suitable for cocktail party conversation, about Bakhtin; rather, I think that it points to a central question in the study of literature and of language generally. In the specific case of this incident, how do we know anything about Bakhtin's book on realism? According to the editors of *Speech genres and other late essays*, "it has been reliably reported" that the lost portions of the book were a formulation of Socialist Realism. Reliably reported, but one wonders by whom. As it pertains to the study of literature and to the problem of knowledge through linguistic material, one might ask the question this way: given, as Bakhtin asserts, that human cognition takes place through linguistic material, and since – in a sense – the language that comprised Bakhtin's book on Socialist Realism disappeared (quite literally) in a cloud of smoke, is there a way to have any knowledge of the existence of that book? If not, then is the account we have from the editors of *Speech genres* simply a construction among others? Or, if so, how do we obtain it and what does it allow us to do (if anything)?

Bakhtin's first given is that language is always already there. Even before we are conceived, humans are thought about and spoken of – are "in dialogue" – linguistically. We are "children," we are given names, we are "daddy's little helper" or "the biggest infant I've ever seen." Humans interiorize language and formulate connections between those signs. This "language background" is the difference between one person's understanding of "Have a nice day" (for example) as a mindless protocol of shop assistants and another's understanding of it as a sincere greeting meriting a response.

How one moves from "Have a nice day" as a phrase that is meaningful to one that is meaningless depends on the ways in which that utterance is placed into contexts by various speaking subjects. This agency is what Bakhtin says allows me to utter "Have a nice day" as already spoken (that is, as I have heard it uttered in contexts before), or as dialogized (that is, by changing the "spin" of the utterance). A more interesting example might be the use of a term like "color" used with reference to the tint of a person's skin. Depending on whether I choose to use the term "colored person" or "person of color," I use the term (in the first case) to show my political and cultural naiveté, or (in the second) to take part in a current political or cultural discussion.

This last example is also interesting in the way that it shows rather clearly how language is ideological material. There is always a history to words and utterances. Subjects can use that history to their own ends – as has the African-American community in connection with other people of color, actively working to change the notion of color over the last thirty years, or as the homosexual community is now working to change the "spin" of the word "queer" from a pejorative term to a politically loaded and powerful term of self-identification. Or subjects can (naively) choose not to see language's history – as some people continue to use the term "black" with reference to a person's skin color without examining the web of connotation that is involved in using the term. Yet regardless of the "interested" or "naive" uses of language and its history, subjects cannot go *outside* of that history: it is always already there. Things either exist in the world in terms of certain sign-relations, or – if signs-relations "don't exist" to describe a certain phenomenon – language is dialogized in such a way as to "create" a sign for it, as it were. You can't, using the term "color" with reference to a person's skin color, avoid the connotations implied by a word's history. It is always already there and so any use (by the speaker) or understanding (by an interlocutor or, in Bakhtin's terms, "other") of the term has prefigured within it some resultant resituation. For the phenomenological Bakhtin, the process functions thus: there cannot be an occurrence outside of language, which means that in negotiating the utterance containing the term "color," the inter-locutors also negotiate the "event" or context itself. Moreover, the event of utterance changes and this in turn changes the uttering subjects: depending upon the way they consummate the utterance, they may become *more* naive or *more* aware of the history of the term and their subsequent use of it.

In order to return to the question of Bakhtin and his rolling papers, we have to ask how we know what was on the paper that Bakhtin used to roll tobacco. It is evident – it has been "reliably reported" – that the language Bakhtin wrote existed in a certain articulation. But how do we know anything about it, since, having been destroyed, we have no access to it? In a sense, it is *outside of language*. So how, using language, do we know what was there? I liken this conundrum to a question that has begun many a first-year philosophy class: If a tree falls in a forest, but you did not hear or see it, then how do you know that it really fell? The obvious answer is that you talk to someone who did see or hear it fall. Or, better still, you listen to an account told by the person who witnessed the event, and then go to the forest and look for the turned-over stump. The problem with these alternatives is that all you have to go on is "their word." The tree either did or did not really fall over, but all you have got to go on is their version of the occurrence. Without their word for it, there's no way to judge. Or, to take the case of Anita Hill's testimony to the Senate Judiciary Committee on her harassment by Clarence Thomas, all you've got is the testimony. You can get people up to testify in support of Hill or Thomas; and you can have experts testify as to whether is makes sense that Hill would wait to tell of the harassment, or whether someone of the Judge's "character" would "do such a thing." But all the Committee members had to go on – from within their various "interpretive communities" – was language, and it gets played against the background of previously interiorized signs.

What we have is a problem of epistemology: by simply referring to questions that are by nature linguistic – asking someone to "tell" you whether they were harassed, or whether they saw a tree fall, or whether they read a manuscript – we have not yet ascertained the *material existence* of the event. If we know about our world lingusitically, then we be able to have knowledge of a tree falling in a forest or of an act of sexual harassment that we ourselves have been witness to. But if we let someone else know – if we tell them – that this tree has fallen or that someone has harassed me, all they have to go on is words: I can construct the "context" with the language I choose to use, and the listener also reconstructs that context according to what he knows. We construct and reconstruct, but the event is over, and I am the only one who had access to it. Though it happened, there is no way to explain it without resorting to the potential boundlessness of language. It works the same way with the anecdote of Bakhtin's manuscript: is there a way to draw logical or valid conclusions about Bakhtin's book on Socialist Realism now that the word has been let out of the bag?

There are two ways to answer this question, each of which addresses the tension I have pointed to in Bakhtin's work and, more broadly, in the academy. The first of these, because it rests on the assumption that there's a way to reconcile the phenomenological and the materialist Bakhtins (and the phenomenological/hermeneutic and materialist tendencies in the academy), is insufficient. One might call it the "philosophy of language" resolution, and it goes like this. Bakhtin certainly would not deny the existence of extra-linguistic events (objective phenomena). What he *does* question is the possibility that we can create knowledge of those events extra-linguistically. The problem runs along the lines of the question which is perenially posed by historical materialism: (how) is it possible to create scientific knowledge of the material forces of production when all we have to work with is language, and when this language (at least for Bakhtin, and it would seem for theorists like Michel Pecheux and Louis Althusser as well) is specifically ideological? If science is a subjectless discourse (Althusser, *Reading capital* 271), while language in a sense defines subjects, then how can you produce knowledge of a subjectless world – a world of forces and phenomena – by way of language without letting ideological concerns creep in?

For Pecheux and for Bakhtin, at least, the answer is that you cannot. There are ways in which to "dialogize" language in such a way as to discern its ideological baggage, its "previous life" as it were. But this doesn't let the subjects who perceive this ideological bind to escape the bind itself. For Pecheux, his "third modality" of abolishing the subject-form of discourse (in which subjects believe themselves to be free from ideological constraints) takes place when the subject form is worked upon itself. In effect, by recognizing their placement in material reality, subjects recognize that placement as *social* placement, and can work from inside that placement (see also Fish, *Doing* 141–61, 315–41; Bakhtin/Voloshinov, *Marxism and the philosophy of language* 11, 19–24).

This suggests, in other words, that there are phenomena that occur outside of considerations of the subject – the forces of history, the workings of the economy, planetary motion and gravity, thermo-dynamics and so on – but we can't know how they work subjectlessly. (This differs from Althusser's formulation, which claims that there *can* be scientific knowledge of these forces.) We know that trees fall silently in forests somewhere, or that women are sexually harassed on the job, but we can't know anything about these events *unless* we actually talk to someone who was there – which communications are acts of language – or unless we are able to view the material results of such events (and again, we understand these results linguistically). For Pecheux and for Bakhtin, scientific knowledge is the knowledge gained of an event and, at the same time, that this very knowledge is ideologically formulated. That is, you understand an event, but you also understand that this very knowledge is interested in a particular way. And all of this takes place at the level of language. But this knowledge *does not* let us out of our placement in that interested language, since there is always some *other* sign-relation that potentially draws us back into the ideological bind. Americans may have thought that their "dispassionate" observation of the Judiciary Committee hearings would lead them – and eventually their representatives in Congress – to weigh the material results of sexual harassment and thus come to some conclusions about the suitability of Clarence Thomas to sit on the Supreme Court. But at the very moment we understand "dispassionate" observation as a way of "escaping" the ideological baggage each Committee member uses in evaluating verbal material (not to mention our own ideological baggage in such an evaluation), we understand that the very notion of "escape" signals that we are not free of the ideology of inside outside, which is at play in the issue of whether Hill was harassed, and so on. (After all, Thomas now sits on the bench, the question of his harassment of Hill notwithstanding.)

So – to return to our anecdote – Bakhtin may or may not have written *The novel of education and its significance in the history of realism*, and he may or may not have smoked it, but that is something about which we can have no knowledge. All we have knowledge of is the language that exists, namely the beginnings of the section on Goethe. Any considerations of the language that no longer exists are purely speculative (that is, ideological), and in a sense aren't valid questions in an objective science of textual analysis.

But this doesn't really matter, since what I'm doing right now is, in effect, placing even the possibility of the actual language of Bakhtin's text on Socialist Realism having existed *into dialogue* with my own language (as well as that of Michael Holquist, Katerina Clark, Caryl Emerson, Gary Saul Morson, Don Bialostosky, Allon White, Ken Hirschkop, and all those others who have speculated on the works of Bakhtin). I am *making something* of it – I am making some "other" language, making my self into a "new" self. I am "inventing" language (sign-relations) out of previously uttered language in such a way as to make the possibility of Bakhtin's texts more real. I am (we are) taking educated guesses about ("authoring" or reorienting) language that does not exist in such a way as to create something new and potential. This is, however, no guarantee that this newly created "potential" is anywhere near to what Bakhtin's book on Realism was like before German bomber- and mortar-fire annihilated the publishing house and the manuscripts in it. Or, in the case of Anita Hill, the newly created "potential" (by Senator Orrin Hatch and others) suggests that Hill read *The exorcist* and "dialogized" its language with language she heard in the office; and thus we "re-created" an Anita Hill that is troubled, that is a jilted lover, and that would do anything to bring a Supreme Court Justice down. But the potential object is not necessarily anything near to what the object of knowledge is.

In fact, the lack of guarantee holds true to the kind of multivalence of potential Bakhtin constructed in his schema of "monologue" and "dialogue" in "From the prehistory of novelistic discourse" (66, 67). At the moment language might be said to be "dialogized," there is always a centripetal force of monologism at work that counters that language and that might "deaden" or "de-socialize" it. Bakhtin gives no guarantees of "progress" in the way language works to create and re-orient selves. To cite an example I've used before, one can't dialogize poverty into plenty; what one can do is reorient language in such a way as to discern one's ideological placement. This doesn't put food on the table, nor does it guarantee that anything that one will do based on new knowledge of poverty – change jobs, join a dem-onstration, take up arms, whatever – will lead to improvement in the situation (one's extra-ideological or extra-linguistic material con-ditions). But it does effectively lead to change of the ideological material of one's life – language – which, for Bakhtin at least, *comprises* the real social world.

As for the value of studying literary language, this solution suggests that Bakhtin sought not to repudiate the existence of objective phenomena that occur outside of linguistic understanding of them. Rather, his problem – particularly with Formalism in Russia – was with categorical divisions between what goes on in "art" and what goes on in "life," between the aesthetic/linguistic and the practical/political worlds. Bakhtin in effect blurs this distinction. More recent theoretical attempts to deal with the aesthetic's articulation with the real maintain just such a dinstinction (see Shepherd). In order to bridge the gap between the two realms – objective and subjective, real and imaginary, scientific and ideological – we are told that literature allows a glimpse into the way "life" functions. Yet as we view the history of literary studies, this distinction – and the prizing of literature and literary analysis as a way to dissolve the distinction – is clearly unsustainable.

In the end, this reduces literary studies and analysis to "ways of reading" or of experiencing the world, as Fish and Rorty do. Subjective reading is seen as a way to see how social conflict is set up, but it doesn't offer social praxis as a solution (or even as an exacerbation) of such a conflict (see Fish, *Doing* 141–61), since without some way to see how ideological struggle is linked to real social struggle, negotiation simply reasserts the terms of the conflict, and social change is thus impossible. We can never agree on meaning, since there's nothing outside subjective, community decisions, and it's these kinds of decisions by which critics (both literary and social) judge whose meaning is off the mark and whose isn't.

This, clearly, is *not* the kind of revolutionary change that some have suggested is possible by way of theory. As I've said, by changing language, one doesn't change a language-using subject's material placement. A reader of an early draft of this conclusion suggested that I point the reader to those places where Bakhtin provides useful models for the kind of analysis that produces social change. The problem is that Bakhtin doesn't provide such models (see White). Bakhtin provides the groundwork for the analysis of literary aesthetic objects (in *Art and answerability*, the Dostoevsky, Rabelais, and *Dialogic imagination* books); and he points to how such analyses might lead to useful models of social movement (in *Marxism and the philosophy of language* and *The formal method*). Yet the work of linking the ideological material in literature to the material which forms the subjects who read and write it is never fully done.

The phenomenological version of Bakhtin's language theory suggests that it is virtually impossible to have access to the material conditions of language, since those material conditions are embedded linguistically. Throwing away epistemological questions is one way to do away with this difficulty, but in the end it exchanges the problem of the possibility of knowledge for the problem of the value of the contingent (hermeneutic) knowledge one has as a result. It is difficult – if not impossible, if you listen to Fish, Rorty and "the phenomenological Bakhtin" – to have access to certain knowledge: if it is approachable at all, it certainly is not approachable linguistically. But the contingent knowledge left over, since it is contingent, does not satisfactorily answer questions like "How do we know that racist readings of certain laws *are not* productive" or "Is it really sexual harassment if a man talks about his penis in front of women co-workers" or "Do we really know that it's a problem when we exclude women or people of color or homosexuals from the literary canon." Though our common sense tells us that racism and sexism are materially harmful, it doesn't give us a way to suggest how such readings can be changed, and how the material circumstances that produce those readings can be replaced.

The other way of looking at the question of the availability of knowledge follows. Before I begin, though, I think it important to note two things. First, what I am proposing here is not new, except to say that it has not been proposed with reference to the theory of Mikhail Bakhtin. In fact, what I am proposing is something Aristotle proposed within the framework of a philosophy of rhetoric a couple thousand years ago. Second, this proposal is derived from the work of Bakhtin, but cannot be said to be culled directly from his work, and this is the result of his ambivalence toward completely letting go of phenomenology. I am *not* suggesting here that, had only Bakhtin given up on the neo-Kantian beginnings of his work, he'd have been able to more completely construct a materialist theory of language that avoided the problems you get when you eliminate epistemology. I *am* suggesting that, in giving up on epistemology and claiming a never-ending process of subject- and text-production, you replace one difficulty (the problem of how you can have access to the material conditions) with another, namely, that one never is able to tell whether one reading is definitively any better than any other.

Though it is the materialism of Bakhtin that is most productive of a workable language theory, this materialism is dependent in large part upon his phenomenological starting point, because it is precisely this phenomenological starting point that suggests that there are two different kinds of knowledge: the certain and the contingent. Phenomenology suggests that contingent knowledge is available only through hermeneutics; the certain is available through science. The two realms – at least for Fish and for Rorty – are not compatible: scientists do science, readers do hermeneutics. What materialism suggests is that the two realms are not incompatible at all (as I have tried to suggest by citing Bhaskar). In fact, both provide access to the same world, but in different ways and through different mediums: science tests observable data through repeatable procedures, while hermeneutics examines contingent information that takes place in unique situations. Both science and hermeneutics depend upon the approximation to the materials of existence.

As I have said, readers who would like me here to point to where Bakhtin suggests this or that will be disappointed, because the glaring deficiency in Bakhtin's work – other than the tensions between phenomenology and Marxism, which can be seen as a strength rather than a weakness – is that the materialism that he lays out in the co-authored texts is far from fleshed out. What I want to propose here is a way of looking at the divergence between the "hermeneutic" and "materialist" Bakhtins as productive of what one could call a "materialist rhetoric," a theory that maintains a distinction between rhetorical (that is, linguistically-embedded) knowledge and material (that is, extra-linguistic) knowledge, but that nevertheless functions with relation to – and reveals valid information about – both.

It is Aristotle's rhetorical model which suggests a classical starting point for what I have dubbed a materialist rhetoric. For Aristotle, rhetoric moved the polis to action, but it did so given certain constraints (that is, *law, politics, ethics*, for example) and these were always considered to be in place prior to the rhetorical situation. Aristotle considers rhetoric only as a means of local persuasion in a given polis. More global political changes (such as changes in government) took place *materially* – through war, revolution, invasion, the changing of laws, and so on. (One notes, for example, that in the *Rhetoric*, a great deal of attention is given to the rhetorical tropes to be used under certain forms of government, but that these forms are presupposed; rhetoric does not change them [see Book I, Chapters 4–15].) So, material constraints are presupposed – since war and brute means generally are associated with the "irrational" for Aristotle, and it is these brute impulses which must be subdued first – and these form an ethos within which persuasion is possible. "Once the lowest part of the soul has been subdued, the rhetorician can appeal to that part of the soul that can be persuaded by reason" (Arnhart 6). What you have, in effect, are two realms. The realm of the *contingent* is that in which rhetorics argue what is probable, but not entirely knowable since the objects of contingent knowledge are produced by humans whose view is necessarily local. The realm of the *certain* encloses this former, and it is comprised by laws, "the good," and so on. In *The Rhetoric* these were demonstrably provable by logical syllogisms. *Both* rhetoric and logic are valid forms of reasoning: logic, because it is based on demonstrability and approximation to certainty or truth; rhetoric, because it is based on demonstrability and approximation to common sense observations. What is important to note both with respect to Aristotle and with respect to the current question is that, though the realms operate in relation to one another, and though the material realm can affect change in the rhetorical, one cannot affect change in the material realm by way of rhetoric. In other words, rhetoric can move the polis, but only *within* certain material constraints. This is because language (the tool of rhetoric) works upon reason, but is ineffective upon brute force. Material forces thus operate independently of the force of language. Language may *approximate* certain material states of affairs, but does not *change* them. So the force of language (for Aristotle, rhetoric) affects local praxes, but not broader social change. To put this another way, rhetoric is a way of formulating local truths (a necessarily contingent means) by analyzing contingent social constructions (that is, the articulation of the polis) and to promote certain praxes – no less contingent but more or less valid based on the best available knowledge. Science is way to formulate general truths by analyzing objects and develop observations of them. There *does* exist in this scheme a mind-independent reality having entities that take part in causal interactions, and this suggests that, though the objects of scientific and rhetorical knowledge operate in relative autonomy, they are both still objects of knowledge. In other words, though the realms of science and language (or, in Rorty's terminology, hermeneutics) are distinct, we nevertheless do have knowledge of both, even though this knowledge is different and not necessarily affective from the rhetorical to the scientific realm. One *must* in this scheme have knowledge of extra-rhetorical (that is, historical) fact within which rhetorical knowledge operates.

As I have suggested, "revolutions" in the philosophy of science (notably by Kuhn and more recently by Rorty) demote scientific knowledge that seeks to demonstrate the existence of such "mind-independent reality" which take part in causal interactions (that is, science) by subsuming it to the realm of the "human sciences" (see

Sokel). One cannot have knowledge of the noumena, the Truth of things independent of the mind. Rorty says, "Truth cannot be out there – cannot exist independently of the human mind – because sentences cannot so exist, or be out there. The world is out there, but descriptions of the world are not. Only descriptions of the world can be true or false. The world on its own – unaided by the describing activities of human beings – cannot" (*Contingency, irony, solidarity* 5). That is, we may be constrained by certain objective – scientific, extra-conceptual (that is, extra-rhetorical) – material conditions, but we know them only through rhetorical means (that is, at the level of "description"), so the only means whereby we can "change" our situation is by means of redescription. This subsumption does two things. First, it dissolves the autonomy of scientific and rhetorical knowledge – and the impossibility of affecting "brute fact" by way of language – by suggesting that "brute fact" is a linguistic category; second, it allows rhetorical action to affect "brute fact." In other words, Rorty here wishes to allow social action and affect (progressive) social change through rhetoric, something that, on a large scale, is impossible in the scientifically rhetorical view.

But as I have tried to suggest, the result of this subsumption is that the kind of praxis or social change that rhetoric might enact is impossible. If there is nothing but human-constructed knowledge, and since it's all biased, it's not consequent. That is, if the force of language only enacts contingent (that is, local, praxes), then one can only have one's mind "changed" to something one already held previously. It's just another spin to the same thing but it doesn't change what one does.

The reason the "revolutionary" hermeneutic view doesn't allow change is because it doesn't adequately theorize subject-construction. Subjects are always already inside a world of language (and the material world is also linguistically constructed by subjects). Any social movement thus occurs within these rhetorical parameters. But you can't adjudicate meanings – say between sexist representations of families in advertisements (for example, women enjoying the ease allowed by a new Rubbermaid kitchen product) and more egalitarian notions of family labor – for better or for worse, because you can't ever get outside of language and the realm of the contingent. Without some notion of "brute material facts" that exist outside (though not necessarily independent of) language – that women are not, as a class or gender, predisposed to menial labor, or that such labor is oppressive when relegated mainly or only to women. One could easily say that ads for Rubbermaid, in which are depicted women in tea-length dresses dancing about the kitchen scrubbing cabinets with a new and improved dustrag, are simply one among many versions of representations of women, with its own valid history. In the case I mentioned earlier of Anita Hill's testimony before the Senate Judiciary Committee, there's no way to decide whether Justice Thomas's assertions that he "would never do something like" harassing a co-worker, or Hill's that her testimony was delayed because of Thomas's hierarchical postion with relation to hers, because there's no way to get outside of either testimony's *language*. Quite simply, by discarding the possibility of acquiring "material knowledge," hermeneutic theorists have discarded along with it the possibility of knowing which rhetorical strategies work to improve the placement of human subjects and which don't. In throwing out the dirty bathwater of the (originally Aristotelian) notion of unmediated scientific knowledge, they've also thrown out the crucial (and also Aristotelian) baby, namely that the construction of human subjects linguistically is constrained by material facts. If one maps a rhetorical hermeneutic (see Mailloux), or discusses the distinct vocabularies historically called for in a particular situation, one needs to find out how that language in fact constructs those subjects, yet one must also examine the material placement of those subjects, and begin to explain how that placement contributes (and perhaps generates) their utterances. One needs to do more than simply examine the the different languages that comprise the Rubbermaid commercial as well as the Thomas–Hill testimony. Finally it isn't enough to subsume "scientific" knowledge to rhetorical analysis simply because (as Rorty suggests) such knowledge is not axiomatic. Both rhetorical and scientific knowledge operate by way of approximating general principles from observable data. That scientific data do not yield objective truth does not make such knowledge useless or less valid.

What needs to be recovered is a kind of "materialist rhetoric," which rests on the notion that there exist two realms of knowledge, the demonstrable (the realm of science or "brute material fact") and the probable (the realm of rhetoric), and that these realms are relatively autonomous. Yet language is a *material fact*, and as such it constructs subjects as much as it constructs meaning. That is, language is at once part of the constraining physical world as it is a tool through which subjects build the boundless context of utterance. In this way, language affects, in a very real sense, one's material conditions since language is part of those very conditions.

This last principle is one on which Bakhtin builds his notion of subjectivity (*Marxism and the philosophy of language* 9). Though Bakhtin claims that all knowledge is in fact context-bound (in Fish's terms, contingent), he does not dismiss it as biased and therefore incapable of having some kind of value (as Fish does), but rather sets up a way to see how such knowledge is formed. He does this by suggesting one must inquire into the material histories of those binding contexts by setting up a way to see how subjects are formed in language.

For Bakhtin, there *does* exist a mind-independent reality in the history of the utterance – its social construction. Yet the knowledge we gain from it is *not* axiomatic, since it is mediated by linguistic inscription. (One can see this in Bakhtin's suggestion that literary analysis – and by this I take, by extension, any rhetorical (that is, linguistic) analysis – "is one branch of the study of ideologies," and that it operates similarly to science [*The formal method* 3].) Nevertheless, there are scientific methods of analysis for non-linguistic (non-rhetorical, that is empirical) phenomena; these methods *function* rhetorically, since they're always already embedded in ideological constructions. Scientific knowledge is proximate: we develop methods that better and better describe a given process insofar as possible. "Rhetorical" or mediated knowledge is per se ideological. That is, it is *material*, yet it is explicitly context-bound since it is of human construction, and moreover is linguistically constructed. In a sense, then, for Bakhtin utterances require two levels of inquiry whereas observable, scientific data require only one. A person must perform a rhetorical analysis of the utterance itself (somewhat like Mailloux's rhetorical hermeneutics), and the "history of its baggage;" and one must also try to reproduce the proximate knowledge of the *material construction* of the utterance in addition to its social context (see *The formal method* 18). Part of this work is the discernment of subject placement and construction.

There is one component of a "scientific rhetoric" that Bakhtin proposes which is left largely left incomplete, and it is this component which must be taken up in order to ensure for rhetoric a useful political function: to enable an analysis of an utterance's (and the subject/author's as well as a reader's) material construction so that one can in fact progressively change that construction (see Hirschkop, White). This is the analysis and reconstruction of the histories which in part constitute (interpellate) the subjects involved. This will be a necessarily proximate construction, since it at once hangs somewhere between a scientific analysis and a rhetorical one. The reason for this is that we're dealing with the histories of utterances, but also the material placement of the uttering and hearing subjects. What this materialist rhetoric recognizes is that – unlike hermeneutic language theories – human subject positions are not constructed sweepingly, as in various "communities" or generic conexts or histories, but that they are construced fractiously. That is, human subjects are constrained materially and lingusitically as amalgams: they operate from among any number of distinct (and sometimes contradictory) subject positions. In the negotiation of utterances – and through the interiorization and reutterance of them, either monologically or dialogically – language re-interpellates human subjects and through this process resituates them materially. This occurs since language which is uttered in any contexts carries with it the "residue" of various other contexts, and can be interiorized and re-uttered variously (either monolgically as "already understood" or dialogically by replacing one "understanding" of the utterance or parts of it with different understandings from previous discourses). To put this concretely, if through a rhetorical analysis of context and speakers, a person comes to understand a term like "sexual harassment" as having to do with her own situation – rather than as an abstract term – by linking it with language contexts not previously understood, then that analysis can lead to action *through those newly understood contexts*. The person given to understand her physical condition differently through a reorientation of a word or phrase can now act – in newly defined contexts, without the constraint of already-perceived contingencies – by redefining those very "contingencies." Rather than simply understanding the ways that the languages of harassment interpellate and situate her in a system of hierarchy (both professional and sexual), a woman should also seek to understand the material underpinnings of the situation – sex as commodity, to use only one obvious example – and work to change those material underpinnings.

The singular advantage Bakhtin's theory offers over current antifoundational strategies is that it does not do away with the world of brute material fact, and in fact offers some kind of access to it (though certainly not directly, since words are "double reflections" of material reality – see *Marxism and the philosophy of language* 23). Following Bakhtin's suggestion, if one has access to this material world, and if one is able to gather some knowledge from this material world, then one in fact can know that poverty is in fact uncomfortable, that there is some material alternative to it, and that the access to this alternative is possible – though, again, I have to stress that access to the alternative and possession of it are two very different things, and that the two are not necessarily causally related.

I conclude by citing one of my previous examples: there is a recourse to the sexist interpretation of a Rubbermaid commercial. In dialogue with some other, one can accept the version of "the feminine" in that commercial monologically (that is, as already given), and thus accept the brute material fact that women in fact enjoy housework, accept it unquestioningly (why else would the woman dance about with her Rubbermaid rag?), and that any alternative to this view – if an alternative exists – is simply on a par with it, and not necessarily superior to it. The recourse to such a monologic reading of the commercial would be to negotiate, in dialogue with some other, the ideological (and necessarily material) history of the rhetorical strategy of the commercial. One could examine, for example, the contradictory messages of the tea-length dress (a generic "party" costume) and of the kitchen (one usually does work in the kitchen, or – given the tea-length dress – one has one's housekeeping staff do it), and begin to match the material baggage of the messages with one's own material placement. How much do I enjoy housework? Is it anything like dancing? Is this the kind of dancing I do? Do I own a tea-length dress? Answering these questions and others like them begins to uncover some of the material contradictions that comprise the commercial's rhetoric, and begins to affect social change on the "viewer" and, in relation to her, the commercial's "author."

What I am suggesting, deriving from Bakhtin, is that the "realm of rhetoric" exists along with the world of brute material fact, and that the two are in relation to one another. Thus one has, in this proposed "Bakhtinian materialist rhetoric," access to the material world through the force of language. But the difference between a Bakhtinian materialist rhetoric and an Aristotelian rhetoric is that, in the former, both the rhetorical and the "historical" (if you will) are comprised by language, and that this language – unlike the Rortyan or Fishean view – is as much a material fact as rocks or trees. And one can in fact change one's subject position within the material world through a rhetorical analysis of that language, and this because language is material, and because a subject's construction is complex, contradictory, and always in negotiation. In short, one can begin, in such a materialist rhetoric, to move beyond the fact that all human subjects are rhetorically situated, and begin to see how that situation is constructed materially.

Bibliography

Althusser, Louis, *For Marx*. London: New Left Books, 1977.
  Lenin and philosophy. London: Monthly Review Press, 1971.
Althusser, Louis and Etienne Balibar, *Reading capital*. London: New Left
  Books, 1970.
Aristotle, *Rhetoric*. Cited in *The rhetorical tradition*, eds. P. Bizzel and B.
  Herzberg. New York: St. Martin's Press, 1990.
Arnhart, Larry, *Aristotle on political reasoning*. DeKalb: Northern Illinois
  University Press, 1981.
Austin, J. L., *How to do things with words*. Cambridge, MA: Harvard
  University Press, 1962.
Badiou, Alain, "Le (re)commencement du matérialisme dialectique,"
  Critique 240 (1967): 37–65.
Bakhtin, Mikhail M., *Art and answerability*, trans. Vadim Liapunov and
  Kenneth Brostrom. Austin: University of Texas Press, 1990.
  "Author and hero in aesthetic activity," in *Art and answerability*, 4–256.
  The dialogic imagination, trans. Caryl Emerson and Michael Holquist.
  Austin: University of Texas Press, 1981.
  "Discourse in life, discourse in art" in *Freudianism: A critical sketch*. New
  York: The Literary Press, 1976, 94–115.
  "Discourse in the novel," in *The dialogic imagination*, 239–422.
  "Epic and novel," in *The dialogic imagination*, 3–40.
  "From the prehistory of novelistic discourse," in *The dialogic
  imagination*, 41–83.
  "The problem of content, material and form in verbal artistic creation,"
  in *Art and answerability*, 257–326.
  Problems of Dostoevsky's poetics, ed. and trans. Caryl Emerson.
  Minneapolis: University of Minnesota Press, 1984.
  "The problem of speech genres," in *Speech genres and other late essays*,
  60–102.
  Rabelais and his world, trans. Hélène Iswolsky. Bloomington: University
  of Indiana Press, 1965.
  Speech genres and other late essays, trans. Vern McGee. Austin: University
  of Texas Press, 1984.

Bibliography

Bakhtin, Mikhail M./Pavel Medvedev, *The formal method in literary scholarship: A critical introduction to sociological poetics*, trans. Albert J. Wehrle. Cambridge, MA: Harvard University Press, 1978.

Bakhtin, Mikhail M./Valentin Voloshinov, *Marxism and the philosophy of language*, trans. Ladislav Matejka and I. R. Titunik. Cambridge, MA: Harvard University Press, 1986.

Bennett, Tony. *Formalism and Marxism*. London: Methuen, 1979.

Bernard-Donals, Michael, Review of *Art and answerability* (Austin: University of Texas Press, 1990). *MLN* 105:5 (December) 1990, 1117–20.

Benton, Ted, *The rise and fall of structural Marxism: Althusser and his influence*. London: Macmillan, 1984.

"Natural science and cultural struggle," in D. H. Ruben and J. Mepham, eds., *Issues in Marxist philosophy*, vol. II. Brighton: Harvester Press, 1979, 101–42.

Benveniste, Emile, *Problems in general linguistics*. Coral Gables: University of Miami Press, 1971.

Bhaskar, Roy, *The possibility of naturalism*. Brighton: Harvester Press, 1979.
Scientific realism and human emancipation. London: Verso, 1986.
Reclaiming reality. London: Verso, 1989.

Bialostosky, Don, "Dialogics as an art of discourse in literary criticism," in *PMLA* 101:5 (September 1986), 788–97.
Wordsworth, dialogics and the practice of criticism. Cambridge University Press, 1992.

Bleich, David, "Negotiated knowledge of language and literature," *Studies in the literary imagination* 12:1 (1979), 73–92.

Booth, Wayne, *The rhetoric of fiction*. University of Chicago Press, 1961.

Brenkman, John, *Culture and domination*. Ithaca: Cornell University Press, 1987.

Clark, Katerina and Michael Holquist, *Mikhail Bakhtin*. Cambridge, MA: Harvard University Press, 1986.

Coward, Rosalind and John Ellis, *Language and materialism*. Boston: Routledge and Kegan Paul, 1977.

Culler, Jonathan, *Structuralist poetics*. Ithaca: Cornell University Press, 1975.

Dallmyr, Fred and Thomas McCarthy, *Understanding and social inquiry*. South Bend, IN: University of Notre Dame Press, 1977.

de Man, Paul, *The resistance to theory*. Minneapolis: University of Minnesota Press, 1986.

Derrida, Jacques, "Signature, event, context," in *The margins of philosophy*. University of Chicago Press, 1982, 307–330.

Eagleton, Terry, *Criticism and ideology*. London: Verso, 1976.
Walter Benjamin or toward a revolutionary criticism. London: Verso, 1981.
Literary theory: An introduction. Minneapolis: University of Minnesota Press, 1983.

Eichenbaum, Boris, *Literatura. Theory, criticism, polemic*. Leningrad: n.p. 1927.

Bibliography

Elliott, Gregory, *Althusser: The detour of theory*. London: Verso, 1987.

Emerson, Caryl, "The outer world and inner speech: Bakhtin, Vygotsky, and the internalization of language," in *Bakhtin: Essays and dialogues on his work*, ed. Gary Saul Morson. University of Chicago Press, 1986, 21–40.

Erlich, Victor, *Russian Formalism: history-doctrine*. New Haven: Yale University Press, 1965.

Fish, Stanley. *Is there a text in this class?* Cambridge, MA: Harvard University Press, 1983.

    Doing what comes naturally: Change, rhetoric, and the practice of theory in literary and legal studies. Durham, NC: Duke University Press, 1989.

    "Why no one's afraid of Wolfgang Iser," *Diacritics* 11:3 (1981), 2–13.

Gadamer, Hans-Georg, *Truth and method*. London: Sheed and Ward, 1975.

    Philosophical hermeneutics. Berkeley: University of California Press, 1976.

Galan, F. W., *Historic structures*. Austin: University of Texas Press, 1985.

Godzich, Wlad, "Correcting Kant: Bakhtin and intercultural interactions," *boundary 2* 18:1 (Spring 1991), 5–17.

Habermas, Jurgen, *Philosophical hermeneutics*, ed. David Linge. Berkeley: University of California Press, 1976.

    "A review of Gadamer's *Truth and method*," in Dallmyr, Fred and Thomas McCarthy, *Understanding and social inquiry*, 34–51.

Hirschkop, Ken, "Bakhtin, discourse and democracy," *New left review* 160:6 (1986), 92–111.

    "Response to the Bakhtin forum," in *Bakhtin: Essays and dialogues on his work*, ed. Gary Saul Morson, University of Chicago Press, 1986, 73–80.

Hirschkop, Ken and David Shepherd, eds., *Bakhtin and cultural theory*. University of Manchester Press, 1989.

Holquist, Michael, "The politics of representation," in *Allegory and representation: Papers from the English institute*, ed. Stephen Greenblatt. Baltimore: The Johns Hopkins University Press, 1981, 163–83.

    "Answering as authoring," in *Bakhtin: Essays and dialogues on his work*. ed. Gary Saul Morson.

Holquist, Michael and Katerina Clark, "The influence of Kant in the early work of M. M. Bakhtin." *Literary theory and criticism*, Part I, ed. Joseph P. Strelka. Bern: Peter Lang, 1984, 299–313.

Holub, Robert C, *Reception theory: A critical introduction*. New York: Methuen, 1984.

Husserl, Edmund, *The Cartesian meditations: An introduction to phenomenology*, trans. Dorion Cairns. The Hague: Nijhoff, 1960.

    Ideas, trans. W. Boyce Gibson. New York: Collins, 1962.

    Logical investigations, trans. J. N. Findlay. London: Routledge and Kegan Paul, 1970.

Ingarden, Roman, *The literary work of art*. Evanston, IL: Northwestern University Press, 1979.

Cognition of the literary work of art. Evanston, IL: Northwestern University Press, 1973.

Iser, Wolfgang, *The act of reading*. Baltimore: The Johns Hopkins University Press, 1978.

The implied reader. Baltimore: The Johns Hopkins University Press, 1974.

"Talk Like Whales," *Diacritics* 11:3 (1981), 82–7.

"Indeterminacy and the reader's response to prose fiction," in *Aspects of narrative*, ed. J. Hillis Miller. New York: Columbia University Press, 1971, 1–45.

"The current situation in literary theory: Key concepts and the imaginary," *New literary history* 11:1 (1979), 1–20.

Jakobson, Roman, *Selected works*. Bloomington: University of Indiana Press, 1976.

Jameson, Fredric, *The political unconscious*. Ithaca: Cornell University Press, 1982.

"Science Versus Ideology," *Humanities in society* 7:1 (1984), 283–302.

Jauss, Hans Robert, "Die Appelstruktur der Texte," in *Aspects of narrative*, ed. J. Hillis Miller. New York: Columbia University Press, 1971, 46–77.

"The idealist embarrassment: Observations on Marxist aesthetics," *New literary history* 7:1 (1975), 191–208.

Towards an aesthetics of reception, Minneapolis: University of Minnesota Press, 1982.

"Literary history as a challenge to literary theory," in *Towards an aesthetics of reception*, 3–45.

"History of art and pragmatic history," in *Towards an aesthetics of reception*, 46–75.

Aesthetic experience and literary hermeneutics. Minneapolis: University of Minnesota Press, 1983.

Johnson, Barbara, *The critical difference*. Baltimore: The Johns Hopkins University Press, 1980.

Kanaev, I. I., "Contemporary Vitalism." *Celovek i priroda* 1:33–42; 2:9–23 (1920).

Kant, Immanuel, *The critique of pure reason*, trans. N. K. Smith. New York: n.p., 1933.

The critique of practical reason, trans. L. W. Beck. New York: n.p., 1949.

Lemon, L. and M. Reis, *Russian Formalist criticism*. Lincoln: University of Nebraska Press, 1965.

Mailloux, Stephen, *Interpretive conventions*. Ithaca: Cornell University Press, 1986.

Rhetorical power. Ithaca: Cornell University Press, 1989.

Marx, Karl, *Grundrisse: Foundations of the critique of political economy*. London: Harmondsworth, 1973.

Miller, J. Hillis, ed. *Aspects of narrative: Selected papers from the English institute*. New York: Columbia University Press, 1971.

Bibliography

Morson, Gary Saul, "The heresiarch of the *Meta,*" *PTL* 3 (1978).

Morson, Gary Saul and Caryl Emerson, *Mikhail Bakhtin: Creation of a prosaics.* Stanford University Press, 1990.

eds., *Rethinking Bakhtin.* Evanston: Northwestern University Press, 1989.

Mukarovsky, Jan, *Structure, sign and function,* trans. John Burbank and Peter Steiner. New Haven: Yale University Press, 1978.

Pecheux, Michel, *Language, semantics and ideology: Stating the Obvious.* London and New York: St. Martin's Press: 1982.

Perlina, Nina, "Bakhtin-Medvedev-Voloshinov: An apple of discourse," *University of Ottawa Quarterly* 53:1 (January–March 1983), 67–84.

Radhakrishnan, R., *Theory in an uneven world.* London: Basil Blackwell, 1991.

Rorty, Richard, *Philosophy and the mirror of nature.* Princeton University Press, 1979.

Contingency, irony, and solidarity. Cambridge University Press, 1989.

Saussure, Ferdinand, *Course in general linguistics.* New York: Random House, 1966.

Shepherd, David, "Bakhtin and the reader," in *Bakhtin and cultural theory,* ed. Ken Hirschkop and David Shepherd.

Shklovsky, Victor, "Art as Technique," in *Russian Formalist criticism.* ed. L. Lemon and M. Reis.

Sokel, Walter H., "Dilthey and the debate between the human and natural sciences," in *The history and philosophy of rhetoric and political discourse,* vol. 1, ed. K. W. Thompson. Lanham, MD: University Press of America, 1987.

Sprinker, Michael. *Imaginary relations.* London: Verso, 1986.

"Boundless Context," *Poetics today* 7:1 (1986), 117–28.

"Knowing, believing, doing: Or, how can we study literature and why should we anyway?" *ADE Bulletin* 98 (Spring 1991), 46–55.

Stallybrass, Peter and Allon White, *The politics and poetics of transgression.* Ithaca: Cornell University Press, 1986.

Stam, Robert, "Mikhail Bakhtin and left cultural critique," in *Postmodernism and its discontents: Theories, practices,* ed. E. Ann Kaplan. New York: Verso, 1988.

Steiner, Peter, *Russian Formalism: A metapoetics.* Ithaca: Cornell University Press, 1984.

Stewart, Susan, "Shouts in the street: Bakhtin's anti-linguistics," in *Bakhtin: Essays and dialogues on his work,* ed. Gary Saul Morson, 41–58.

Tompkins, Jane, *Reader response criticism.* Baltimore: The Johns Hopkins University Press, 1980.

Van Buuren, Maarten, "Quelques aspects du dialogisme." *Degres* 24–5 (1980–81), 34–57.

Vygotsky, Lev, *Thought and language,* ed. and trans. Eugenia Hanfmann and Gertrude Vakar. Cambridge, MA: Harvard University Press, 1962.

Mind in society: The development of higher psychological processes, ed. Michael Cole et al. Cambridge, MA: Harvard University Press, 1978.

Wess, Robert, "Class, Hegemony, Hierarchy? – Laclau, Mouffe, and the trajectory of the Althusserian theory of ideology." Paper delivered at *The politics of knowledge* conference. Ljubljana, Yugoslavia, 16–18 June 1988.

White, Allon, "The struggle over Bakhtin: A fraternal reply to Robert Young," *Cultural critique* 8 (Fall 1988), 217–41.

Index

Index

Index

Kuhn, Thomas 153, 172

Laclau, Ernesto 127–8
language theory, impure 146, 147, 148
language theory, pure 146–7, 155
linguistics 5
literariness 3, 4
Lukacs, Georg 73

Mailloux, Stephen 59 n. 2, 67, 71, 72, 140, 174, 175
Marburg 18, 22
material 4, 5–6, 8, 10, 12, 15, 16, 28
Marx, Karl 88, 110, 129, 130
Medvedev, Pavel 2, 7, 8, 9, 10, 11, 13, 17, 28, 89–95, 122, 124, 138, 159
Merleau-Ponty, Maurice 2 n. 1
Mikhail Bakhtin (Katerina Clark and Michael Holquist) 11, 23, 88, 118, 132 n. 15, 162
Miller, J. Hillis 53
monologic, monologism 16, 27, 81, 86, 98, 106–9, 113, 118, 119, 120, 122, 125–6, 131, 139, 159, 161, 162, 166, 168, 170, 176, 177
Morson, Gary Saul 1, 2, 31 n. 4, 108, 167
Mouffe, Chantal 127–9
Mukarovsky, Jan 91, 92

Natorp, Paul 20
novel 108

ontology 148, 153
overdetermination 69, 111–14, 120, 126, 129, 151, 155

Pecheux, Michel 115–20, 124, 126, 130, 133, 148, 151, 166, 167, 168
Perlina, Nina 2, 128 n. 13
persuasion 81, 82, 171
philosophy, Hegelian 131
philosophy, Husserlian 2, 7, 14, 47, 56, 74, 76
philosophy, neo-Kantian 2, 18–46, 92, 99, 134, 170
positivism 20
Poulet, Georges 56
prosaic(s) 36, 37
Putnam, Hilary 146, 147
Pynchon, Thomas 64

Rabelais, François 16, 24, 103
reception 16, 48–60, 68
Rezeptionsaesthetik 47, 55, 67–76, 78
Rhadakrishnan, R. 63, 133
rhetoric 90, 128 n. 13, 144, 145, 150, 151, 152, 156–7, 162, 170–8

Rorty, Richard 105, 123, 136, 141, 146–7, 148, 149, 152–5, 159, 160, 169, 170, 172, 173, 174, 177
Russia 1, 8, 18, 40, 81, 112, 113, 168

Said, Edward 66
Schmidt, Conrad 131
science 3, 40–1, 43, 88, 89, 90, 94–5, 103, 105, 109, 120–7, 147, 153–4, 160, 161, 166, 167, 169, 170–1, 172, 173, 175, 176
semiotics 75–6, 96, 99
Shepherd, David 16, 39, 169
Shklovsky, Victor 4, 5, 6
sign 3, 29, 32, 43–5, 90, 96–7, 98, 99, 114–15, 122, 163, 165
Socialist realism 163, 165, 167
Solzhenitsyn, Aleksandr 81
Soviet Union 1, 40, 81, 96, 113, 162
speech genres 37, 62, 65, 70, 79, 80–1, 93, 103, 122
Spet, Gustav 4, 6, 39
Sprinker, Michael 37–8, 57, 68, 152 n. 4
Stalinism 81, 88
Stallybrass, Peter 133
Steiner, Peter 40, 43, 44
Sterne, Laurence 5
Stewart, Susan 140
Structuralism 49–52
structure 54
superstructure 90, 101, 102, 111, 112, 113, 114, 120, 123, 127–8

Thackeray, William M. 58
theory (Fish) 144–5, 148, 156, 169
Thomas, Clarence 161, 165, 167, 174
Tolstoy, Leo 5, 118, 119
Tompkins, Jane 152
tradition 80, 81, 85
transcendental ego (Husserl) 76, 84
transitive dimension 121–2, 124

utterance 9–11, 16, 21, 34, 35, 36, 37, 116, 117, 164

Van Buuren, Martin 108
vitalism 23
Voloshinov, Valentin 2, 7, 28, 66, 90, 91, 93–103, 109, 159, 166
Vygotsky, Lev 30–1 n. 4, 90

we-experience 116
Wess, Robert 127 n. 11, 128–9
White, Allon 88, 133, 167

Zhirmunski, Victor 4